The *Educational Psychology* Guide to Preparing for the PRAXIS II™ Principles of Learning and Teaching Exam

Nancy Defrates-Densch
Northern Illinois University

Veronica Rowland
University of California, Irvine

Boston   Burr Ridge, IL   Dubuque, IA   Madison, WI   New York   San Francisco   St. Louis
Bangkok   Bogotá   Caracas   Kuala Lumpur   Lisbon   London   Madrid   Mexico City
Milan   Montreal   New Delhi   Santiago   Seoul   Singapore   Sydney   Taipei   Toronto

The McGraw·Hill Companies

McGraw-Hill Higher Education

The Educational Psychology Guide to Preparing for the PRAXIS II™
Principles of Learning and Teaching Exam

1 2 3 4 5 6 7 8 9 0 QPD/QPD 0 9 8 7 6 5 4

ISBN 0-07-298151-2

www.mhhe.com

Contents

Part IV: Practice Tests

Part I

Introduction

Introduction to *The Educational Psychology Guide to Preparing for the PRAXIS II™ Principles of Learning and Teaching Exam*

This guide is designed to help students use *Educational Psychology*, by John W. Santrock, to prepare for the Praxis II™ Principles of Learning and Teaching exam. While this study resource tests students on content covered in the exam, it should not be considered an exhaustive study guide. It is not the only resource that students will need. *The* Educational Psychology *Guide to Preparing for the PRAXIS II™ Principles of Learning and Teaching Exam* tests only material covered in *Educational Psychology*. The exam will cover additional material. To help students prepare for the Praxis II™ Principles of Learning and Teaching exam, we recommend that they visit the ETS Web site at www.ets.org/praxis for a full description of the exam, a listing of content covered, sample questions, and information about study resources available.

The Educational Psychology *Guide to Preparing for the PRAXIS II™ Principles of Learning and Teaching Exam*

The Educational Psychology *Guide to Preparing for the PRAXIS II™ Principles of Learning and Teaching Exam* consists of five sections designed to help students master knowledge from *Educational Psychology* that will be covered in PRAXIS II™ Principles of Learning and Teaching exam and to allow them to take practice tests with questions that use a format similar to that used in the PRAXIS II™ exam.

1. The ***Educational Psychology*/PRAXIS II™ Topic Matrix** shows where to review in *Educational Psychology* content covered[1] in the PRAXIS II™ Principles of Learning and Teaching Exam.

2. **Content Practice Quizzes by *Educational Psychology* Chapter** presents objective quizzes to allow students to practice with key content. This is organized by the *Educational Psychology* table of contents.

3. **Content Practice Quizzes by PRAXIS II™ Subject Category** presents objective quizzes to allow students to practice with key content. These quizzes are organized by the PRAXIS II™ Principles of Learning and Teaching Subject Categories.[2]

---

[1] Content referenced as covered in the PRAXIS II™ Principles of Learning and Teaching Exam is based on the information presented in the ETS Principles of Learning and Teaching *Tests at a Glance*, located at *ftp://ftp.ets.org/pub/tandl/0522.pdf*.

[2] See the Principles of Learning and Teaching *Tests at a Glance*, located at *ftp://ftp.ets.org/pub/tandl/0522.pdf*, for a full listing of the subject categories.

4. **Practice Multiple-Choice Test Based on the PRAXIS II™ Principles of Learning and Teaching Format** provides test questions based on the format of the PRAXIS II™ Principles of Learning and Teaching Exam.

5. **Practice Short-Answer Test Based on the PRAXIS II™ Principles of Learning and Teaching Format** provides test questions based on the format of the PRAXIS II™ Principles of Learning and Teaching Exam.

Test-taking Tips

Many students have problems on standardized exams because they do not take the time to read carefully. *Take your time and read each item.* For the essay items, it is essential that you answer the questions that are asked. While you could probably write about other aspects of the cases, be sure to focus your responses on the questions as they are asked.

Educational Psychology/ PRAXIS II™ Topic Matrix

PRAXIS II™ TOPICS[1]	Where to Review in *Educational Psychology*
I. STUDENTS AS LEARNERS	
A. *Student Development and the Learning Process*	
1. Theoretical foundations about how learning occurs: how students construct knowledge, acquire skills, and develop habits of mind.	Chapters 7–11, and 13
Examples of important theorists:	
• Jean Piaget	• Ch 2: 39–50, 54–55
• Lev Vygotsky	• Ch 2: 51–56; Ch 10: 314–315
• Howard Gardner	• Ch 4: 111–116
• Robert Sternberg	• Ch 4: 110–111, 116
• Albert Bandura	• Ch 7: 226–229
Important terms that relate to learning theory:	
• Conservation	• Ch 2: 43–44
• Constructivism	• Ch 10: 314; Ch 11: 356–357, 360–363, 366–368
• Equilibration	• Ch 2; 40
• Co-construction	• Ch10: "social constructivism"
• Private speech	• Ch 2: 52–53
• Scaffolding	• Ch 10: 316–317
• Zone of proximal development	• Ch 2: 51–52
• Learning	• Ch 7: 210–218; 226–239
• Knowledge	• Ch 8: 267, 273
• Memory	• Ch 8: 248–265
• Schemas	• Ch 2: 39; Ch 8: 260–261
• Transfer	• Ch 9: 304–308
2. Human development in the physical, social, emotional, moral, and cognitive domains	Chapters 2 and 3
Contribution of important theorists:	
• Jean Piaget	• Ch 2: 39–50, 54–55; Ch 3: 94–95
• Lev Vygotsky	• Ch 2: 51–56
• Erik Erikson	• Ch 3: 71–73
• Lawrence Kohlberg	• Ch 3: 95–97
• Carol Gilligan	• Ch 3: 97

---

[1] Topics covered are based on those listed in ETS' The Principles of Learning and Teaching *Tests at a Glance*, located at *ftp://ftp.ets.org/pub/tandl/0522.pdf*. Listed in this matrix are only PRAXIS II™ PLT topics, as presented at *ftp://ftp.ets.org/pub/tandl/0522.pdf*, that are covered in *Educational Psychology*. Students should reference to the ETS Web site and publications for the most accurate and comprehensive information.

PRAXIS II™ TOPICS[1]	Where to Review in *Educational Psychology*
Major progressions in each developmental domain and the ranges of individual variation within each domain	Chapters 2 and 3
Impact of students' physical, social, emotional, moral, and cognitive development on their learning and how to address these factors when making decisions	Chapters 2 and 3
How development in one domain, such as physical, may affect performance in another domain, such as social	Chapters 2 and 3
B. Students as Diverse Learners	
1. *Differences in the ways students learn and perform*	Chapter 4
Learning styles	Ch 4: 123–125
Multiple intelligences	Ch 4: 111–117
Performance modes • Concrete operational thinking • Visual and aural learners	Ch 2: 45–46
Gender differences	Ch 3: 153–165
Cultural expectations and styles	Ch 5: 134–142
2. *Areas of exceptionality in students' learning*	Chapter 6
Special physical or sensory challenges	Ch 6: 175–178
Learning disabilities	Ch 6: 182–186
ADHD	Ch 6: 186–188
Functional and mental retardation	Ch 6: 178–181
3. *Legislation and institutional responsibilities relating to exceptional students*	Chapter 6
Americans with Disabilities Act (ADA); Individuals with Disabilities Education Act (IDEA); Section 504 Protections for Students	Ch 6: 191–192, 198
Inclusion, mainstreaming, and "least restrictive environment"	Ch 6: 192–197
4. *Approaches for accommodating various learning styles, intelligences, or exceptionalities*	Chapter 4: 113–114, 134–135 Chapter 6
Alternative assessment	Ch 15: 510–511 Ch 16: 536–545
Testing modifications	Ch 6: 198–200 "Assistive Technologies"
5. *Process of second language acquisition and strategies to support the learning of students*	Chapter 5: 143–145

PRAXIS II™ TOPICS[1]	Where to Review in *Educational Psychology*
6. *Understanding of influences of individual experiences, talents, and prior learning, as well as language, culture, family, and community values on students' learning*	Chapters 3 and 5
Multicultural backgrounds	Ch 5: 134–142
Age-appropriate knowledge and behavior	Ch 3: 84–85
The student culture at school	Ch 3: 84–90
Family backgrounds	Ch 3: 74–81
Linguistic patterns and differences	Ch 5: 143–145
C. Student Motivation and the Learning Environment	
1. *Theoretical foundations of human motivation and behavior*	Chapter 13
Important terms that relate to motivation and behavior	Chapter 13
2. *How knowledge of human motivation and behavior should influence strategies for organizing and supporting individual and group work in the classroom*	Chapter 13
3. *Factors and situations that are likely to promote or diminish student's motivation to learn, and how to help students to become self-motivated*	Chapter 7: 232–238 Chapter 13
4. *Principles on effective classroom management and strategies to promote positive relationships, cooperation, and purposeful learning*	Chapter 14
Establishing daily procedures and routines	Ch 14: 460–462, 473
Establishing classroom rules	Ch 14: 460–462, 473
Using natural and logical consequences	Ch 14: 472–474
Providing positive guidance	Ch 14: 459, 462–467
Modeling conflict resolution, problem solving, and anger management	Ch 14: 476–480
Using objective behavior descriptions	Ch 14: 472
Responding to student behavior	Ch 14: 459, 472–476
Arranging classroom space	Ch 14: 454–458
Pacing and structuring the lesson	Ch 14: 460

PRAXIS II™ TOPICS[1]	Where to Review in *Educational Psychology*
II. INSTRUCTION & ASSESSMENT	
a. Instructional Strategies	
1. *Major cognitive processes*	Chapters 8 & 9
Critical thinking	Ch 9: 288–290
Creative thinking	Ch 9: 293–297
Higher-order thinking	Ch 9
Inductive and deductive thinking	Ch 9: 287–288
Problem structuring and problem solving	Ch 9: 290–293, 298–304
Memorization and recall	Ch 8: 248–265
Social reasoning	Ch 3: 93–100
Representation of ideas	Ch 9: 283–286
2. *Major categories, advantages, and appropriate uses of instructional strategies*	Chapters 10, 11, and 12
Cooperative learning	Ch 10: 321–324
Direct instruction	Ch 12: 382–384
Discovery learning	Ch 2: 397–398
Whole-group discussion	Ch 12: 386–387
Concept mapping	Ch 8: 269 Ch 9: 284
Questioning	Ch 12: 386–387
Learning centers	Ch 12: 389
Small-group work	Ch 10: 324–327
Project approach	Ch 10: 331–333
3. *Principles, techniques, and methods associated with major instructional strategies*	Chapters 10 and 12
Direct instruction	Ch 12: 383–384
Student-centered models	Ch 12: 396–398
4. *Methods for enhancing student learning through the use of a variety of resources and materials*	
Computers, internet resources, Web pages, e-mail	Ch 12: 399–406 Technology & Education Features
Service learning	Ch 3: 98–99

PRAXIS II™ TOPICS[1]	Where to Review in *Educational Psychology*
b. Planning Instruction	
1. *Techniques for planning instruction, including addressing curriculum goals, selecting content topics, incorporating learning theory, subject matter, curriculum development, and student development and interests*	Chapter 12
Behavioral objectives: affective, cognitive, psychomotor, speech/language	Ch 12: 378–383
Learner objectives and outcomes	Ch 16: 523–524
Antibias curriculum	Ch 5: 150–151, 164–165
2. *Techniques for creating effective bridges between curriculum goals and students' experiences*	
Modeling	Ch 7: 232–232 Ch 10: 317, 329–330 Ch 11: 346–347
Independent practice, including homework	Ch 12; 388–391
Activating students' prior knowledge	Ch 12: 384–385
Encouraging exploration and problem solving	Ch 11: 349–350
c. Assessment Strategies	Chapters 15 and 16
1. *Types of assessments*	Chapters 15 and 16
2. *Characteristics of assessments*	Chapters 15 and 16
3. *Scoring assessments*	Chapters 15 and 16
4. *Uses of assessments*	Chapters 15 and 16
5. *Understanding of measurement theory and assessment-related issues*	Chapters 15 and 16
6. *Interpreting and communicating results of assessments*	Chapters 15 and 16

PRAXIS II™ TOPICS[1]	Where to Review in *Educational Psychology*
III—COMMUNICATION TECHNIQUES	
a. *Basic, effective verbal and nonverbal communication techniques*	*Chapter 14: 465–471*
b. *Effect of cultural and gender differences on communications in the classroom*	*Chapter 2: 58–59* *Chapter 5: 159*
c. *Types of communications and interactions that can stimulate discussion in different ways for particular purposes*	*Chapter 10*
Probing for learner understanding	Ch 12: 386–387
Helping students articulate their ideas and thinking processes	Ch 12: 386–387
Promoting risk taking and problem solving	Ch 9: 298–304
Facilitating factual recall	Ch 8: 263–264
Encouraging convergent and divergent thinking	Ch 9: 287–288
Stimulating curiosity	Ch 9: 293–297
Helping students to question	Ch 10: 330
Promoting a caring community	Ch 3: 99–100
IV—PROFESSION & COMMUNITY	
a. *The Reflective Practitioner*	
1. *Types of resources available for professional development and learning*	
2. *Ability to read, understand, and apply articles and books about current research, views, ideas, and debates regarding best teaching practices*	*Chapter 1: 15–28*
3. *Ongoing personal reflection on teaching and learning practices as a basis for making professional decisions*	
Code of Ethics	Ch 1: 24–25
b. *The Larger Community*	
1. *Role of the school as a resources to the larger community*	
2. *Factors in the students' environment outside of school (family circumstances, community environments, health and economic conditions) that may influence students' life and learning*	*Chapter 3: 68–70, 73–81* *Chapter 5: 136–140*
3. *Develop and utilize active partnerships among teachers, parents/guardians, and leaders in the community to support educational process*	*Chapter 5; 151–152* *Chapter 6: 197–198*
4. *Major laws related to students' rights and teacher responsibilities*	*Chapter 6: 191–192*
Appropriate education for students with special needs	Ch 6: 191–192

Part II

Content Practice Quizzes by *Educational Psychology Chapter*

CHAPTER 1

Educational Psychology: A Tool For Effective Teaching

1. Current educational reform emphasizes the use of which of the following types of activities or assignments? (Text Hint: See page 8)[1]
   a. Writing reports
   b. Completing worksheets
   c. Working in groups
   d. Using calculators

2. Who was the first individual to use the term "gifted" to describe students who scored exceptionally high on intelligence tests? (Text Hint: See page 6)
   a. Mamie Clark
   b. William James
   c. John Dewey
   d. Leta Hollingsworth

3. An individual who takes a constructivist approach to teaching would most likely encourage students to do which of the following? (Text Hint: See page 8)
   a. Solve math problems
   b. Collaborate with others
   c. Memorize information
   d. Assemble puzzles

4. Effective teachers tend to display which of the following traits? (Text Hint: See page 9)
   a. They do not allow students to ask questions about political issues.
   b. They are knowledgeable about people from different cultural backgrounds.
   c. They discourage students from discussing ethnic issues.
   d. They encourage students to work alone.

5. Which of the following researchers, during the late 1880s, argued for the importance of observing teaching and learning in the classrooms for improving education? (Text Hint: See page 8)
   a. John Dewey
   b. William James
   c. E. L. Thorndike
   d. Leta Hollingsworth

---

[1] All text hint references are to *Educational Psychology,* 2/e, Classroom Update, by John. W. Santrock.

6. A teacher would like to identify students' attitudes about using calculators to complete math assignments. Which of the following research methods would be most appropriate? (Text Hint: See page 17)

   a. Case study

   b. Laboratory observation

   c. Standardized test

   d. Questionnaire

7. When choosing participants for an experiment, an investigator most effectively ensures that the resultant effects are not due to any preexisting group difference by _____. (Text Hint: See page 21)

   a. assigning participants alphabetically to treatment and control conditions

   b. letting participants choose treatment or control groups

   c. assigning participants randomly to either treatment or control groups

   d. assigning students who arrive first to the treatment condition

8. Which of the following refers to an intensive and in-depth study of one individual? (Text Hint: See page 19)

   a. Descriptive research

   b. Ethnography

   c. Case study

   d. Experimental research

9. Which of the following terms refers to an integrated, coherent set of ideas that attempts to explain a phenomenon and to make predictions? (Text Hint: See page 16)

   a. Principle

   b. Theory

   c. Hypothesis

   d. Scientific method

10. A _____ describes how closely two constructs are related. (Text Hint: See page 20)

   a. correlation

   b. hypothesis

   c. theory

   d. principle

11. In a study comparing the effects of studying with music versus no music on reading comprehension, an investigator administers a comprehension test after a reading study period. She finds that scores were higher for the group who listened to classical pieces. What is the independent variable in this study? (Text Hint: See page 20)

   a. Studying

   b. Reading comprehension score

   c. Study period

   d. Presence or absence of music during studying.

12. Ms. Stevenson calculates how correlated her students' final exam scores are with the number of homework assignments during the school year and determines they are positively correlated. Which of the following is true? (Text Hint: See page 20)

    a. When students have less homework, they score lower on the final exam.

    b. Having more homework causes lower scores on the final exam.

    c. Having more homework causes higher scores on the final exam.

    d. When students have more homework, they score lower on the final exam.

13. Which of the following is a descriptive approach to research that consists of in-depth examination of life with a group that includes direct involvement with the participants? (Text Hint: See page 19)

    a. Descriptive research

    b. Ethnography

    c. Case study

    d. Experimental research

14. Which of the following conclusions can be drawn only from an experimental study? (Text Hint: See page 20)

    a. Quantity of trips to the bathroom is associated with lower academic achievement.

    b. High teacher expectations leads to higher academic achievement

    c. High school students think more analytically than elementary students.

    d. When the teacher drinks more caffeine, he/she is much more animated during his/her lectures.

15. A _____ occurs when the researcher becomes a participant in the activity or setting in order to better understand life in that group. (Text Hint: See page 18)

    a. participant observation

    b. ethnography

    c. descriptive research

    d. experimentation

16. Which of the following would be the best example of action research? (Text Hint: See page 23)

    a. Answer a question about whether a school district has an effective classroom management approach.

    b. Improve classroom management practices in a third grade math classroom.

    c. Determine best classroom management practices that can be applied to most school classrooms.

    d. Make decisions about the effectiveness of a particular behavioristic classroom management program.

17. Which of the following is *NOT* true concerning the need to be cautious about what is reported in the popular media? (Text Hint: See page 27)

    a. Views expressed in the media are never grounded in systematic educational research.

    b. Sometimes when information to report is not sensational enough, there is a chance it might be embellished to keep audiences tuned to their programming.

    c. Most journalists are not scientifically trained in educational research, so they may sometimes not make sound decisions about reporting information.

    d. Media often do not go enough into detail about a study, so important specifics may be omitted.

18. According to a recent technology survey in 2001, _____. (Text Hint: See page 12)

    a. about 30 percent of low-income students have a computer at home, compared to almost 90 percent of students from high-income families

    b. students from low-income families are equally likely as high-income students to have a computer at home

    c. about 10 percent of all students have high-speed Internet access in their classrooms

    d. about 30 percent of students report they have no interest in technology use

19. All of the following traits are characteristics of "worst" teachers EXCEPT _____. (Text Hint: See page 13)

    a. having a dull/boring class

    b. making unclear or confusing explanations

    c. treating students like adults

    d. lacking control

20. Effective teachers typically exhibit _____. (Text Hint: See page 8)

    a. rigidity in their teaching methods

    b. solid professional knowledge and skills

    c. predictability in their lesson plans and curriculum

    d. control over every aspect of the classroom

Answer Key

1. C—Feedback: Subject Category: II. Instruction and Assessment: Instructional Strategies: Major categories, advantages, and appropriate uses of instructional strategies: Cooperative learning

2. D—Feedback: Subject Category I. Students as Learners: Student Development and the Learning Process: Theoretical foundations about how learning occurs—how students construct knowledge, acquire skills, and develop habits of mind: Examples of important theorists

3. B—Feedback: Subject Category I. Students as Learners: Student Development and the Learning Process: Theoretical foundations about how learning occurs—how students construct knowledge, acquire skills, and develop habits of mind: Examples of important theorists: Important terms that relate to learning theory: Constructivism

4. B—Feedback: Subject Category I. Students as Learners: Students as Diverse Learners: Differences in the ways students learn and perform: Cultural expectations and styles

5. B—Feedback: Subject Category I. Students as Learners: Student Development and the Learning Process: Theoretical foundations about how learning occurs—how students construct knowledge, acquire skills, and develop habits of mind: Examples of important theorists

6. D—Feedback: Subject Category IV. Profession and Community: The Reflective Practitioner: Why personal reflection on teaching practices is critical, and approaches that can be used to achieve this

7. C—Feedback: Subject Category IV. Profession and Community: The Reflective Practitioner: Why personal reflection on teaching practices is critical, and approaches that can be used to achieve this

8. C—Feedback: Subject Category IV. Profession and Community: The Reflective Practitioner: Why personal reflection on teaching practices is critical, and approaches that can be used to achieve this

9. B—Feedback: Subject Category IV. Profession and Community: The Reflective Practitioner: Why personal reflection on teaching practices is critical, and approaches that can be used to achieve this

10. A—Feedback: Subject Category IV. Profession and Community: The Reflective Practitioner: Why personal reflection on teaching practices is critical, and approaches that can be used to achieve this

11. D—Feedback: Subject Category IV. Profession and Community: The Reflective Practitioner: Ability to read and understand articles about current views, ideas, and debates regarding best teaching practices

12. A—Feedback: Subject Category IV. Profession and Community: The Reflective Practitioner: Why personal reflection on teaching practices is critical, and approaches that can be used to achieve this

13. B—Feedback: Subject Category IV. Profession and Community: The Reflective Practitioner: Why personal reflection on teaching practices is critical, and approaches that can be used to achieve this

14. B—Feedback: Subject Category IV. Profession and Community: The Reflective Practitioner: Why personal reflection on teaching practices is critical, and approaches that can be used to achieve this

15. A—Feedback: Subject Category IV. Profession and Community: The Reflective Practitioner: Why personal reflection on teaching practices is critical, and approaches that can be used to achieve this

16. B—Feedback: Subject Category IV. Profession and Community: The Reflective Practitioner: Why personal reflection on teaching practices is critical, and approaches that can be used to achieve this

17. A—Feedback: Subject Category IV. Profession and Community: The Reflective Practitioner: Ability to read and understand articles about current views, ideas, and debates regarding best teaching practices

18. A—Feedback: Subject Category IV. Profession and Community: The Larger Community: Factors in the students' environment outside of school (family circumstances, community environments, health, and economic conditions) that may influence students' life and learning

19. C—Feedback: Subject Category I. Students as Learners: Student Motivation and the Learning Environment: Principles of effective management and strategies to promote positive relationships, cooperation, and purposeful learning

20. B—Feedback: Subject Category I. Students as Learners: Student Motivation and the Learning Environment: Principles of effective management and strategies to promote positive relationships, cooperation, and purposeful learning

All Subject Categories are as listed in the ETS Principles of Learning and Teaching, *Tests at a Glance*, located at *ftp://ftp.ets.org/pub/tandl/0522.pdf*.

CHAPTER 2
Cognitive and Language Development

1. Which of the following is an example of a biological process that might be studied by an educational psychologist? (Text Hint: See page 35)
   a. The development of social relationships
   b. The changes in children's motor skills
   c. The changes in children's ability to think logically
   d. The influence of parental nurturing on children's tendency to be aggressive

2. During the period of development known as "middle and late childhood," a child typically does which of the following? (Text Hint: See page 35)
   a. Masters the fundamental skills of writing
   b. Prefers to spend time with parents rather than with peers
   c. Makes important career decisions
   d. Learns to identify letters of the alphabet

3. Myelination of areas in the brain related to hand-eye coordination is typically completed during which stage of an individual's life? (Text Hint: See page 37)
   a. Infancy
   b. Early childhood
   c. Adolescence
   d. Young adulthood

4. _____ occurs when a child incorporates new knowledge into existing knowledge. (Text Hint: See page 39)
   a. Assimilation
   b. Accommodation
   c. Equilibration
   d. Lateralization

5. Patricia demonstrates object permanence when her rattle is taken and hidden under a blanket and she _____. (Text Hint: See page 40)
   a. looks to find something new to play with
   b. lifts the blanket to look for the rattle
   c. begins to play with her mother
   d. cries hysterically

6. The preoperational stage, as described by Piaget, includes individuals in which of the following age groups? (Text Hint: See page 40)
   a. Birth to 2 years
   b. 2 to 7 years
   c. 7 to 11 years
   d. 11 years through adulthood

7. Choose the best example of seriation from the following examples. (Text Hint: See page 45)
   a. Lorna lines her blocks up in a straight row.
   b. Billy lines his blocks by color.
   c. Jermaine lines his blocks from biggest to smallest.
   d. Troy chews on his blocks.

8. According to Piaget, a child is *first* able to understand that sequences or procedures are reversible when the child reaches which of the following stages? (Text Hint: See page 43)
   a. Sensorimotor stage
   b. Preoperational stage
   c. Concrete operational stage
   d. Formal operational stage

9. Tracy examines the possibilities of working with Sam. He is very good at working with computers, so he may be a good partner for helping to complete the research project. However, Tracy also knows that Sam is chronically irresponsible and may neglect the project. Tracy decides to test the waters by talking to other students who have worked with Sam as well as asking Sam a few questions about his ideas about carrying out the project to determine his likelihood of helping out. At which stage of Piaget's theory is Tracy? (Text Hint: See page 46)
   a. Sensorimotor
   b. Preoperational
   c. Concrete Operational
   d. Formal Operational

10. The following emphases are central to Vygotsky's theory. (Text Hint: See page 51)
    a. Zone of proximal development
    b. Sociocultural influences
    c. Language
    d. All the above

11. Which of the following represents Vygotsky's view of the origin of cognitive development? (Text Hint: See page 51)
    a. Intelligence
    b. Genetics
    c. Social interactions
    d. Self-regulated behavior

12. The teacher notices Shawn cannot solve a problem on his own, but can when he is given either adult or peer guidance. This guidance is called _____. (Text Hint: See page 51)

    a. assisted performance

    b. the zone of proximal development

    c. preoperational thinking

    d. lateralization

13. Which one of the following is the best example of scaffolding? (Text Hint: See page 52)

    a. Mr. Christiansen takes every opportunity to nurture students' individual strengths.

    b. Mrs. Jackson has students write their term papers on an area of each student's interests.

    c. Ms. Alicia always provides a detailed lesson on the Civil War before giving students their term paper assignments.

    d. Mr. Thompson demonstrates how to write the letter "z" in cursive at the blackboard before having students do so.

14. Vygotsky's stage in the development of speech characterized by silent "self-talk" is called _____. (Text Hint: See page 52)

    a. private speech

    b. personal speech

    c. egocentric speech

    d. social speech

15. Kylie's parents are so proud because Kylie has just said her first word. Having only this information, how old would you guess Kylie is? (Text Hint: See page 62)

    a. 3–6 months

    b. 10–13 months

    c. 18–24 months

    d. at least 36 months

16. Critics of Piaget assert all of the following EXCEPT _____. (Text Hint: See page 49)

    a. children's cognitive development does not occur in synchronous stages

    b. children at one cognitive stage can be trained to reason at a higher cognitive stage

    c. children go through cognitive stages at the same rate

    d. culture and education exert strong influences on children's cognitive development

17. Which of the following is the best example of an argument for environmental influences on language? (Text Hint: See page 57)

    a. Humans are prewired to learn language.

    b. Even if parents do not speak to children, children still demonstrate language acquisition.

    c. Parents' reinforcement of children's linguistic attempts helps them to fine-tune their use of language.

    d. Children have an inborn propensity to figure language out all on their own.

18. Effective teachers who work with formal operational thinkers do all of the following EXCEPT _____. (Text Hint: See page 48)

    a. realize that many adolescents are not full-fledged formal operational thinkers

    b. present a problem that has one, clear approach to solving it

    c. propose a problem and invite students to form hypotheses about how to solve it

    d. develop projects and investigations for students to carry out

Answer Key

1. B—Feedback: Subject Category I. Students as Learners: Student Development and the Learning Process: Human development in the physical, social, emotional, moral, and cognitive domains: Impact of students' physical, social, emotional, moral, and cognitive development on their learning and how to address these factors when making decisions

2. A—Feedback: Subject Category I. Students as Learners: Student Development and the Learning Process: Human development in the physical, social, emotional, moral, and cognitive domains: Major progressions in each developmental domain and the ranges of individual variation within each domain

3. B—Feedback: Subject Category I. Students as Learners: Student Development and the Learning Process: Human development in the physical, social, emotional, moral, and cognitive domains: Major progressions in each developmental domain and the ranges of individual variation within each domain

4. A—Feedback: Subject Category I. Students as Learners: Student Development and the Learning Process: Important terms that relate to learning theory

5. B—Feedback: Subject Category I. Students as Learners: Student Development and the Learning Process: Human development in the physical, social, emotional, moral, and cognitive domains: Major progressions in each developmental domain and the ranges of individual variation within each domain

6. B—Feedback: Subject Category I. Students as Learners: Student Development and the Learning Process: Human development in the physical, social, emotional, moral, and cognitive domains: Contributions of important theorists: Jean Piaget

7. C—Feedback: Subject Category I. Students as Learners: Student Development and the Learning Process: Theoretical foundations about how learning occurs—how students construct knowledge, acquire skills, and develop habits of mind: Important terms that relate to learning theory: Seriation

8. C—Feedback: Subject Category I. Students as Learners: Student Development and the Learning Process: Human development in the physical, social, emotional, moral, and cognitive domains: Contributions of important theorists: Jean Piaget

9. D—Feedback: Subject Category I. Students as Learners: Student Development and the Learning Process: Human development in the physical, social, emotional, moral, and cognitive domains: Contributions of important theorists: Jean Piaget

10. D—Feedback: Subject Category I. Students as Learners: Student Development and the Learning Process: Human development in the physical, social, emotional, moral, and cognitive domains: Contributions of important theorists: Lev Vygotsky

11. C—Feedback: Subject Category I. Students as Learners: Student Development and the Learning Process: Human development in the physical, social, emotional, moral, and cognitive domains: Contributions of important theorists: Lev Vygotsky

12. A—Feedback: Subject Category I. Students as Learners: Student Development and the Learning Process: Important terms that relate to learning theory

13. D—Feedback: Subject Category I. Students as Learners: Student Development and the Learning Process: Important terms that relate to learning theory

14. A—Feedback: Subject Category I. Students as Learners: Student Development and the Learning Process: Important terms that relate to learning theory

15. B—Feedback: Subject Category I. Students as Learners: Student Development and the Learning Process: Human development in the physical, social, emotional, moral, and cognitive domains: Major progressions in each developmental domain and the ranges of individual variation within each domain

16. C—Feedback: Subject Category I. Students as Learners: Student Development and the Learning Process: Human development in the physical, social, emotional, moral, and cognitive domains: Contributions of important theorists: Carol Gilligan

17. C—Feedback: Subject Category I. Students as Learners: Students as Diverse Learners: Understanding of influences of individual experiences, talents, and prior learning, as well as language, culture, family, and community values on students' learning: Linguistic patterns and differences

18. B—Feedback: Subject Category I. Students as Learners: Student Development and the Learning Process: Human development in the physical, social, emotional, moral, and cognitive domains: Impact of students' physical, social, emotional, moral, and cognitive development on their learning and how to address these factors when making decisions

All Subject Categories are as listed in the ETS Principles of Learning and Teaching, *Tests at a Glance*, located at *ftp://ftp.ets.org/pub/tandl/0522.pdf.*

CHAPTER 3

Social Contexts and Socioemotional Development

1. Which of the following provides the best example of the microsystem, as described in Bronfenbrenner's ecological theory? (Text Hint: See page 68)

   a. Students interact directly with their teacher.

   b. A parent attends a parent-teacher conference without the student.

   c. Local government approves increased funding for public school libraries.

   d. Society progresses toward acceptability of females serving in more administrative roles in the schools.

2. The link between the home and the school is an example of a (an) _____. (Text Hint: See page 68)

   a. microsystem

   b. mesosystem

   c. exosystem

   d. macrosystem

   e. chronosystem

3. The school board passes a new rule that limits the number of students allowed in each classroom in order to enhance teacher-student relationships. This is an example of which environmental system? (Text Hint: See page 69)

   a. Microsystem

   b. Mesosystem

   c. Exosystem

   d. Macrosystem

   e. Chronosystem

4. Which of the following provides the best example of the macrosystem, as described in Bronfenbrenner's ecological theory? (Text Hint: See page 70)

   a. Students interact directly with their teacher.

   b. A parent attends a parent-teacher conference without the student.

   c. Local government approves increased funding for public school libraries.

   d. Society progresses toward acceptability of females serving in more administrative roles in the schools.

5. Which of the following is the final stage of development, as proposed by Erikson? (Text Hint: See page 72)

   a. Autonomy versus shame and doubt

   b. Trust versus mistrust

   c. Integrity versus despair

   d. Identity versus identity confusion

6. According to Erikson's life-span development theory, at approximately what age does a person undergo the stage of autonomy versus shame and doubt? (Text Hint: See page 71)
    a. The first year
    b. The second year
    c. Age 6 to puberty
    d. Adolescence

7. On the basis of Erikson's life-span development theory, which of the following strategies would best enable a teacher to stimulate identity exploration in adolescents? (Text Hint: See page 73)
    a. Encourage individuals to express their views freely.
    b. Structure activities around success rather than failure.
    c. Provide opportunities for fantasy play.
    d. Evaluate students' opinions carefully and critically.

8. Children are most likely to have high self-esteem and get along well with their peers when raised with which of the following styles of parenting? (Text Hint: See page 74)
    a. Indulgent
    b. Neglectful
    c. Authoritarian
    d. Authoritative

9. Researchers who study peer relations among children have noted that "popular" children typically display which of the following characteristics? (Text Hint: See page 81)
    a. They listen carefully.
    b. They are conceited.
    c. They engage in delinquent behavior.
    d. They are aggressive.

10. Of the following activities, which is most "developmentally appropriate" for school children between 5 and 8 years of age? (Text Hint: See page 84)
    a. Highly structured activity
    b. Reading silently while sitting at a desk
    c. Teacher-directed lesson
    d. Pursuit of student-selected project

11. Which of the following actions by teachers would most likely increase the self-esteem of an elementary school child? (Text Hint: See page 91)
    a. Complimenting the student for being polite toward others
    b. Criticizing the student for making a mistake on a homework assignment
    c. Punishing the student for interrupting somebody else
    d. Showing little interest in the student's work

12. Which of the following statements best describes a student with identity diffusion? (Text Hint: See page 92)
    a. The student has explored career paths and made a commitment toward a goal.
    b. The student has accepted someone else's idea for a career path and made a commitment toward that goal.
    c. The student has not explored career paths and lacks a goal.
    d. The student has explored career paths but has made no commitments toward any path.

13. Alina, a high school student, loves to work with computers. She is also very active in student government. She would like to pursue a career that involves interacting with people. She is considering careers in computer programming and computer sales, as well as careers in politics and law. She hopes to make a final decision by the end of this school year. Which of the following labels best describes Alina's identity status? (Text Hint: See page 92)
    a. Identity diffusion
    b. Identity moratorium
    c. Identity achievement
    d. Identity foreclosure

14. A high school student who feels it is wrong to cheat because if he gets caught he will be sent to the office is revealing which level of Kohlberg's moral reasoning? (Text Hint: See page 95)
    a. Preconventional
    b. Conventional
    c. Postconventional

15. An individual in the conventional level of Kohlberg's theory would turn to which of the following when making a moral decision? (Text Hint: See page 96)
    a. Family expectations
    b. Potential punishment involved
    c. Individual values
    d. Personal needs and desires

16. An individual in the postconventional level of Kohlberg's theory would turn to which of the following when making a moral decision? (Text Hint: See page 96)
    a. Family expectations
    b. Potential punishment involved
    c. Individual values
    d. Personal needs and desires

17. Kohlberg's second level of morality, reflecting an internalization of standards created by other people in society, is called _____. (Text Hint: See page 96)
    a. preconventional
    b. conventional
    c. midconventional
    d. postconventional

18. Individuals who evaded the draft due to fear for their lives would be considered _____; while those who did so out of principles of peace would be _____. (Text Hint: See page 95)
    a. preconventional; postconventional
    b. conventional; preconventional
    c. postconventional; conventional
    d. conventional; postconventional

19. Mr. Johnson utilizes an activity within his social studies class that involves students volunteering in the community. Students are given the option of helping the elderly, working in a hospital, or assisting Habitat for Humanity. This is a good example of _____ (Text Hint: See page 98)
    a. character education
    b. values clarification
    c. cognitive moral education
    d. service learning

20. Kohlberg and Gilligan have proposed theories of moral development. Kohlberg's focuses on _____; Gilligan's focuses on _____. (Text Hint: See page 97)
    a. justice; care
    b. care; justice
    c. rightness; wrongness
    d. relationships; abstract reasoning

21. Researchers have found that in some ethnic groups, aspects of the authoritarian parenting style may be associated with _____. (Text Hint: See page 75)
    a. pro-social behaviors
    b. identity diffusion
    c. positive child outcomes, such as high academic achievement
    d. enhanced language development

22. The current controversy about early childhood education is largely comprised of three groups: advocates of a constructivist approach, advocates of an instructivist approach, and _____. (Text Hint: See page 86)
    a. advocates of programs that emphasize children's intellectual development
    b. advocates of home-based programs
    c. advocates of culture-based curriculum
    d. advocates of authoritarian instruction

23. The NAEYC states that standards in early childhood education are useful when they _____. (Text Hint: See page 86)
    a. guide disciplinary consequences for children
    b. are developed by local governments
    c. emphasize developmentally appropriate content
    d. are used to rank and place children

24. A child's low self-esteem may be caused by _____. (Text Hint: See page 91)
    a. competence in an area
    b. family conflict
    c. emotional support
    d. social approval

25. To improve her students' prosocial behavior, Ms. Tilly moderates whole-group discussions when there are disagreements or misunderstandings among students. She asks questions that help students understand one another's needs, feelings, and perspectives. Which type of question would Ms. Tilly most likely ask her students? (Text Hint: See page 99)
    a. How would you feel if someone messed up your desk like that?
    b. Would you like to go to the principal's office?
    c. Why are you so destructive?
    d. Who messed up Jerome's desk?

Answer Key

1. A—Feedback: Subject Category I. Students as Learners: Student development and the learning process: Human development in the physical, social, emotional, moral, and cognitive domains: Contributions of Bronfenbrenner

2. B—Feedback: Subject Category I. Students as Learners: Student development and the learning process: Important terms that relate to learning theory: Mesosystem

3. C—Feedback: Subject Category I. Students as Learners: Student development and the learning process: Important terms that relate to learning theory: Exosystem

4. D—Feedback: Subject Category I. Students as Learners: Student development and the learning process: Important terms that relate to learning theory: Macrosystem

5. C—Feedback: Subject Category I. Students as Learners: Student development and the learning process: Human development in the physical, social, emotional, moral, and cognitive domains: The major progressions in each developmental domain and the ranges of individual variation within each domain

6. B—Feedback: Subject Category I. Students as Learners: Student development and the learning process: Human development in the physical, social, emotional, moral, and cognitive domains: The major progressions in each developmental domain and the ranges of individual variation within each domain

7. A—Feedback: Subject Category I. Students as Learners: Student development and the learning process: Human development in the physical, social, emotional, moral, and cognitive domains: The impact of students' physical, social, emotional, moral, and cognitive development on their learning and how to address these factors when making instructional decisions

8. D—Feedback: Subject Category I. Students as Learners: Students as Diverse Learners: How students' learning is influenced by individual experiences, talents, and prior learning, as well as language, culture, family, and community values: Family backgrounds

9. A—Feedback: Subject Category I. Students as Learners: Students as Diverse Learners: How students' learning is influenced by individual experiences, talents, and prior learning, as well as language, culture, family, and community values

10. D—Feedback: Subject Category I. Students as Learners: Students as Diverse Learners: How students' learning is influenced by individual experiences, talents, and prior learning, as well as language, culture, family, and community values: Age-appropriate knowledge and behavior

11. A—Feedback: Subject Category I. Students as Learners: Student motivation and the learning environment: Factors and situations that are likely to promote or diminish students' motivation to learn; how to help students become self-motivated

12. C—Feedback: Subject Category I. Students as Learners: Student development and the learning process: Human development in the physical, social, emotional, moral, and cognitive domains: The major progressions in each developmental domain and the ranges of individual variation within each domain

13. B—Feedback: Subject Category I. Students as Learners: Student development and the learning process: Human development in the physical, social, emotional, moral, and cognitive domains: The major progressions in each developmental domain and the ranges of individual variation within each domain

14. A—Feedback: Subject Category I. Students as Learners: Student development and the learning process: Human development in the physical, social, emotional, moral, and cognitive domains: Theoretical contributions of important theorists: Lawrence Kohlberg

15. A—Feedback: Subject Category I. Students as Learners: Student development and the learning process: Human development in the physical, social, emotional, moral, and cognitive domains: Theoretical contributions of important theorists: Lawrence Kohlberg

16. C—Feedback: Subject Category I. Students as Learners: Student development and the learning process: Human development in the physical, social, emotional, moral, and cognitive domains: Theoretical contributions of important theorists: Lawrence Kohlberg

17. B—Feedback: Subject Category I. Students as Learners: Student development and the learning process: Human development in the physical, social, emotional, moral, and cognitive domains: Theoretical contributions of important theorists: Lawrence Kohlberg

18. A—Feedback: Subject Category I. Students as Learners: Student development and the learning process: Human development in the physical, social, emotional, moral, and cognitive domains: Theoretical contributions of important theorists: Lawrence Kohlberg

19. D—Feedback: Subject Category II. Instruction and Assessment: Instructional Strategies: Methods for enhancing student learning through the use of a variety of resources and materials: Service learning and PRAXIS Feedback: Subject Category IV. Profession and Community: The Larger Community: The role of the school as a resource to the larger community

20. A—Feedback: Subject Category I. Students as Learners: Student development and the learning: Human development in the physical, social, emotional, moral, and cognitive domains: Theoretical Contributions of important theorists: Lawrence Kohlberg and Carol Gilligan

21. C—Feedback: Subject Category I. Students as Learners: Students as Diverse Learners: Differences in the ways students learn and perform: Cultural expectations and styles

22. A—Feedback: Subject Category I. Students as Learners: Students as Diverse Learners: How students' learning is influenced by individual experiences, talents, and prior learning, as well as language, culture, family, and community values: Age-appropriate knowledge and behavior

23. C—Feedback: Subject Category I. Students as Learners: Students as Diverse Learners: How students' learning is influenced by individual experiences, talents, and prior learning, as well as language, culture, family, and community values: Age-appropriate knowledge and behavior

24. B—Feedback: Subject Category IV. Profession and Community: The Larger Community: Factors in the students' environment outside of school (family circumstances, community environments, health and economic conditions) that may influence students' life and learning

25. A—Feedback: Subject Category III. Communication Techniques: Types of questions that can stimulate discussion in different ways for different purposes: Promoting a caring community

All Subject Categories are as listed in the ETS Principles of Learning and Teaching, *Tests at a Glance*, located at *ftp://ftp.ets.org/pub/tandl/0522.pdf*.

CHAPTER 4

Individual Variations

1. According to William Stern's 1912 definition of intelligence quotient (IQ), a person would have an IQ greater than 100 under which of the following conditions? (Text Hint: See page 107)

    a. A person's chronological age is greater than his or her own mental age.

    b. A person's mental age is greater than his or her own chronological age.

    c. A person earns average scores on an intelligence test, as compared to other individuals of the same chronological age.

    d. A person earns a higher than average score on an intelligence test, as compared to other individuals of the same chronological age.

2. William Stern's (1912) intelligence quotient is defined as which of the following? (Text Hint: See page 107)

    a. A person's chronological age divided by the person's mental age, multiplied by 100

    b. A person's mental age divided by the person's chronological age, multiplied by 100

    c. A person's mental age divided by a standard value for their age, multiplied by 100

    d. A person's mental age divided by the average mental age for other people of the same chronological age, multiplied by 100

3. Which is the truest representation of a normal distribution? (Text Hint: See page 107)

    a. Distribution where most scores fall in the middle and some scores fall higher and lower.

    b. Distribution of normal people's scores

    c. Distribution where some scores fall in the middle but most fall toward the extremes

    d. There is no "normal" distribution when dealing with the social sciences.

4. Which of the following individuals proposed that there are eight types of intelligence and developed Project Spectrum to apply this information to classroom teaching? (Text Hint: See page 111)

    a. Robert Sternberg

    b. William Stern

    c. Alfred Binet

    d. Howard Gardner

5. Which of the following descriptions of students reveals the greatest level of "analytical" intelligence, as proposed by Sternberg? (Text Hint: See page 110)

    a. Carlos has won numerous awards for his ability to play the piano.

    b. Mika is a champion tennis player.

    c. Anna won the science fair for designing an irrigation system.

    d. Kara earned a perfect score on her midterm history exam.

6. All of the following skills are included in Howard Gardner's eight types of intelligence except which one? (Text Hint: See page 111)
   a. Sensory skills
   b. Movement skills
   c. Verbal skills
   d. Intrapersonal skills

7. Which of Gardner's intelligences is involved in an activity calling for self-reflection and setting life goals? (Text Hint: See page 111)
   a. Verbal skills
   b. Interpersonal skills
   c. Intrapersonal skills
   d. Naturalist skills

8. A psychologist who wants to emphasize the importance of nature in the nature-nurture debate would cite which of the following factors as being most influential in an individual's intelligence? (Text Hint: See page 117)
   a. The individual attended preschool.
   b. The individual enjoys reading books.
   c. The individual does well in school.
   d. The individual's parents have high IQs.

9. Which of the following best describes a criticism of tracking? (Text Hint: See page 121)
   a. Slower students in each track "hold back" the progress of the class.
   b. Better students in each track set the pace at which topics are covered.
   c. Students in the low-track group are stigmatized.
   d. A small percentage of students in each track are destined to fail.

10. Which of the following would be the best example of an impulsive student? (Text Hint: See page 124)
    a. Lamar actively sets his own learning goals.
    b. Rhonda performs poorly in school yet is good at problem-solving when it is in an area of her interest.
    c. Jonathan is an above-average student who has a knack for quickly and accurately coming up with the answers.
    d. Sheila resolves problems in interpersonal relationships through thoughtful introspection.

11. Which of the following would be the best example of a surface style learner? (Text Hint: See page 124)
    a. Uses systematic reasoning and logic when making decisions
    b. Enjoys working in small groups rather than working alone
    c. Evaluates and criticizes other people's points of view
    d. Relies on intuition when solving problems

12. Which of the following is the most accurate way to conceptualize learning and thinking styles? (Text Hint: See page 125)
    a. They are heavily dependent on intelligence.
    b. They may be dependent on the content domain.
    c. They are reliably consistent across content domains.
    d. You've either got them or you don't.

13. A student who is emotionally stable would most accurately be described as which of the following? (Text Hint: See page 127)

    a. Careful, organized, and disciplined

    b. Sociable, fun-loving, and affectionate

    c. Calm, secure, and self-satisfied

    d. Imaginative, interested in variety, and independent

14. Rolanda generally responds to new experiences negatively, is impulsive, and is sometimes aggressive. How would you characterize Rolanda's temperament? (Text Hint: See page 127)

    a. Easy

    b. Difficult

    c. Slow-to-warm-up

15. Which of the following would be the best example of a slow-to-warm-up child? (Text Hint: See page 127)

    a. Lily is fairly accommodating but is often not interested in doing things.

    b. Reece is a happy child who gets along with acquaintances of the family but can be hesitant around complete strangers.

    c. Peter is aggressive and usually rejects new people in his life.

16. To help surface learners think more deeply, teachers can _____. (Text Hint: See page 125)

    a. give assignments that require students to fit information into a larger framework

    b. set up a system that rewards deep thinking and punishes surface thinking

    c. ask questions that require memory and recall

    d. Surface learners are "hardwired" to think in this manner. Nothing can be done to alter this style

17. Imagine a teacher who prefers that her classroom is quiet and controlled. How would this teacher most likely label her bodily-kinesthetic and extroverted students?. (Text Hint: See pages 127–128)

    a. Temperamental

    b. Easy

    c. Slow-to-warm-up

    d. Difficult

18. To avoid using information about a student's intelligence in negative ways, teachers should _____. (Text Hint: See pages 109–110)

    a. base their expectations of students on IQ scores

    b. consider the students' intellectual competence in a wide range of areas

    c. develop advanced curriculum to meet the needs of students with high IQ scores

    d. not gain access to students' IQ scores

Answer Key

1. B—Feedback: Subject Category I. Students as Learners: Student Development and the Learning Process: Theoretical foundations about how learning occurs: Important terms that relate to learning theory: Intelligence

2. B—Feedback: Subject Category I. Students as Learners: Student Development and the Learning Process: Theoretical foundations about how learning occurs: Important terms that relate to learning theory: Intelligence

3. A—Feedback: Subject Category II. Instruction and Assessment: Assessment Strategies: Scoring Assessments: Reporting assessment results: Normal distribution

4. D—Feedback: Subject Category I. Students as Learners: Student Development and the Learning Process: Theoretical foundations about how learning occurs: Examples of important theorists: Howard Gardner

5. D—Feedback: Subject Category I. Students as Learners: Student Development and the Learning Process: Theoretical foundations about how learning occurs: Examples of important theorists: Robert Sternberg

6. A—Feedback: Subject Category I. Students as Learners: Students as Diverse Learners: Differences in the ways students learn and perform: Multiple intelligences

7. C—Feedback: Subject Category I. Students as Learners: Students as Diverse Learners: Differences in the ways students learn and perform: Multiple intelligences

8. D—Feedback: Subject Category I. Students as Learners: Student development and the learning process: Theoretical foundations about how learning occurs: How students construct knowledge, acquire skills, and develop habits of mind

9. C—Feedback: Subject Category I. Students as Learners: Students as Diverse Learners: Approaches for accommodating various learning styles, intelligences, or exceptionalities: Differentiated instruction

10. C—Feedback: Subject Category I. Students as Learners: Students as Diverse Learners: Differences in the ways students learn and perform: Learning styles

11. D—Feedback: Subject Category I. Students as Learners: Students as Diverse Learners: Differences in the ways students learn and perform: Learning styles

12. B—Feedback: Subject Category I. Students as Learners: Students as Diverse Learners: Differences in the ways students learn and perform: Learning styles

13. C—Feedback: Subject Category I. Students as Learners: Students as Diverse Learners: Differences in the ways students learn and perform: Learning styles

14. B—Feedback: Subject Category I. Students as Learners: Student Development and the Learning Process: Impact of students' physical, social, emotional, moral, and cognitive development on their learning and how to address these factors when making decisions

15. A—Feedback: Subject Category I. Students as Learners: Student Development and the Learning Process: Impact of students' physical, social, emotional, moral, and cognitive development on their learning and how to address these factors when making decisions

16. A—Feedback: Subject Category II. Instruction and Assessment: Planning Instruction: Techniques for creating effective bridges between curriculum goals and students' experiences: Encouraging exploration and problem solving

17. D—Feedback: Subject Category I. Students as Learners: Student Development and the Learning Process: Impact of students' physical, social, emotional, moral, and cognitive development on their learning and how to address these factors when making decisions

18. B—Feedback: Subject Category II. Instruction and Assessment: Assessment Strategies: Uses of assessments

All Subject Categories are as listed in the ETS Principles of Learning and Teaching, *Tests at a Glance*, located at *ftp://ftp.ets.org/pub/tandl/0522.pdf*.

CHAPTER 5
Sociocultural Diversity

1. Research suggests that people in all cultures have a tendency to do all of the following except which one? (Text Hint: See page 135)
   a. Believe that what happens in other cultures is unnatural and incorrect.
   b. Behave in ways that favor their own cultural group.
   c. Prefer to associate with individuals from different cultural groups.
   d. Feel proud of their own cultural group.

2. Which of the following strategies would be most appropriate in helping an individualist teacher interact effectively with students from a collectivist culture? (Text Hint: See page 136)
   a. Emphasize cooperation rather than competition.
   b. Encourage students to work independently rather than in groups.
   c. Avoid becoming friendly with students or parents.
   d. Boast about one's own accomplishments frequently.

3. Currently in the United States, what percent of African-American children live below the poverty line? (Text Hint: See page 136)
   a. Less than 20 percent
   b. Approximately 25 percent
   c. Approximately 30 percent
   d. More than 40 percent

4. Critics of bilingual education have voiced concern that bilingual education fails to do which of the following? (Text Hint: See page 143)
   a. Enhance students' self-esteem.
   b. Increase the likelihood of academic success.
   c. Prepare students for the workplace.
   d. Show respect for students' family and community.

5. Which of the following statements best represents a sexist attitude? (Text Hint: See page 156)
   a. In a recent study of eighth graders, boys scored higher on science tests than girls.
   b. Since women do poorly in math, they should not become engineers.
   c. Boys are more active than girls and therefore are more likely to fidget.
   d. Hormonal changes of puberty lead to increased body fat for girls.

6. Which of the following teachers is exhibiting an individualist teaching strategy? (Text Hint: See page 136)
   a. Mr. Randall stresses cooperation in his classroom, especially in group assignments.
   b. Mrs. Simone thinks that students work best if they work independently rather than in groups.
   c. Mr. Tamishi avoids criticism of students in public, he'd rather express criticism in private.
   d. Ms. Ohara thinks that cultivating long-term relationships with parents and students is very effective.

7. Weyne Hill High School has few resources, a large number of students, lower achievement scores, lower graduation rates, and lower percentage of students going to college. According to the information provided in this scenario, where is Weyne Hill High School most likely to be located? (Text Hint: See page 137)

   a. In a higher-income neighborhood

   b. In a lower-income neighborhood

   c. In a collectivist society

   d. none of the above are correct

8. Which of the following teachers is using a teacher strategy that is recommended for students from impoverished backgrounds? (Text Hint: See page 140)

   a. Mrs. Rall is a disciplinarian; she thinks restricting freedom creates a good working environment.

   b. Mr. Mesing disregards motivation as a priority; he thinks it does not effectively impact achievement.

   c. Mr. Amista teaches to improve thinking skills.

   d. Ms. Rysra looks for ways to bring in guest speakers from non-impoverished backgrounds.

9. Ms. Williams is reading over her students' names as listed on her attendance record. Although she has not met any of her future students because the school year will not officially begin until the following day, Ms. Williams is already classifying some of her students as being more intelligent, less competent, or more responsible on the basis of their ethnic names. What is Ms. Williams engaging in? (Text Hint: See page 142)

   a. Creating a hierarchy based on genders

   b. Creating ineffective teaching strategies

   c. Preparing for a collectivist teaching year

   d. Creating stereotypes based on ethnicity

10. Mrs. Perez is a teacher at Springfield Elementary School. She teaches academic subjects to immigrant children in their native languages, while gradually adding English instruction. What type of teacher is Mrs. Perez? (Text Hint: See page 143)

    a. A bilingual education teacher

    b. A special education teacher

    c. A regular classroom teacher

    d. A resource education teacher

11. Hugo and Javier are brothers whose parents moved to the U.S. from a Latin American country a few years ago. Hugo is fourteen and Javier is six. Although both boys can speak and write the English language, Hugo made faster progress than Javier initially. However, Hugo has more difficulty pronouncing the English accent, and he scores significantly lower than his brother on tests of grammar. What is likely to account for the differences in language acquisition of these two brothers? (Text Hint: See page 144)

    a. Javier is more motivated than Hugo and therefore learned the language better.

    b. Javier probably got more individual attention because he is the younger one.

    c. Hugo is older than Javier, and although he can become competent at a second language, it is a more difficult task than that of learning it as a child like his brother.

    d. Hugo probably has a lower IQ than Javier and thus cannot be as competent as his brother at learning a second language.

12. Mr. Denosting wants to empower his students. Which of the following would he need to begin doing in his classroom? (Text Hint: See page 146)

   a. Better representing minorities and cultural groups

   b. Giving students the opportunity to learn about the struggles of different ethnic groups

   c. Helping white and students of color develop multiple perspectives within their curricula

   d. All of the above are correct

13. Ms. Rogers asks her students to write down their family histories so that she may include parts of each of the student's family's past in the class's history lesson. Ms. Rogers is engaging in _____ education. (Text Hint: See page 147)

   a. minority

   b. culturally-relevant

   c. issues-centered

   d. moral

14. Mrs. Guenero is careful of the behaviors that she exhibits in her class because she believes that gender development occurs through observation and imitation of gender behavior. She is also aware of the reinforcement and punishment that she gives her students for gender behavior. She uses _____.(Text Hint: See page 154)

   a. psychoanalytic theory of gender

   b. cognitive developmental theory of gender

   c. gender schema theory

   d. social learning theory

15. Susan and Jerry's teacher has noticed that Susan, like most other female students in her class, enjoys establishing connections and negotiating when she is engaged in talking relationships; whereas Jerry, like most other male students in the class, prefers talk that gives information. This is because _____is usually preferred by females more than by males and _____ is usually preferred by males more than by females. (Text Hint: See page 159)

   a. sexism; gender stereotypes

   b. rapport talk; report talk

   c. report talk; rapport talk

   d. prejudice; discrimination

16. Thirteen-year old Diane is feminine and nurturing yet assertive and commanding. Diane is demonstrating the concept of_____. (Text Hint: See page 160)

   a. androgyny

   b. gender stereotypes

   c. discrimination

   d. prejudice

17. Exposure to more family conflict and violence, less social support, polluted air and water, and inferior schools are factors representative of _____. (Text Hint: See pages 136, 137)

   a. high socioeconomic status

   b. culture bias

   c. gender discrimination

   d. an impoverished childhood environment

18. Parents in impoverished communities _____. (Text Hint: See pages 136, 137)
    a. typically exhibit indulgent parenting styles
    b. are less involved in their children's school activities
    c. are equally likely to read to their children as their counterparts in economically advantaged communities
    d. rarely give their children access to TV

19. Although boys are more physically aggressive than girls, girls are more likely to engage in verbally aggressive behavior such as _____. (Text Hint: See pages 159)
    a. relational aggression
    b. rapport talk
    c. report talk
    d. gender bias

20. Gender-role critics believe that parents should raise their children to be competent individuals, not masculine, feminine, or androgynous. This view is known as _____. (Text Hint: See page 162)
    a. gender denial
    b. sex-typing
    c. gender equity
    d. gender-role transcendence

21. Research shows that teachers communicate differently with girls and boys in the classroom. All of the following suggests that classrooms are biased against girls EXCEPT: (Text Hint: See page 163)
    a. Boys demand more attention, while girls are more likely to quietly wait their turn.
    b. In many classrooms, teachers spend more time watching and interacting with boys while girls work and play quietly on their own.
    c. Teachers often give boys more time to answer a question, more hints at the correct answer, and further tries if they give the wrong answer.
    d. School personnel tend to ignore that many boys clearly have academic problems.

22. Evidence suggests that classroom environments are biased against boys because _____. (Text Hint: See page 163)
    a. teachers tend to identify more girls than boys as having learning problems
    b. teachers value behaviors such as hyperactivity, which is typically associated with boys
    c. teachers are more likely to criticize boys than girls and stereotype boys' behavior as problematic
    d. teachers are more likely to promote boys to the next grade than girls

23. Mrs. Williams' classroom is filled with books, posters, and other resources related to different American cultures. She communicates high expectations for all of her students, regardless of ethnicity or social background. Mrs. Williams is implementing effective teaching strategies for _____. (Text Hint: See page 153).
    a. multicultural education
    b. culture bias
    c. second-language learning
    d. mentoring

24. Mrs. Jenkins brought copies of letters written by Revolutionary War soldiers to her social studies classroom. After reading the letters aloud, she asked her students to select one soldier and write a letter back to him. The war letters are examples of _____. (Text Hint: See page 149)

    a. jigsaw classroom materials

    b. state-mandated curriculum

    c. biased materials

    d. primary documents

25. Mr. Newell's classroom displays pictures of children from around the world and his bookshelves contain a wide range of books and magazines. The majority of his students come from diverse backgrounds and one of Mr. Newell's class rules is that no child may be teased or excluded on the basis of race, ethnicity or gender. Mr. Newell is implementing which kind of classroom curriculum? (Text Hint: See page 149)

    a. Anti-bias curriculum

    b. State curriculum

    c. Emergent curriculum

    d. Subject matter curriculum

Answer Key

1. C—Feedback: Subject Category I. Students as Learners: Students as Diverse Learners: Differences in the ways students learn and perform: Cultural expectations and styles

2. A—Feedback: Subject Category I. Students as Learners: Students as Diverse Learners: Differences in the ways students learn and perform: Cultural expectations and styles

3. D—Feedback: Subject Category IV. Profession and Community: The Larger Community: Factors in the students' environment outside of school (family circumstances, community environments, health, and economic conditions) that may influence students' life and learning

4. C—Feedback: Subject Category I. Students as Learners: Students as Diverse Learners: Process of second language acquisition and strategies to support the learning of students

5. B—Feedback: Subject Category I. Students as Learners: Students as Diverse Learners: Differences in the ways students learn and perform: Gender differences

6. B—Feedback: Subject Category II. Instruction and Assessment: Instructional Strategies: Major categories, advantages, and appropriate uses of instructional strategies: Independent study

7. B—Feedback: Subject Category IV. Profession and Community: The Larger Community: Factors in the students' environment outside of school (family circumstances, community environments, health, and economic conditions) that may influence students' life and learning

8. C—Feedback: Subject Category II. Instruction and Assessment: Instructional Strategies: Major cognitive processes associated with student learning: Critical thinking and creative thinking

9. D—Feedback: Subject Category I. Students as Learners: Students as Diverse Learners: Differences in the ways students learn and perform: Cultural expectations and styles

10. A—Feedback: Subject Category I. Students as Learners: Students as Diverse Learners: Process of second language acquisition and strategies to support the learning of students

11. C—Feedback: Subject Category I. Students as Learners: Students as Diverse Learners: Process of second language acquisition and strategies to support the learning of students

12. D—Feedback: Subject Category I. Students as Learners: Student Development and the Learning Process: Understanding of influences of individual experiences, talents, and prior learning, as well as language, culture, family, and community values on students' learning: Multicultural backgrounds and the student culture at the school

13. B—Feedback: Subject Category I. Students as Learners: Students as Diverse Learners: Understanding of influences of individual experiences, talents, and prior learning, as well as language, culture, family, and community values on students' learning: Family backgrounds

14. D—Feedback: Subject Category I. Students as Learners: Students as Diverse Learners: Differences in the ways students learn and perform: Gender differences

15. B—Feedback: Subject Category I. Students as Learners: Students as Diverse Learners: Differences in the ways students learn and perform: Gender differences

16. A—Feedback: Subject Category I. Students as Learners: Students as Diverse Learners: Differences in the ways students learn and perform: Gender differences

17. D—Feedback: Subject Category IV. Profession and Community: The Larger Community: Factors in the students' environment outside of school (family circumstances, community environments, health, and economic conditions) that may influence students' life and learning

18. B—Feedback: Subject Category I. Students as Learners: Students as Diverse Learners: Understanding of influences of individual experiences, talents, and prior learning, as well as language, culture, family, and community values on students' learning: Family backgrounds

19. A—Feedback: Subject Category I. Students as Learners: Students as Diverse Learners: Differences in the ways students learn and perform: Gender differences

20. D—Feedback: Subject Category I. Students as Learners: Students as Diverse Learners: Differences in the ways students learn and perform: Gender differences

21. D—Feedback: Subject Category III. Communication Techniques: The effect of cultural and gender differences on communications in the classroom

22. C—Feedback: Subject Category III. Communication Techniques: The effect of cultural and gender differences on communications in the classroom

23. A—Feedback: Subject Category III. Communication Techniques: The effect of cultural and gender differences on communications in the classroom

24. D—Feedback: Subject Category II. Instruction and Assessment: Instructional Strategies: Methods for enhancing student learning through the use of a variety of resources and materials: Primary documents and artifacts

25. A—Feedback: Subject Category II. Instruction and Assessment: Planning Instruction: Techniques for planning instruction to meet curriculum goals, including the incorporation of learning theory, subject matter, curriculum development, and student development: Anti-bias curriculum

All Subject Categories are as listed in the ETS Principles of Learning and Teaching, *Tests at a Glance*, located at *ftp://ftp.ets.org/pub/tandl/0522.pdf*.

CHAPTER 6

Learners Who Are Exceptional

1. Of children with disabilities, approximately what percent are considered mentally retarded? (Text Hint: See page 175)

   a. 6%

   b. 11%

   c. 18%

   d. 23%

2. A student with epilepsy will most likely display which of the following behaviors? (Text Hint: See page 177)

   a. Staring and/or convulsions

   b. Complaining of nasal congestion and earaches

   c. Difficulty learning to spell

   d. Shaking and unclear speech

3. A student whose speech is hoarse, harsh, or too loud has which of the following disorders? (Text Hint: See page 181)

   a. Voice disorder

   b. Language disorder

   c. Fluency disorder

   d. Articulation disorder

4. Hannah has difficulty working independently. When asked to sit in her seat for long periods of time, she frequently gets up to sharpen her pencil, look out the window, or flip through books on the bookshelf. She does poorly on repetitive tasks such as math drills. And she rarely completes her homework. Hannah most likely has which of the following conditions? (Text Hint: See page 186)

   a. Mental retardation

   b. Attention deficit/hyperactivity disorder

   c. Down's syndrome

   d. Dyslexia

5. An enrichment program is a standard option for teaching which of the following groups of children? (Text Hint: See page 202)

   a. Children with attention deficit/hyperactivity disorder

   b. Children with autism

   c. Children who are gifted

   d. Children who are mentally retarded

6. Maria keeps rubbing her eyes during the teacher's lesson, which takes place through the use of an overhead. She also holds books close to her face when she reads and she has even complained to her parents that sometimes things on a page appear to be moving around. Maria has a _____. (Text Hint: See page 176)

   a. receptive disorder

   b. expressive disorder

   c. visual impairment

   d. attention deficit/hyperactivity disorder

7. Joey is once again not following directions. The teacher notices that Joey usually has no problems following directions if he turns one ear toward her or if he asks several times to have the directions repeated. Joey most likely has one of these conditions: (Text Hint: See page 176)

   a. Visual impairment.

   b. Hearing impairment.

   c. Articulation problem.

   d. Mental retardation.

8. A child in your class is identified as being mentally retarded. In addition to having low intelligence, the child will also likely exhibit: (Text Hint: See page 178)

   a. Deficits in adapting to everyday life.

   b. Deficits with regard to social responsibility.

   c. Deficits in skills such as toileting, feeding, and self-control.

   d. Deficits with regard to peer interaction.

   e. All of the above are correct.

9. Erin has problems pronouncing sounds correctly and as a result, she avoids communicating with her peers and is often embarrassed by having to discuss anything with the teacher. Erin's parents have begun to take her to a speech therapist and Erin's speech is slowly improving. Erin is most likely to have_____. (Text Hint: See page 181)

   a. autism

   b. visual impairment

   c. articulation disorder

   d. voice disorder

   e. fluency disorder

10. Tera finds it difficult to communicate with her peers and her teacher. She easily understands what they are saying to her but when she tries to communicate her response and express her thoughts she finds it very difficult. Tera is most likely to have _____. (Text Hint: See page 181)

    a. expressive language disorder

    b. articulation disorder

    c. receptive language disorder

    d. voice disorder

    e. fluency disorder

11. Mrs. Chiden has just been informed that she will have several students in her class next school year with learning disabilities. Mrs. Chiden can expect these students to all _____. (Text Hint: See page 182)

    a. have normal intelligence or above

    b. have difficulty in at least one academic area and usually in several

    c. have no other diagnosed problem or disorder that can be attributing as the cause of the disability.

    d. all of the above are correct

12. Mr. Sanders is concerned about one of his students. The student, Mateo, has serious and persistent problems concerning his relationships with other students; he displays aggression and is often out of control. Mateo displays signs of depression that can last up to several weeks, and he experiences fears that are often school related and interfere with his learning. Mateo is most likely to be suffering from _____. (Text Hint: See page 188)

    a. mental retardation

    b. attention deficit/hyperactivity disorder

    c. emotional and behavioral disorders

    d. sensory disorders

13. Ms. Meyers is a regular classroom teacher who has just begun working with children with special needs. Her principal has advised that she be familiarized with the Individuals with Disabilities Education Act (IDEA), since she will now be interacting with parents whose children have special needs and she will have to create individualized education plans (IEP). Which of the following is not true and therefore not one of the items that Ms. Meyers will be learning about regarding IDEA's specific provisions that relate to the parents of a child with a disability? (Text Hint: See page 191)

    a. Schools are required to send notices to parents of proposed actions.

    b. Parents are not allowed to attend meetings regarding the child's individualized education plans (IEP).

    c. Parents are allowed to attend meetings regarding the child's placement.

    d. Parents have the right to appeal school decisions to an impartial evaluator.

14. Mrs. Barone is using technology in her classroom to help children with disabilities function in the classroom environment. The technology she is using consists of various services and devices that include communication aids, alternative computer keyboards, and adaptive services. What type of technology is Mrs. Barone using? (Text Hint: See page 198)

    a. Assistive technology

    b. Instructional technology

    c. Regular education technology

    d. Receptive technology

15. Hugo has been identified as being gifted. What are the program options available for educating children who are gifted? (Text Hint: See page 202)

    a. Special classes

    b. Acceleration and enrichment programs in the regular classroom setting

    c. Enrichment programs in the regular classroom setting

    d. Mentor and apprenticeship programs in or out of the regular classroom setting or work-study programs in the community

    e. All of the above are correct

16. Rodney is on anticonvulsant medication. However he still has episodes in which he loses consciousness, becomes rigid, shakes, and moves jerkily. This episode can last a few minutes. Rodney most likely has _____. (Text Hint: See page 177)

    a. mental retardation

    b. autism

    c. attention deficit/hyperactivity disorder

    d. epilepsy

17. Most of the students who have been diagnosed with a learning disability have which type of disability? (Text Hint: See page 175)

    a. Emotional disturbances

    b. Autism

    c. Hearing impairments

    d. Speech and language impairments

18. To control their behavior, 85–90 percent of children with ADHD _____. (Text Hint: See page 187)

    a. are placed in classes that emphasize rigorous physical activity

    b. are placed in environments with limited structure

    c. are taking stimulation medication such as Ritalin

    d. are placed in special education classes

19. Which of the following statements is true about students with ADHD? (Text Hint: See page 187)

    a. Most physicians refuse to prescribe medication for children with milder forms of ADHD.

    b. The number of children diagnosed and treated for ADHD has increased substantially, by some estimates doubling in the 1990s.

    c. Girls are diagnosed with ADHD equally as often as boys.

    d. Although signs of ADHD are often present in the preschool years, their classification doesn't take place until the middle school years.

20. In 1975, Congress passed the Education for All Handicapped Children Act. What does this law require? (Text Hint: See page 191).

    a. All students with disabilities receive homebound instruction.

    b. All students with disabilities receive life skills training

    c. All students with disabilities placed in separate, special education classes.

    d. All students with disabilities given a free, appropriate public education.

21. The overrepresentation of minorities in special education programs has led to concern among education leaders. The U.S. Office of Education cites all of these as concerns EXCEPT _____. (Text Hint: See page 193)

    a. students may be underserved or receive services that do not meet their needs

    b. students may be misclassified or inappropriately labeled

    c. special education classes are overcrowded

    d. placement in special education classes may be a form of discrimination

22. Children with disabilities can be placed in a variety of settings. Which of the following is the least restrictive environment? (Text hint: See page 192)

    a. Regular classroom with supplementary instruction

    b. Part of time spent in a resource room

    c. Special schools

    d. Homebound instruction

23. Lauren is a hearing-impaired student who is receiving instruction in a regular second-grade classroom. This approach to educating students with disabilities is called _____. (Text hint: See page 192)

    a. collaborative consultation

    b. inclusion

    c. special education

    d. interactive teaming

Answer Key

1. B—Feedback: Subject Category I. Students as Learners: Students as Diverse Learners: Areas of exceptionality in students' learning: Functional and mental retardation

2. A—Feedback: Subject Category I. Students as Learners: Students as Diverse Learners: Areas of exceptionality in students' learning: Special physical or sensory challenges

3. A—Feedback: Subject Category I. Students as Learners: Students as Diverse Learners: Areas of exceptionality in students' learning: Special physical or sensory challenges

4. B—Feedback: Subject Category I. Students as Learners: Students as Diverse Learners: Areas of exceptionality in students' learning: ADHD

5. C—Feedback: Subject Category I. Students as Learners: Students as Diverse Learners: Approaches for accommodating various learning styles, intelligences, or exceptionalities: Differentiated instruction

6. C—Feedback: Subject Category I. Students as Learners: Students as Diverse Learners: Areas of exceptionality in students' learning: Special physical or sensory challenges

7. B—Feedback: Subject Category I. Students as Learners: Students as Diverse Learners: Areas of exceptionality in students' learning: Special physical or sensory challenges

8. E—Feedback: Subject Category I. Students as Learners: Students as Diverse Learners: Areas of exceptionality in students' learning: Functional and mental retardation

9. C—Feedback: Subject Category I. Students as Learners: Students as Diverse Learners: Areas of exceptionality in students' learning: Special physical or sensory challenges

10. A—Feedback: Subject Category I. Students as Learners: Students as Diverse Learners: Areas of exceptionality in students' learning: Special physical or sensory challenges

11. D—Feedback: Subject Category I. Students as Learners: Students as Diverse Learners: Areas of exceptionality in students' learning: Learning disabilities

12. C—Feedback: Subject Category I. Students as Learners: Students as Diverse Learners: Understanding of influences of individual experiences, talents, and prior learning, as well as language, culture, family, and community values on students' learning: Social and emotional issues

13. B—Feedback: Subject Category I. Students as Learners: Students as Diverse Learners: Legislation and institutional responsibilities relating to exceptional students: Americans with Disabilities Act (ADA), Individuals with Disabilities Education Act (IDEA); Section 504 Protections for Students

14. A—Feedback: Subject Category I. Students as Learners: Students as Diverse Learners: Approaches for accommodating various learning styles, intelligences, or exceptionalities: Differentiated instruction

15. E—Feedback: Subject Category I. Students as Learners: Students as Diverse Learners: Approaches for accommodating various learning styles, intelligences, or exceptionalities: Differentiated instruction

16. D—Feedback: Subject Category I. Students as Learners: Students as Diverse Learners: Areas of exceptionality in students' learning: Special physical or sensory challenges

17. D—Feedback: Subject Category I. Students as Learners: Students as Diverse Learners: Areas of exceptionality in students' learning: Learning disabilities

18. C—Feedback: Subject Category I. Students as Learners: Students as Diverse Learners: Areas of exceptionality in students' learning: ADHD

19. B—Feedback: Subject Category I. Students as Learners: Students as Diverse Learners: Areas of exceptionality in students' learning: ADHD

20. D—Feedback: Subject Category IV. Profession and Community: The Larger Community: Major laws related to students' rights and teacher responsibilities: Appropriate education for students with special needs

21. C—Feedback: Subject Category IV. Profession and Community: The Larger Community: Major laws related to students' rights and teacher responsibilities: Equal education and Appropriate treatment of students

22. A—Feedback: Subject Category I. Students as Learners: Students as Diverse Learners: Legislation and institutional responsibilities relating to exceptional students: Least restrictive environment

23. B—Feedback: Subject Category I. Students as Learners: Students as Diverse Learners: Legislation and institutional responsibilities relating to exceptional students: Inclusion

All Subject Categories are as listed in the ETS Principles of Learning and Teaching, *Tests at a Glance*, located at *ftp://ftp.ets.org/pub/tandl/0522.pdf*.

CHAPTER 7

Behavioral and Social Cognitive Approaches

1. Learning is primarily the result of _____. (Text Hint: See page 210)
   a. development
   b. experience
   c. innate abilities
   d. socialization

2. Which of the following is the best example of classical conditioning? (Text Hint: See page 212)
   a. Harold gets hungry each morning about one half hour before lunchtime.
   b. Susan likes to chew gum during class because it helps her to relax.
   c. Isaac cries when he arrives at the doctor's office because he usually gets shots near the end of each visit.
   d. Andrea takes the long way home after school because she likes to avoid a busy intersection.

3. Ms. Alvarez has been teaching for 20 years. She has learned that it is best to structure her class so that students complete the projects and activities that they really do not like first; only after completing these "disliked" activities can they engage in the projects and activities that they do like. This is an example of: (Text Hint: See page 219)
   a. Negative reinforcement.
   b. Time-out.
   c. Premack principle.
   d. Punishment.

4. Mr. Roberts, having to step out of the class for a moment, tells Melody to watch the class. Melody begins to get teased by her classmates for being a goody-goody and the teacher's pet. When Mr. Roberts returns, Melody tells him that she does not ever want to be left in charge of the class again. In this situation, Melody was_____. (Text Hint: See page 216)
   a. positively reinforced by her classmates
   b. negatively reinforced by her classmates
   c. punished by her classmates
   d. punished by the teacher

5. Which of the following scenarios best depicts "extinction"? (Text Hint: See page 216)

    a. Ivan used to bring his lunch to school every day because his mother always praised him for doing so. Now that she has stopped praising him, he often forgets.

    b. Ruby used to get very nervous when she played her violin in public. She recently started practicing relaxation techniques prior to each performance, and now she usually feels calm.

    c. Heather forgot to take off her muddy shoes at the door until recently, when her mother posted a sign in the hallway.

    d. Dennis runs to the door when he hears a truck pull into the driveway because he knows that his father opens the door within moments of when Dennis hears the sound of his father's car.

6. Which of the following scenarios best depicts a punishment? (Text Hint: See page 216)

    a. A student answers a question correctly. The teacher compliments the student. The student continues to raise her hand to answer questions.

    b. A student answers a question correctly. The teacher stops criticizing the student for not paying attention. The student continues to raise her hand to answer questions.

    c. A student answers a question incorrectly. The teacher criticizes the student for not paying attention. The student begins to pay attention and starts answering questions correctly.

    d. A student answers a question incorrectly. The teacher stops asking the student to answer questions. The student starts paying attention during class.

7. Ms. Santos is explaining geometric angles, when she sees Stanley poke his pencil in Sharon's arm. Sharon winces but does not say anything. Ms. Santos immediately tells Stanley that he has lost 10 minutes of recess. In this scenario, Ms. Santos used a _____. (Text Hint: See page 216)

    a. positive reinforcer

    b. negative reinforcer

    c. punishment

    d. none of the above are correct

8. Mr. Elliot is walking around the learning centers in the room helping his students with their activity. Jack tells Mr. Elliot that Jan is not doing her part of the work, in fact, she is distracting them by telling them jokes. Mr. Elliot privately asks Jan to get to work and stop telling jokes or she will have to go back to her seat and work independently. Jan does not cause further problems in her group. In this example, Mr. Elliot used_____, and it was _____. (Text Hint: See page 216)

    a. punishment, ineffective

    b. negative reinforcer, effective

    c. punishment, effective

    d. negative reinforcer, ineffective

9. Mr. Bristol hands his eighth graders an agenda that tells them the due dates for all of their assignments are exactly one month apart. What type of reinforcement schedule did Mr. Bristol put his eighth graders on? (Text Hint: See page 220)

    a. Fixed ratio

    b. Fixed interval

    c. Variable ratio

    d. Variable interval

10. Every half hour or so, a teacher compliments a certain student for staying in his seat and working quietly, unless the student fails to do so. This teacher is using which of the following schedules of reinforcement? (Text Hint: See page 220)

    a. Fixed-interval

    b. Fixed-ratio

    c. Variable-interval

    d. Variable-ratio

11. Which of the following best represents the social cognitive perspective? (Text Hint: See page 226)

    a. The environment causes behaviors.

    b. The environment and behaviors have a reciprocal relationship.

    c. Behavior is the result of cognitive factors, behavioral factors, and environmental factors.

    d. There is no relationship between the environment, behavior, and personal consequences.

12. The first step in self-regulated learning is _____. (Text Hint: See page 236)

    a. goal-setting and strategic planning

    b. monitoring outcomes and refining strategies

    c. putting a plan into action and monitoring the plan

    d. self-evaluation and self-monitoring

13. Kyle's third grade class is watching a presentation by local college students on how to improve reading and writing skills. Kyle is excited about learning how to improve his reading and writing skills. However, even though he paid close attention to the presentation, and he remembers all the tips that were shown and demonstrated, Kyle does not think that he has the skill that the presenters have. In fact, he thinks that these tips are not ones that he would be able to apply. According to observational learning theory, which of the following processes is Kyle having difficulty with? (Text Hint: See page 228)

    a. Attention

    b. Retention

    c. Production

    d. Motivation

14. Mr. Rojas says "what great behavior Daniel is showing, he is standing quietly in line the way he is supposed to be." Soon, all of the third graders in Mr. Rojas class are standing in line quietly like Daniel. Why did all of the third grade students imitate Daniel's behavior? (Text Hint: See page 229)

    a. Because they were classically conditioned to do so.

    b. Because they watched Daniel, a model, be positively reinforced for doing so and thought they would be positively reinforced if they copied Daniel's behavior.

    c. Because Daniel was negatively reinforced by the teacher and they wanted to be negatively reinforced as well.

    d. Because they watched Daniel, a model, be punished for doing so and thought they would be punished if they did not copy Daniel's behavior.

15. Ally just received an A on her spelling test. Her teacher, Mrs. Succo, compliments her on her achievement. Ally continues to do well on her spelling tests. This scenario best depicts a_____. (Text Hint: See page 216)

    a. positive reinforcer

    b. negative reinforcer

    c. punishment

    d. none of the above are correct

16. Marchand is a first grader in Mr. Tobia's class whose homework would sometimes end up in the wrong bin. Mr. Tobia has decided to always ensure that he reinforces Marchand for putting his homework in the bin labeled "Today's homework" and not in the other bins that Mr. Tobias has in the classroom. Marchand has been placing his homework in the right bin every day. In this scenario, what is Mr. Tobia's intention? (Text Hint: See page 216)

    a. To use generalization on Marchand

    b. To use discrimination on Marchand

    c. To use extinction on Marchand

    d. To use punishment on Marchand

17. Mrs. Renir tells her second graders that once they complete their reading assignment, they may go and play on the computers. In this scenario, Mrs. Renir is using _____. (Text Hint: See page 219)

    a. extinction

    b. generalization

    c. Premack Principle

    d. a schedule of reinforcement

18. Mr. Mijuet had been consistently praising Talan for contributing comments in the class discussions. However, Mr. Mijuet has noticed that Talan has become disruptive and that his comments are frequently not pertinent to the discussion that the class is having. Mr. Mijuet decides to ignore Talan's inappropriate comments and behavior during class discussions and give him attention and praise only when his comments are relevant. Talan's contributions to the class discussion are no longer inappropriate. In this scenario, Mr. Mijuet is using _____. (Text Hint: See page 216)

    a. shaping

    b. prompts

    c. Premack Principle

    d. extinction

19. According to Bandura, what is the concept of self-efficacy? (Text Hint: See page 226)

    a. The belief that one can master a situation and produce positive outcomes.

    b. The belief that one can change the outcome of a situation by providing external consequences.

    c. The belief that one can regulate learning by becoming more aware of how it is that we acquire knowledge.

    d. Occurs when a person observes and imitates someone else's behavior.

20. Winston is very anxious when it comes to taking tests. He usually performs poorly on tests because of his anxiety and not his lack of knowledge. Winston's teacher has decided to have Winston associate relaxation with taking tests. She has Winston imagine a relaxing situation and think of it a few days before the test, the morning of the test, right before taking the test, and finally while he is taking his test. In this example, Winston's teacher is using which of the following: (Text Hint: see page 214)

    a. Generalization.

    b. Systematic desensitization.

    c. Discrimination.

    d. Negative reinforcement.

21. As students in U.S. schools have become more ethnically diverse in recent decades, teacher demographics _____. (Text Hint: See page 229)

    a. have changed to reflect their students' ethnic backgrounds

    b. are about 50 percent African-American

    c. are primarily comprised of African-American and Latino males

    d. are overwhelmingly non-Latino White females

22. Mr. Sanchez invites professionals from the local engineering company to serve as after school mentors. These mentors not only provide academic help but also serve as positive role models. This is an example of _____. (Text Hint: See page 231)
    a. positive reinforcement
    b. observational learning
    c. self-regulatory learning
    d. classic conditioning

23. Tanya is working on a book report that is due the next day in school. She is talking to herself saying, "This is a little confusing, but I think I can do it. If I keep working, I know I'll get it done." This is an example of _____. (Text Hint: See page 234)
    a. observational learning
    b. social cognitive approaches to learning
    c. the Premack Principle
    d. a self-instructional method

24. Dillon agrees to stop pushing at the drinking fountain. His teacher agrees to let him be first at the drinking fountain on Friday if he does not push his peers all week. This is an example of _____. (Text Hint: See page 221)
    a. contracting
    b. prompting
    c. a schedule of reinforcement
    d. extinction

Answer Key

1. B—Feedback: Subject Category I. Students as Learners: Student Development and the Learning Process: Theoretical foundations about how learning occurs—how students construct knowledge, acquire skills, and develop habits of mind: Important terms that relate to learning theory: Learning

2. C—Feedback: Subject Category I. Students as Learners: Student motivation and the learning environment: Important terms that relate to motivation and behavior: Classical conditioning

3. C—Feedback: Subject Category I. Students as Learners: Student motivation and the learning environment: How knowledge of human motivation and behavior should influence strategies for organizing and supporting individual and group work in the classroom

4. C—Feedback: Subject Category I. Students as Learners: Student motivation and the learning environment: Important terms that relate to motivation and behavior: Punishment

5. A—Feedback: Subject Category I. Students as Learners: Student motivation and the learning environment: Important terms that relate to motivation and behavior: Extinction

6. C—Feedback: Subject Category I. See Students as Learners: Student motivation and the learning environment: Important terms that relate to motivation and behavior: Punishment

7. C—Feedback: Subject Category I. Students as Learners: Student motivation and the learning environment: Important terms that relate to motivation and behavior: Punishment

8. B—Feedback: Subject Category I. Students as Learners: Student motivation and the learning environment: Important terms that relate to motivation and behavior: Negative reinforcer

9. B—Feedback: Subject Category I. Students as Learners: Student motivation and the learning environment: Important terms that relate to motivation and behavior: Schedules of reinforcement

10. C—Feedback: Subject Category I. Students as Learners: Student motivation and the learning environment: Important terms that relate to motivation and behavior: Schedules of reinforcement

11. C—Feedback: Subject Category I. Students as Learners: Student motivation and the learning environment: Theoretical foundations about human motivation and behavior

12. A—Feedback: Subject Category I. Students as Learners: Student motivation and the learning environment: How knowledge of human motivation and behavior should influence strategies for organizing and supporting individual and group work in the classroom

13. C—Feedback: Subject Category I. Students as Learners: Student motivation and the learning environment: Important terms that relate to motivation and behavior: Production

14. B—Feedback: Subject Category I. Students as Learners: Student motivation and the learning environment: Important terms that relate to motivation and behavior: Positive reinforcement

15. A—Feedback: Subject Category I. Students as Learners: Student motivation and the learning environment: Important terms that relate to motivation and behavior: Positive reinforcement

16. B—Feedback: Subject Category I. Students as Learners: Student motivation and the learning environment: Important terms that relate to motivation and behavior: Discrimination

17. C—Feedback: Subject Category I. Students as Learners: Student motivation and the learning environment: How knowledge of human motivation and behavior should influence strategies for organizing and supporting individual and group work in the classroom

18. D—Feedback: Subject Category I. Students as Learners: Student motivation and the learning environment: Important terms that relate to motivation and behavior: Extinction

19. A—Feedback: Subject Category I. Students as Learners: Student motivation and the learning environment: Theoretical foundations about human motivation and behavior: Albert Bandura

20. B—Feedback: Subject Category I. Students as Learners: Student motivation and the learning environment: How knowledge of human motivation and behavior should influence strategies for organizing and supporting individual and group work in the classroom

21. D—Feedback: Subject Category I. Students as Learners: Students as Diverse Learners: How students' learning is influenced by individual experiences, talents, and prior learning, as well as language, culture, family, and community values: Multicultural backgrounds

22. B—Feedback: Subject Category II. Instruction and Assessment: Instructional Strategies: Methods for enhancing student learning through the use of a variety of resources and materials: Local experts

23. D—Feedback: Subject Category I. Students as Learners: Student motivation and the learning environment: Important terms that relate to motivation and behavior: Self-efficacy

24. A—Feedback: Subject Category I. Students as Learners: Student motivation and the learning environment: Principles of effective classroom management and strategies to promote positive relationships, cooperation, and purposeful learning: Responding to student misbehavior

All Subject Categories are as listed in the ETS Principles of Learning and Teaching, *Tests at a Glance*, located at *ftp://ftp.ets.org/pub/tandl/0522.pdf*.

CHAPTER 8

The Information-Processing Approach

1. All of the following questions reflect a cognitive information processing approach, except which one? (Text Hint: See page 246)
   a. How do children get information into memory, store it, and retrieve it?
   b. How can teachers help children improve their memory and study strategies?
   c. How do environmental factors influence the age at which a child learns to crawl?
   d. What are the best strategies for helping children become better problem solvers?

2. Which of the following scenarios best demonstrates automaticity? (Text Hint: See page 247)
   a. Margie knows that 3 times 4 equals 12 without thinking about it.
   b. Jordan counts the number of apples in a basket.
   c. Kara practices how to print the alphabet.
   d. Harry uses his fingers to add 5 plus 4.

3. Which of the following scenarios presents the best example of encoding? (Text Hint: See page 247)
   a. Tamara is writing a letter.
   b. Brian is practicing how to count.
   c. Joan remembers her first day of school.
   d. Julie is listening to music.

4. Which of the following scenarios best depicts elaboration? (Text Hint: See page 252)
   a. Jose memorized a list of spelling words for a spelling bee.
   b. Kate and Sue brainstormed ideas for a poster.
   c. Taylor practiced writing the numbers and alphabet.
   d. John thought about his vegetable garden when his class studied botany.

5. Which of the following examples best illustrates chunking? (Text Hint: See page 254)
   a. Georgia thinks of personal examples when learning about new concepts in science.
   b. Jodi classifies animals based on common features and differences.
   c. Adam uses symbols to represent words that he has difficulty spelling.
   d. Harold and Mohammed work together when designing a telescope.

6. Which of the following statements best describes the nature of declarative memory? (Text Hint: See page 259)
   a. Karen applies knowledge to perform a certain task.
   b. Scott recognizes a famous person.
   c. Natasha is able to provide specific factual information about an event.
   d. Ivan recalls a specific event from his or her past.

7. Multiple-choice questions assess a student's ability to _____. (Text Hint: See page 263)

   a. recognize the correct answer

   b. recall the correct answer

   c. construct the correct answer

   d. explain the correct answer

8. According to the decay theory, which of the following is the cause of forgetting? (Text Hint: See page 263)

   a. Lack of schema

   b. Disintegration of memory traces

   c. Lack of initial encoding

   d. Interference by new information

9. Mr. Abraham is having a guest speaker come into his first grade class to give his students a lesson on space travel. The guest speaker is very humorous and brought with her attention-grabbing devices and pictures. Immediately upon the speaker's leaving, Mr. Abraham discusses the presentation with his class. He is puzzled to discover that although the students enjoyed the presentation, they did not seem to know the subject matter of the presentation. Most students could not recall what the guest speaker had actually said. They did, however, remember all of the unusual items that the guest speaker brought with her. In this scenario, why did Mr. Abraham's class have trouble recalling the subject matter of the presentation? (Text Hint: See Ch 8, page 249)

   a. Because the students lacked short-term memory

   b. Because the students' attention was drawn away from the lesson by the interesting objects the speaker brought in to the class

   c. Because the students do not have memory traces

   d. Because the students experienced the decay theory

10. Susan is excited about returning to school after summer vacation. Her first day of middle school ended great, and once Susan is at home she begins to recall that day's events. Susan's memory of the day's events is called_____. (Text Hint: See page 259)

    a. procedural knowledge

    b. chunking

    c. episodic memory

    d. semantic memory

11. Brian, an eleventh grader, is taking his French exam. He prepared for this exam and he knows the information; however, while taking the exam Brian is having trouble recalling the information because the teacher did not provide a word bank from which to choose the answer. Brian's forgetting is most likely due to: (Text Hint: See page 263)

    a. Cue-dependent forgetting.

    b. Interference theory.

    c. Decay theory.

    d. Sensory register.

12. Ursula is taking an algebra exam and in order to remember the order in which to perform certain functions on the exam, Ursula aids her memory by writing down the word 'GRUMPY' on her paper. She smiles knowing that this will help her reach the right answers. Ursula is using _____. (Text Hint: See page 264)

    a. the method of loci

    b. rhymes

    c. acronyms

    d. keyword method

13. Todd and Kimberly are seated opposite one another getting ready to begin a game of Scrabble. Todd is 10 years old and Kimberly is 15 years old. Their camp counselor says to Kimberly, "Now Kimberly, go easy on Todd, remember he is younger than you and there are differences in memory ability between the two of you." However, much to Kimberly and the camp counselor's surprise, Todd beats Kimberly at every game he plays with her. In fact, Todd has competed in Scrabble matches and has received awards and trophies. Todd's winning all of the matches against Kimberly was most likely because _____. (Text Hint: See page 266)

    a. Todd's intelligence was greater than Kimberly's

    b. Todd was probably cheating and Kimberly did not notice

    c. Todd was just lucky and Kimberly was not

    d. Todd was an expert in Scrabble and Kimberly was a beginner

14. Mrs. Right wants to ensure that her students remember the information she is presenting in class today. Thus, after she is done with the lesson, she begins a question and answer period in which she asks the students to generate personal examples of the concepts they just learned. What is Mrs. Right using? (Text Hint: See Ch 8, page 252)

    a. Encoding

    b. Elaboration

    c. Retrieval

    d. Chunking

15. Mr. Tyrell wants his tenth grade students to learn a list of Spanish verbs and their conjugations by the following week. He tells them to make sure that they memorize the list by the exam day. According to Mr. Tyrell's instructions, what process are students most likely to use to remember the list of verbs and their conjugations? (Text Hint: See page 251)

    a. Organization

    b. Rehearsal

    c. Elaboration

    d. Attention

16. Mrs. Isadora asks to see Toby during recess to discuss his last test performance. "Toby, I want to know why you did not tell me that you were having difficulties," Mrs. Isadora asks. "I thought I knew that stuff. I always think that but then when I take the test I don't do so well," Toby replies. What is likely to be the cause of Toby's problems? (Text Hint: See page 248)

    a. Toby lacks metacognition.

    b. Toby is exceeding the capacity of the sensory register.

    c. Toby is lacking working memory.

    d. Toby is employing organization.

17. Mrs. Kily's ninth grade science class is learning the difference between the states of matter: solid, gas, and liquid. She tells them to imagine the molecules in these states of matter as Ping-Pong balls. Therefore she tells them to envision a solid as a group of Ping-Pong balls lumped together in a mass, a gas as all of those Ping-Pong balls moving very fast over an area, and a liquid as those ping pong balls moving but slower than they did as a gas. Mrs. Kily is helping her students remember by _____. (Text Hint: See page 253)

    a. metacognition

    b. serial positioning effect

    c. construction of images

    d. mnemonics

18. Quinn tells his teacher that someone in the class took his pencil while he was working with his reading group. He says that several children have explanations for what happened to his pencil, and he would like her to hear them all. Although several of the children claim they saw what happened, they all have different versions of the event. Nathan says that Ron took the pencil just like he took Nathan's eraser yesterday. Keri tells the teacher that it was Ron who took the pencil because he was sitting next to Quinn's desk at the time. Finally, Cecilia says that it was Teresa who took the pencil and then gave it to Ron in exchange for his multicolored pen. The students' various stories of what happened to Ron's pencil are best accounted for by _____. (Text Hint: See page 260)

    a. schema theories

    b. network theories

    c. encoding specificity principle

    d. expertise

19. Experts do all of the following EXCEPT _____. (Text Hint: See page 266)

    a. approach new situations with the same strategies

    b. detect meaningful patterns of information

    c. retrieve key aspects of their knowledge with little effort

    d. acquire extensive knowledge that is organized in a manner that shows a deep understanding of the subject

20. Jake has difficulty in determining which information is central to understanding a concept and which details are peripheral. This is an example of the _____ stage of expertise. (Text Hint: See page 268)

    a. retrieval

    b. encoded

    c. metacognitive

    d. acclimation

21. Rehearsal is a strategy best used when students need to _____. (Text Hint: See page 251)

    a. generate examples of a concept

    b. encode information for long-term memory

    c. remember a list of items for a brief period of time

    d. organize information

22. The three types of memory that vary according to their time frames include all of the following EXCEPT _____. (Text Hint: See page 255)

    a. sensory memory

    b. semantic memory

    c. short-term memory

    d. long-term memory

Answer Key

1. C—Feedback: Subject Category I. Students as Learners: Student Development and the Learning Process: Theoretical foundations about how learning occurs: how students construct knowledge, acquire skills, and develop habits of mind

2. A—Feedback: Subject Category I. Students as Learners: Student Development and the Learning Process: Important terms that relate to learning theory

3. D—Feedback: Subject Category I. Students as Learners: Student Development and the Learning Process: Important terms that relate to learning theory

4. D—Feedback: Subject Category I. Students as Learners: Student Development and the Learning Process: Important terms that relate to learning theory

5. B—Feedback: Subject Category I. Students as Learners: Student Development and the Learning Process: Important terms that relate to learning theory

6. C—Feedback: Subject Category I. Students as Learners: Student Development and the Learning Process: Important terms that relate to learning theory: Memory

7. A—Feedback: Subject Category II. Instruction and Assessment: Instructional Strategies: The major cognitive processes associated with student learning: Memorization and recall

8. B—Feedback: Subject Category I. Students as Learners: Student Development and the Learning Process: Important terms that relate to learning theory: Memory

9. B—Feedback: Subject Category I. Students as Learners: Student Development and the Learning Process: Important terms that relate to learning theory: Memory

10. C—Feedback: Subject Category I. Students as Learners: Student Development and the Learning Process: Important terms that relate to learning theory: Memory

11. A—Feedback: Subject Category I. Students as Learners: Student Development and the Learning Process: Important terms that relate to learning theory: Memory

12. C—Feedback: Subject Category II. Instruction and Assessment: Instructional Strategies: Principles, techniques, and methods associated with various instructional strategies: Direct instruction: Mnemonics

13. D—Feedback: Subject Category I. Students as Learners: Student development and the learning process: Important terms that relate to learning theory: Expert and novice knowledge

14. B—Feedback: Subject Category II. Instruction and Assessment: Instructional Strategies: Principles, techniques, and methods associated with various instructional strategies: Direct instruction: Questioning and Feedback: Subject Category III. Communication Techniques: Types of questions that can stimulate discussion in different ways for different purposes: Probing for learner understanding

15. B—Feedback: Subject Category II. Instruction and Assessment: Instructional Strategies: The major cognitive processes associated with student learning: Memorization and recall

16. A—Feedback: Subject Category II. Instruction and Assessment: Instructional Strategies: Major categories of instructional strategies: Reflection

17. C—Feedback: Subject Category II. Instruction and Assessment: Instructional Strategies: Major cognitive processes associated with student learning: Representation of ideas

18. A—Feedback: Subject Category I. Students as Learners: Student development and the learning process: Important terms that relate to learning theory: Schemata

19. A—Feedback: Subject Category I. Students as Learners: Student development and the learning process: Theoretical foundations about how learning occurs: how students construct knowledge, acquire skills, and develop habits of mind

20. D—Feedback: Subject Category I. Students as Learners: Student development and the learning process: Important terms that relate to learning theory: Acclimation

21. C—Feedback: Subject Category II. Instruction and Assessment: Instructional Strategies: The major cognitive processes associated with student learning: Memorization and recall

22. B—Feedback: Subject Category I. Students as Learners: Student Development and the Learning Process: Important terms that relate to learning theory: Memory

All Subject Categories are as listed in the ETS Principles of Learning and Teaching, *Tests at a Glance*, located at *ftp://ftp.ets.org/pub/tandl/0522.pdf*.

CHAPTER 9

Complex Cognitive Processes

1. All of the following are steps used in the rule-sample strategy, except which one? (Text Hint: See page 283)

   a. Define the concept.

   b. Clarify terms in the definition.

   c. Give examples to illustrate the key features or characteristics.

   d. Do not provide additional examples, as it confuses the students.

2. Theo is creating a _____, which is a visual representation of a concept that is filled with connections and hierarchical organizations pertinent to each concept. Theo is including examples and non-examples of the concept in order to gain a more sound understanding of the concept. (Text Hint: See page 284)

   a. hypothesis testing

   b. concept map

   c. fixation

   d. prototype matching

3. Which of the following scenarios presents the best example of prototype matching? (Text Hint: See page 285)

   a. Tyler is deciding whether an item is a member of a category by comparing it with the most typical item(s) of the category.

   b. Brianna is naming all of the non-examples of a concept.

   c. Joseph is writing all of the examples of a concept on the board.

   d. Jana is listening to the teacher list all of the defining features of a concept.

4. Which of the following scenarios best depicts a student or students thinking critically? (Text Hint: See page 288)

   a. Abdul memorized a list of spelling words for a spelling bee.

   b. Felix and Sue are thinking reflectively and productively, as well as evaluating the evidence.

   c. Gabriel and Todd are brainstorming ideas for the class play.

   d. Martin is trying to think of all of the examples of the concept "vegetable."

5. Which of the following examples best illustrates problem solving? (Text Hint: See page 298)

   a. Athena thinks of personal examples when learning about new concepts in geometry.

   b. Isabella classifies animals based on common features.

   c. Cheryl uses made-up symbols to represent words that she is memorizing.

   d. Mona and Asha work together to find an appropriate way to attain a goal.

6. A type of formal reasoning that involves four parts, with the relation of the last two parts being the same as the relation of the first two parts is called _____. (Text Hint: See page 287)

    a. an analogy

    b. deductive reasoning

    c. inductive reasoning

    d. critical thinking

7. If a student has belief perseverance, which of the following would he or she most likely display? (Text Hint: See page 291)

    a. A tendency to search for and use information that supports rather than refutes their ideas

    b. A tendency to falsely report, after the fact, that he or she accurately predicted an event

    c. A tendency to have more confidence in judgment and decisions than he or she should based on probability or past occurrence

    d. A tendency to hold onto a belief even in the face of contradictory evidence

8. Mr. Allport has shown his first grade class four different shapes drawn on a large piece of poster board. He has secretly selected one of these shapes and he will now ask his students to develop educated guesses about what concept he has selected. Students begin asking questions related to the different shapes and by eliminating non-examples, they will be able to identify what concept Mr. Allport has chosen. In this scenario, what is Mr. Allport's class taking part in? (Hint: See page 284)

    a. Concept mapping

    b. Analogies

    c. Subgoaling

    d. Hypothesis testing

9. Swen is not excited about having to read another Shakespearean play. He has already read two of Shakespeare's plays and he concluded from reading those two plays that he dislikes the general nature of Shakespeare's plays. Swen is engaging in _____. (Text Hint: See page 287)

    a. inductive reasoning

    b. deductive reasoning

    c. critical thinking

    d. decision making

10. Alex and Brian are engaging in a detective game in which they must gather and sort through all of the clues in order to determine who has committed a crime. Alex and Brian are engaging in _____ when playing this detective game. (Text Hint: See page 287)

    a. inductive reasoning

    b. deductive reasoning

    c. critical thinking

    d. decision making

11. Uma is trying to decide whether next year she should take calculus, which is considered an advanced mathematics class for her grade level, or algebra II, which is the regular mathematics for her grade level. In making this decision, Uma is weighing the costs and the benefits of this decision by creating a plus and minuses list. Uma is using _____. (Text Hint: See page 290)

    a. subgoaling

    b. hypothesis testing

    c. decision making

    d. belief perseverance

12. Mrs. Kombly encourages her students to brainstorm, to be internally motivated, to be flexible and playful in their thinking. She is also careful that she does not become overcontrolling of her students. Mrs. Kombly is fostering _____ in her classroom. (Text Hint: See page 293)

    a. intelligence

    b. decision making

    c. creativity

    d. problem solving

13. Ronald is very good at being able to think about something in novel and unusual ways and come up with unique solutions to the problem. This means that Ronald is very_____. (Text Hint: See page 293)

    a. good at problem solving

    b. good at analogies

    c. good at thinking critically

    d. creative

14. Ronnie's history teacher has just given an extra credit assignment consisting of a research project. Ronnie decides to assess her current situation, which is that she has some possible ideas for this project. She then sketches out a plan to reduce the difference between her current state and the goal of doing the project. She knows that she must now reduce the number of topic ideas down to one, research that idea by going to the library, and asking her uncle, who is a historian, if he has any books on the topic. What is Ronnie using to solve her problem? (Text Hint: See page 299)

    a. An algorithm

    b. Subgoaling

    c. Means-end analysis

    d. Fixation

15. Mrs. Moran's geometry class is learning how to prove theorems. Mrs. Moran instructs them on this concept and then will test her students in the same setting in which the concept was learned. In Mrs. Moran's class, what type of transfer are her students involved in? (Text Hint: See page 305)

    a. Near

    b. Far

    c. Low-road

    d. High-road

16. Mr. Vista always encourages his students to think about how they can apply information that they have already learned to a new context. What type of transfer is Mr. Vista encouraging his students to do? (Text Hint: See page 306)

    a. Forward-rearing transfer

    b. Backward-rearing transfer

    c. Near transfer

    d. Far transfer

17. Which of the following statements about creativity is true? (Text Hint: See page 294)
    a. Creative students are able to generate a single, best way to solve a problem.
    b. Students who are creative in math are also creative in other disciplines such as language arts, science, and the visual arts.
    c. Creative students think about things in novel and unusual ways.
    d. Most highly intelligent students are very creative.

18. Mrs. Daniels' students are building a model of the rainforest in the classroom. They are making trees using twisted, brown paper as well as a variety of tropical flowers and birds. What is Mrs. Daniels fostering in her students? (Text Hint: See page 268)
    a. Concept mapping
    b. Problem based learning
    c. Convergent thinking
    d. Creativity

19. Mr. Berman is moderating a classroom debate about year-round schooling. Students in Group 1 are in favor of year-round schools and Group 2 is opposed to year-round schools. Group 2 is sharing research that refutes the position of Group 1. A Group 2 student is passionately speaking against a point that was made by a Group 1 student. Which statement best describes what is happening in Mr. Berman's classroom? (Text Hint: See page 289)
    a. The students are engaging in a critical thinking activity.
    b. Mr. Berman is in danger of losing control of his classroom.
    c. Students are being encouraged to give a single, correct answer about year-round schooling.
    d. Mr. Berman is pitting students against each other and will ultimately undermine friendships.

20. When students are having fun in the classroom, _____. (Text Hint: See page 296)
    a. they are less likely to absorb and retain information
    b. they are less attentive and less motivated to learn
    c. they are more likely to engage in disruptive and dangerous behavior
    d. they are more likely to consider creative solutions to problems

Answer Key

1. D—Feedback: Subject Category II. Instruction and Assessment: Instructional Strategies: Major categories of instructional strategies: Direct instruction

2. B—Feedback: Subject Category II. Instruction and Assessment: Instructional Strategies: Major categories of instructional strategies: Concept mapping

3. A—Feedback: Subject Category II. Instruction and Assessment: Instructional Strategies: Major cognitive processes associated with student learning: Critical thinking

4. B—Feedback: Subject Category II. Instruction and Assessment: Instructional Strategies: Major cognitive processes associated with student learning: Critical thinking

5. D—Feedback: Subject Category II. Instruction and Assessment: Instructional Strategies: The major cognitive processes associated with student learning: Problem-structuring and problem-solving

6. A—Feedback: Subject Category II. Instruction and Assessment: Instructional Strategies: The major cognitive processes associated with student learning: Representation of ideas

7. D—Feedback: Subject Category II. Instruction and Assessment: Planning Instruction: Techniques for creating effective bridges between curriculum goals and students' experiences: Anticipating preconceptions

8. D—Feedback: Subject Category II. Instruction and Assessment: Instructional Strategies: Major categories of instructional strategies: Whole-group discussion and Questioning

9. A—Feedback: Subject Category II. Instruction and Assessment: Instructional Strategies: Major cognitive processes associated with student learning: Inductive and deductive thinking

10. B—Feedback: Subject Category II. Instruction and Assessment: Instructional Strategies: Major cognitive processes associated with student learning: Inductive and deductive thinking

11. C—Feedback: Subject Category II. Instruction and Assessment: Instructional Strategies: Major cognitive processes associated with student learning: Higher-order thinking

12. C—Feedback: Subject Category II. Instruction and Assessment: Instructional Strategies: Major cognitive processes associated with student learning: Creative thinking

13. D—Feedback: Subject Category II. Instruction and Assessment: Instructional Strategies: Major cognitive processes associated with student learning: Creative thinking

14. C—Feedback: Subject Category II. Instruction and Assessment: Instructional Strategies: The major cognitive processes associated with student learning: Problem-structuring and problem-solving

15. A—Feedback: Subject Category I. Students as Learners: Student Development and the Learning Process: Important terms that relate to learning theory: Transfer

16. B—Feedback: Subject Category I. Students as Learners: Student Development and the Learning Process: Important terms that relate to learning theory: Transfer

17. C—Feedback: Subject Category II. Instruction and Assessment: Instructional Strategies: Major cognitive processes associated with student learning: Creative thinking

18. D—Feedback: Subject Category II. Instruction and Assessment: Instructional Strategies: Major cognitive processes associated with student learning: Creative thinking

19. A—Feedback: Subject Category II. Instruction and Assessment: Instructional Strategies: Major cognitive processes associated with student learning: Critical thinking

20. D—Feedback: Subject Category II. Instruction and Assessment: Instructional Strategies: The major cognitive processes associated with student learning: Play

All Subject Categories are as listed in the ETS Principles of Learning and Teaching, *Tests at a Glance*, located at *ftp://ftp.ets.org/pub/tandl/0522.pdf*.

CHAPTER 10

Social Constructivist Approaches

1. Constructivism emphasizes that individuals learn best when they _____. (Text Hint: See page 314)
   a. work in collaborative groups
   b. actively put together knowledge and understanding
   c. learn effective strategies for retrieving information
   d. solve real world problems

2. Unlike Piaget's model of child development, Vygotsky's model emphasizes the importance of social interactions in shaping children's knowledge. (Text Hint: See page 314)
   a. True
   b. False

3. Situated cognition is best described as _____. (Text Hint: See page 316)
   a. thinking that is located in social and physical contexts
   b. a technique for changing the level of support over the course of a teaching session
   c. a social constructivist program that encourages reflection and discussion through using adults as role models, children teaching children, and online computer consultation
   d. the importance of gleaning knowledge from different contexts

4. Three of the following teachers are using scaffolding to help their students learn. Which one is *NOT* a good example of scaffolding? (Text Hint: See page 316)
   a. Ms. Lilly gives her class some hints about how to solve an especially difficult algebra problem.
   b. Mrs. Branson teaches a golf swing by gently guiding each student through the correct movement a few times.
   c. Ms. Niles gives John a structure to follow when he writes his first poem.
   d. Mr. Johnson takes his students to the computer lab.

5. Cognitive apprenticeship is a tool that involves _____. (Text Hint: See page 317)
   a. an expert stretching and supporting a novice's understanding and use of a culture's skills
   b. a technique for changing the level of support over the course of a teaching session
   c. a social constructivist program that encourages reflection and discussion through using adults as role models, children teaching children, and online computer consultation
   d. thinking that is located in social and physical contexts

6. Which of the following examples is the best use of tutoring? (Text Hint: See page 317)
   a. Two students working on teacher-made worksheets.
   b. A parent volunteer assisting a student with the alphabet.
   c. A parent volunteer circling the room to ensure students are on task.
   d. Both A and B are correct.

7. Who might serve as effective tutors for students? (Text Hint: See page 317)
   a. Peers
   b. Volunteers
   c. Mentors
   d. All the above

8. Which of the following is NOT true of peer tutoring? (Text Hint: See page 319)
   a. Using students of different grade levels to serve as mentors for students.
   b. Alternating the tutor and tutee roles between students.
   c. Delegating the responsibility of testing to tutors.
   d. Communicating to parents your use of peer tutoring in the classroom.

9. Group rewards are essential for the effective use of cooperative learning. Which of the following is (are) good examples of group rewards? (Text Hint: See page 322)
   a. Ms. Jackson recognizes winning teams in the class newsletter.
   b. Mr. Randall writes individual notes home to praise each student.
   c. Mr. Wallace takes the time to praise each student individually after class.
   d. Mrs. Chen raises each student's unit grade with an improved test score.

10. Which of the following is an example of social loafing? (Text Hint: See Ch 10, page 322)
    a. Ryan is not doing his work because he knows his group will complete it.
    b. Grant is not feeling well today and is having trouble staying on task.
    c. Miranda's group is disagreeing over which topic to pursue and has reached a stalemate.
    d. Miles is known for his lack of social skills and is not well liked by his peers.

11. Mrs. Little wants to use the Group Investigation method in her history class. Which of the following would be the best activity to employ? (Text Hint: See page 323)
    a. Group members decide which historical figures they want to study and break up to meet with students from other groups.
    b. Groups decide which historical figure they want to study and delegate responsibilities for initial legwork within the group before getting together to summarize the findings.
    c. Students work together at tables on teacher prepared worksheets.
    d. Each student signs up for a historical figure to research at the library.

12. When a group member is given part of the material to be learned, becomes an expert on that material, and then teaches it to others, this is called _____. (Text Hint: See page 323)
    a. reciprocal teaching
    b. jigsaw
    c. student-teams-achievement divisions
    d. group investigation

13. When heterogeneous cooperative groups are formed, students of which ability level(s) are most likely to feel left out? (Text Hint: See page 325)
    a. High ability
    b. Medium ability
    c. Low ability
    d. Both low and high ability

14. Mr. Weiss takes time at the beginning of the school year to put students into groups to help students become better listeners, get used to contributing to a team product, and get experience with handling problem situations. Mr. Weiss is attempting to use _____. (Text Hint: See page 326)

    a. team-building skills

    b. scaffolding

    c. cognitive apprenticeship

    d. a collaborative school

15. When working in cooperative groups, the role of the praiser is best described as _____. (Text Hint: See page 327)

    a. thinking about and evaluating the group's progress

    b. equalizing the participation of students in the group

    c. helping with academic content

    d. showing appreciation for each student's contributions

16. Shanice is in charge of writing down ideas the group has and who is responsible for each task. Which group role has she been assigned? (Text Hint: See page 327)

    a. Encourager

    b. Recorder

    c. Materials monitor

    d. Reflector

17. Which of the following assignments is most consistent with the social constructivist approach to writing? (Text Hint: See page 314)

    a. Writing a book report about a novel read aloud during class.

    b. Creating an outline to summarize main events studied during history class.

    c. Writing a term paper about a topic studied during science class.

    d. Writing an essay about a recent significant personal event.

18. "Schools for Thought" emphasizes the importance of infusing real-world problems into the curriculum. Which of the following is an example of a real-world problem appropriate for academic content? (Text Hint: See page 331)

    a. How cities can reduce population.

    b. The United States' role in reducing world hunger.

    c. How to resolve a conflict of opinion.

    d. All the above

19. Mr. Azaria is conducting a mock trial in his social studies class to teach students about the judicial branch of government. This activity exemplifies which of the following concepts? (Text Hint: See page 316)

    a. Situated cognition

    b. Scaffolding

    c. Cognitive apprenticeship

    d. Peer tutoring

20. On Fridays, sixth grade students spend one hour with kindergarten children. The older students help the younger children with math or reading work. Which of the following terms best describes this example? (Text Hint: See page 319)

    a. The Jigsaw Classroom

    b. Cross-age peer tutoring

    c. Group investigation

    d. Reciprocal teaching

21. When composing groups of students for small-group work, teachers should _____. (Text Hint: See page 325)

    a. place students with their friends

    b. create groups with diversity in ability, ethnicity, socioeconomic status, and gender

    c. place students of the same ability-level in the same group

    d. separate boys from girls

22. Which of the following conclusions is not true? To develop students' team-building skills, teachers should _____. (Text Hint: See page 326)

    a. help students to become better listeners

    b. give students some practice in contributing to a common product as part of a team

    c. discuss the value of having a group leader and different roles

    d. let teams solve problem situations independently

Answer Key

1. B—Feedback: Subject Category I. Students as Learners: Student Development and the Learning Process: Important terms that relate to learning theory: Constructivism

2. A—Feedback: Subject Category I. Students as Learners: Theoretical foundations about how learning occurs: how students construct knowledge, acquire skills, and develop habits of mind: Examples of important theorists: Lev Vygotsky

3. A—Feedback: Subject Category I. Students as Learners: Important terms that relate to learning theory: Situated cognition

4. D—Feedback: Subject Category I. Students as Learners: Important terms that relate to learning theory: Scaffolding

5. A—Feedback: Subject Category I. Students as Learners: Important terms that relate to learning theory: Cognitive apprenticeship

6. B—Feedback: Subject Category IV. Profession and Community: The Larger Community: Basic strategies for involving parents/guardians and leaders in the community in the educational process

7. D—Feedback: Subject Category IV. Profession and Community: The Larger Community: Basic strategies for involving parents/guardians and leaders in the community in the educational process

8. C—Feedback: Subject Category I. Students as Learners: Student Motivation and the Learning Environment: How knowledge of human emotion and behavior should influence strategies for organizing and supporting individual and group work in the classroom

9. A—Feedback: Subject Category I. Students as Learners: Student Motivation and the Learning Environment: Principles of effective management and strategies to promote positive relationships, cooperation, and purposeful learning: Establishing classroom rules, punishments, and rewards

10. A—Feedback: Subject Category II. Instruction and Assessment: Instructional Strategies: Major categories, advantages, and appropriate uses of instructional strategies: Cooperative learning

11. B—Feedback: Subject Category II. Instruction and Assessment: Instructional Strategies: Principles, techniques, and methods associated with major instructional strategies: Student-centered models: Project-based learning

12. B—Feedback: Subject Category II. Instruction and Assessment: Instructional Strategies: Principles, techniques, and methods associated with major instructional strategies: Student-centered models: Cooperative learning (pair-share, jigsaw, STAD, teams, games, tournaments)

13. B—Feedback: Subject Category II. Instruction and Assessment: Instructional Strategies: Major categories, advantages, and appropriate uses of instructional strategies: Cooperative learning

14. B—Feedback: Subject Category I. Students as Learners: Student Motivation and the Learning Environment: How knowledge of human emotion and behavior should influence strategies for organizing and supporting individual and group work in the classroom

15. D—Feedback: Subject Category II. Instruction and Assessment: Instructional Strategies: Major categories, advantages, and appropriate uses of instructional strategies: Cooperative learning

16. B—Feedback: Subject Category II. Instruction and Assessment: Instructional Strategies: Major categories, advantages, and appropriate uses of instructional strategies: Cooperative learning

17. D—Feedback: Subject Category II. Instruction and Assessment: Instructional Strategies: The major cognitive processes associated with student learning: Social reasoning

18. D—Feedback: Subject Category II. Instruction and Assessment: Instructional Strategies: Major cognitive processes associated with student learning: Problem structuring and problem solving

19. A—Feedback: Subject Category II. Instruction and Assessment: Instructional Strategies: Major cognitive processes associated with student learning: Critical and Creative thinking

20. B—Feedback: Subject Category II. Instruction and Assessment: Planning Instruction: Techniques for creating effective bridges between curriculum goals and students' experiences: Modeling

21. B—Feedback: Subject Category II. Instruction and Assessment: Instructional Strategies: Major categories, advantages, and appropriate uses of instructional strategies: Cooperative learning

22. D—Feedback: Subject Category II. Instruction and Assessment: Instructional Strategies: Major categories of instructional strategies: Small group work

All Subject Categories are as listed in the ETS Principles of Learning and Teaching, *Tests at a Glance*, located at *ftp://ftp.ets.org/pub/tandl/0522.pdf*.

CHAPTER 11

Learning and Cognition in the Content Areas

1. A cognitive approach to reading that emphasizes instruction in strategies, especially metacognitive strategies, is which of the following? (Text Hint: See page 345)
   a. Everyday mathematics
   b. Whole language approach
   c. Reciprocal teaching
   d. Transactional strategy instruction approach

2. Which of the following is a 4-year, problem-based high school math curriculum that emphasizes solving math problems in context? (Text Hint: See page 357)
   a. Connected mathematics program.
   b. Interactive Mathematics Program.
   c. Everyday mathematics.
   d. Interactive demonstration strategy.

3. Mr. Perez is teaching in the field that seeks to promote civic competence with the goal of helping students make informed and reasoned decisions for the public good as citizens of a culturally diverse, democratic society in an interdependent world. What field is Mr. Perez teaching in? (Text Hint: See page 364)
   a. Mathematics
   b. Social studies
   c. Science
   d. Reading

4. Mrs. Treble is using a form of teaching in which she initially explains strategies and then models how to use them in making sense of the text. Then she asks her students to demonstrate the strategies, giving them support as they learn. What teaching strategy is Mrs. Treble using? (Text Hint: See page 346)
   a. Whole language approach
   b. Interactive demonstration strategy
   c. Reciprocal Teaching
   d. HUMBIO

5. Ms. Tesda thinks that the program developed by Stanford University scientists in collaboration with middle school teachers, which integrates the study of ecology, evolution, genetics, physiology, human development, culture, health, and safety is very effective. What program is Ms. Tesda referring to? (Text Hint: See page 362)
   a. Transactional strategy instruction approach
   b. HUMBIO
   c. Interactive demonstration strategy
   d. Reciprocal teaching

6. The interactive demonstration strategy helps students to _____. (Text Hint: See page 360)

    a. construct meaningful strategies

    b. integrate ecology, evolution, genetics, physiology, human development, culture, health, and safety

    c. work on everyday problems

    d. overcome misconceptions in science in which the teacher introduces the demonstration, asks students to discuss the demonstration with the neighbors and predicts its outcome, and then performs the demonstration

7. Sam is excited about returning to school after summer vacation. He will be learning to read. According to research findings presented in your text, what approach is best to teach reading? (Text Hint: See page 342)

    a. Whole language approach is best

    b. Basic skills and phonetics approach is best

    c. Both approaches were found to benefit children

    d. Neither approach was found beneficial

8. Mr. Brians is teaching his students to read by emphasizing that they decode and comprehend words. He thinks metacognitive skills as well as general automaticity are important. What approach to teaching reading is Mr. Brians using? (Text Hint: See page 343)

    a. A cognitive approach

    b. A social constructivist approach

    c. The whole language approach

    d. The interactive approach

9. Enrique is learning to read; his teacher understands the contribution of the social context in helping children to read. Being that Enrique is Hispanic, his teacher wants to be informed about how much emphasis the culture places on reading, and the extent to which his parents have exposed him to books before he entered formal schooling. Enrique's teacher wants to give him and all of the other students the opportunity to discuss what they have read with the class. Enrique's teacher is using_____ approach to reading. (Text Hint: See page 345)

    a. a cognitive approach

    b. a social constructivist approach

    c. the whole language approach

    d. the interactive approach

10. Ty and Amy-Lynn are involved in a book club, which will involve peer learning and student-led discussions. In a book club, what is the role of the teacher? (Text Hint: See page 347)

    a. To serve as a guide but to give students responsibility for how the discussions will evolve

    b. To remain completely uninvolved

    c. To be completely in charge of the discussion, topics, and learning

    d. The teacher is not present during book clubs

11. Mrs. Shimm always has her students outline and organize content information prior to beginning their writing. She gives them feedback for their efforts, which is beneficial because it gives the students confidence. What approach to writing is Mrs. Shimm using? (Text Hint: See page 349)

    a. Problem solving

    b. Planning

    c. Revising

    d. Metacognition

12. Ms. Rydell has her students learn about social studies so that they will take what they learned and use it in school and also outside of school. She stresses meaningful learning and thinking critically about values. What approach to social studies is Ms. Rydell taking? (Text Hint: See page 367)

    a. A cognitive approach

    b. A constructivist approach

    c. The traditional approach

    d. The interactive approach

13. Mr. Ortiz will be teaching social studies in an elementary school. How is Mr. Ortiz likely to teach social studies? (Text Hint: See page 364)

    a. As an interdisciplinary course

    b. As a focused single discipline

    c. Integrated across several disciplines

    d. None of the above

14. Ms. Mott's ninth grade science class is taught with an emphasis on discovery and hands-on laboratory investigation; thus her students are helped to construct their own knowledge. What approach to science teaching is Ms. Mott's using? (Text Hint: See page 360)

    a. Cognitive approach

    b. HUMBIO

    c. Social approach

    d. Constructivist approach

15. Genevieve in entering high school; she will be enrolled in science classes. How is Genevieve going to be taught science now? (Text Hint: See page 363)

    a. In the sequence: biology, chemistry, and physics

    b. In the sequence: chemistry, biology, and physics

    c. In the sequence: physics, chemistry, biology

    d. None of the above

16. Which statement best describes the controversy in math education? (Text Hint: See page 356)

    a. Educators currently debate whether math should be taught in the elementary grades.

    b. Educators currently debate whether math should be taught online.

    c. Educators currently debate whether math should be taught using a cognitive, constructivist approach or a practice, computational approach.

    d. Educators currently debate whether the NCTM math standards should be replaced with the standards used in Japan.

17. Wiring a doll house, making replicas of boats for a regatta, and dropping eggs are examples of _____. (Text Hint: See page 363)

    a. HumBio science curriculum

    b. gender-based science activities

    c. drill and practice

    d. a cognitive, constructivist approach to science

18. Recent research in math shows that _____. (Text Hint: See page 356)
    a. teachers in the U.S. should emphasize basic skills and formulas
    b. teachers in the U.S. are less likely to assign math homework than teachers in most other countries
    c. teachers in the U.S. are more likely to assign math homework than teachers in most other countries
    d. assigning math homework has no positive affect on students' overall learning and performance

19. According to the recent National Assessment of Educational Progress, in the fourth grade, frequent calculator use was associated with _____. (Text Hint: See page 358)
    a. lower national achievement test scores in math
    b. higher national achievement test scores in math
    c. expert math knowledge in eighth grade
    d. full mastery of basic math skills

20. Mr. Anthony frequently invites local writing experts, such as journalists and authors, to his classroom. He also regularly schedules student-teacher writing conferences to discuss students' writing. Mr. Anthony emphasizes _____. (Text Hint: See page 351)
    a. planning and problem solving in writing
    b. the social context of writing
    c. a cognitive approach to writing
    d. prewriting activities

21. The National Science Teachers Association, the National Council for the Social Studies, The National Council of Teachers of English, and the National Council of Teachers of Mathematics are all examples of _____. (Text Hint: See Ch 11)
    a. online newsgroups
    b. professional development institutes
    c. teachers' unions
    d. professional associations

22. In an effort to improve the literacy of its students, Washington Elementary School holds family literacy seminars for parents twice a month. The seminars include English-as-a-Second-Language classes and information about sharing language-related activities with children. This program is an example of _____. (Text Hint: See page 347)
    a. character education
    b. a social constructivist approach to reading
    c. reciprocal teaching
    d. metacognitive strategies

Answer Key

1. D—Feedback: Subject Category II. Instruction and Assessment: Instructional Strategies: Major categories of instructional strategies: Reflection and Metacognition

2. B—Feedback: Subject Category II. Instruction and Assessment: Instructional Strategies: Major cognitive processes associated with student learning: Problem-structuring and problem-solving

3. B—Feedback: Subject Category II. Instruction and Assessment: Planning Instruction: Techniques for planning instruction to meet curriculum goals, including the incorporation of learning theory, subject matter, curriculum development, and student development: Scope and sequence in specific disciplines

4. C—Feedback: Subject Category II. Instruction and Assessment: Planning Instruction: Techniques for creating effective bridges between curriculum goals and students' experiences: Modeling and Guided Practice

5. B—Feedback: Subject Category II. Instruction and Assessment: Instructional Strategies: Major categories of instructional strategies: Interdisciplinary instruction

6. D—Feedback: Subject Category II. Instruction and Assessment: Instructional Strategies: Principles, techniques, and methods associated with various instructional strategies: Direct instruction: Demonstrations

7. C—Feedback: Subject Category II. Instruction and Assessment: Instructional Strategies: Principles, techniques, and methods associated with various instructional strategies

8. A—Feedback: Subject Category II. Instruction and Assessment: Instructional Strategies: Principles, techniques, and methods associated with various instructional strategies: Direct Instruction

9. B—Feedback: Subject Category I. Students as Learners: Students as Diverse Learners: How students' learning is influenced by individual experiences, talents, and prior learning, as well as language, culture, family, and community values: Multicultural backgrounds and Family backgrounds

10. A—Feedback: Subject Category II. Instruction and Assessment: Instructional Strategies: Principles, techniques, and methods associated with various instructional strategies: Student-centered models: Discussion models

11. B—Feedback: Subject Category I. Instruction and Assessment: Instructional Strategies: Principles, techniques, and methods associated with various instructional strategies: Direct Instruction: Outlining and Note-taking

12. B—Feedback: Subject Category II. Instruction and Assessment: Instructional Strategies: Major cognitive processes associated with student learning: Critical thinking and Social reasoning

13. C—Feedback: Subject Category II. Instruction and Assessment: Instructional Strategies: Major categories of instructional strategies: Interdisciplinary instruction

14. D—Feedback: Subject Category II. Instruction and Assessment: Instructional Strategies: Principles, techniques, and methods associated with various instructional strategies: Student-centered models: Laboratories

15. A—Feedback: Subject Category II. See answer 3

16. C—Feedback: Subject Category IV. Profession and Community: The Reflective Practitioner: Ability to read and understand articles about current views, ideas, and debates regarding best teaching practices

17. D—Feedback: Subject Category II. Instruction and Assessment: Instructional Strategies: Major cognitive processes associated with student learning: Invention

18. B—Feedback: Subject Category IV. Profession and Community: The Reflective Practitioner: Ability to read and understand articles about current views, ideas, and debates regarding best teaching practices

19. A—Feedback: Subject Category IV. Profession and Community: The Reflective Practitioner: Ability to read and understand articles about current views, ideas, and debates regarding best teaching practices

20. B—Feedback: Subject Category II. Instruction and Assessment: Instructional Strategies: Methods for enhancing student learning through the use of a variety of resources and materials: Local experts

21. D—Feedback: Subject Category IV. Profession and the Community: The Reflective Practitioner: Types of resources available for professional development and learning: Professional associations

22. B—Feedback: Subject Category IV. Profession and Community: The Larger Community: The role of the school as a resource to the larger community

All Subject Categories are as listed in the ETS Principles of Learning and Teaching, *Tests at a Glance*, located at *ftp://ftp.ets.org/pub/tandl/0522.pdf*.

CHAPTER 12

Planning, Instruction, and Technology

1. Ms. Alice must set instructional goals for her class, plan activities, prioritize tasks, make time estimates, and create schedules while remaining flexible. How would you characterize Ms. Alice's activity? (Text Hint: See page 377)

    a. Planning

    b. Prioritizing

    c. Creating a lesson plan

    d. Scaffolding

2. Teachers are attending a workshop offering strategies on establishing general content, creating basic curriculum sequence, and ordering and reserving materials. What might an appropriate title for such a workshop be? (Text Hint: See page 379)

    a. Yearly Planning

    b. Term Planning

    c. Unit Planning

    d. Weekly Planning

    e. Daily Planning

3. According to Robert Yinger, which of the following goals is recommended for term planning? (Text Hint: See page 379)

    a. Establishing general content

    b. Detailing of content in three-month segments

    c. Developing a sequence of related and well-organized learning experiences

    d. Laying out activities within the framework of the weekly schedule

4. Which of the following is the best example of a behavioral objective according to Robert Mager? (Text Hint: See page 378)

    a. Students will complete the test with 85% accuracy.

    b. Students will correctly employ the "i" before "e" rule with 85% accuracy.

    c. Given a 15-item teacher-made test, students will correctly employ the "i" before "e" rule with 85% accuracy.

    d. Given a 15-item teacher-made test, students will complete the test with 85% accuracy.

5. Which of the following scenarios depicts "application"? (Text Hint: See page 380)

    a. Melinda plants a garden after reading about how to grow plants.

    b. Jerry identifies the assumptions of the theory of the origin of the universe.

    c. Ingrid disagrees with her teacher's interpretation of a story.

    d. Francisco learns about common features of all mammals.

6. Which of the following statements provides the best description of evaluation? (Text Hint: See page 380)

    a. To combine elements to create new information

    b. To break down complex information into smaller parts

    c. To make judgments about ideas or theories

    d. To remember information accurately

7. Which of the following is a category of the affective domain in Bloom's taxonomy? (Text Hint: See page 380)

    a. Application

    b. Valuing

    c. Perception

    d. Comprehension

8. Objectives pertaining to reflex movements, basic fundamental movements, perceptual abilities, physical abilities, skilled movements, and nondiscussive behaviors pertain to which taxonomy? (Text Hint: See page 381)

    a. Cognitive

    b. Affective

    c. Psychomotor

9. Which of the following characteristics is most consistent with direct instruction? (Text Hint: See page 383)

    a. It is a student-centered approach.

    b. The classroom environment is typically unstructured.

    c. Academic learning time is kept to a minimum.

    d. The teacher expects students to reach high levels of academic excellence.

10. Before Mr. Nielson begins his lecture, he reviews the previous day's lesson, discusses its relevance to the day's topic, and provides clear instructions for students' work. Which behavior is Mr. Nielson engaging in? (Text Hint: See page 384)

    a. Orienting

    b. Lecturing

    c. Explaining

    d. Reciting

11. When using questions in the classroom, all of the following strategies are recommended, EXCEPT which one? (Text Hint: See page 386)

    a. Avoiding questions that can be answered with yes or no.

    b. Using fact-based questions to lead into thinking-based questions.

    c. Allowing plenty of time for students to think about answers.

    d. Asking leading questions that suggest the desired answer.

12. Advocates for the teacher-centered approach feel that it is the best strategy for teaching _____. (Text Hint: See page 392)

    a. critical thinking

    b. metacognition

    c. basic skills

    d. high school students

13. The learner-centered principle described as "the goals of learning" refers to _____. (Text Hint: See page 393)

    a. thinking creatively and critically

    b. making long-term and short-term plans

    c. improving self-esteem and appreciating one's own talents

    d. developing shared construction of important skills

14. Ms. Martha has students get into groups for their next activity. She instructs students to work with the paint provided at each table in order to find out how we get green paint. Ms. Martha is using which learner-centered strategy? (Text Hint: See page 397)

    a. Discovery learning

    b. Guided discovery learning

    c. Problem-based learning

    d. Mastery learning

15. Supporters of learner-centered instruction feel it leads to students' _____. (Text Hint: See page 398)

    a. active construction of learning

    b. positive self-esteem

    c. internal motivation

    d. all of the above

16. Mr. Stevenson has decided to create a location on the Web in order to post: contact information, students' homework, upcoming field trips, and requests for parental involvement. What has Mr. Stevenson created? (Text Hint: See page 400)

    a. An e-mail address

    b. A Web site

    c. Electronic monitoring

    d. A wireless network

17. What does The Educator's Reference Desk provide? (Text Hint: See page 402)

    a. Provides free information about a wide range of educational topics

    b. Monitors education websites

    c. Offers information on developing technology into the classroom

    d. All the above

18. Which grade level should be able to use keyboards and other common input, discuss common uses of technology in daily life, use technology tools (such as Web tools and scanners), and use telecommunications and online resources? (Text Hint: See page 403)

    a. Prekindergarten—2nd grade

    b. Grades 3–5

    c. Grades 6–8

    d. Grades 9–12

19. Which statement best describes an effective teaching strategy for delivering lectures? (Text Hint: See page 385)

    a. Simplify the lecture focus and present a single point of view.

    b. Make the lecture interesting and motivate students' interest in a topic.

    c. Ask students to save their questions until after the conclusion of the lecture.

    d. Avoid using visual aids as they distract students from the lecture focus.

20. Knowledge, comprehension, application, analysis, synthesis, and evaluation are objectives from which of the following domains? (Text Hint: See page 380)

    a. Behavioral domain

    b. Psychomotor domain

    c. Affective domain

    d. Cognitive domain

21. Eric wants to conduct research about dolphins on the Web. Which tool should he use to find information on the Internet? (Text Hint: See page 400)

    a. A search engine like Google or Yahoo!

    b. A wireless network

    c. Instant messenger

    d. Email

22. Which of the following statements describes the social inequities associated with technology? (Text Hint: See page 401)

    a. Students from middle- and upper-income families are far more likely to have computers at home.

    b. Schools with high percentages of low-income minority students tend to use computers for drill-and-practice exercises.

    c. Boys are more likely to use computers for math and science applications while girls are more likely to use computers for word processing.

    d. All of the above.

23. Mr. Noble frequently develops integrated curriculum units based on essential questions. His students create charts on which they mark their experiences in language and literacy, mathematics, science, social studies, music, and art. Which of the following is the best example of an essential question? (Text Hint: See 396)

    a. Who was the first president of the United States?

    b. How does a prism work?

    c. What is the effect of World War I?

    d. Does life exist on another planet?

24. Which of the following Bloom's Taxonomy objectives is most appropriate for encouraging students to think critically? (Text Hint: See page 380)

    a. Knowledge

    b. Comprehension

    c. Application

    d. Evaluation

25. Numerous resources are available on the Internet for teachers. What does The Educator's Reference Desk provide? (Text Hint: See page 402)

    a. Provides free, online information, articles, and research about a wide range of educational topics

    b. Free access to online encyclopedias

    c. Online professional development courses

    d. None of the above

26. _____ involves learning one concept or topic thoroughly before moving on to a more difficult one. (Text Hint: See page 387)

    a. Mastery learning

    b. Discovery learning

    c. Guided discovery learning

    d. Metacognition

27. _____ are used at the beginning of a lesson to orient students and help them see "the big picture" of what is to come and how information is connected to what they already know. (Text Hint: See page 384)

    a. Visual aids

    b. Early assessment

    c. Advance organizers

    d. Essential questions

28. At the conclusion of a lecture, teachers should _____. (Text Hint: See page 386)

    a. tell students which parts of the lecture will be on the test

    b. select inattentive students to repeat key lecture points

    c. save students' questions until the next day

    d. summarize the main ideas and make connections to future lectures or activities

Answer Key

1. A—Feedback: Subject Category II. Instruction and Assessment: Planning Instruction: Techniques for planning instruction to meet curriculum goals, including the incorporation of learning theory, subject matter, curriculum development, and student development: Scope and sequence in specific disciplines

2. A—Feedback: Subject Category II. Instruction and Assessment: Planning Instruction: Techniques for planning instruction to meet curriculum goals, including the incorporation of learning theory, subject matter, curriculum development, and student development: Scope and sequence in specific disciplines

3. B—Feedback: Subject Category II. Instruction and Assessment: Planning Instruction: Techniques for planning instruction to meet curriculum goals, including the incorporation of learning theory, subject matter, curriculum development, and student development: Scope and sequence in specific disciplines

4. C—Feedback: Subject Category II. Instruction and Assessment: Planning Instruction: Techniques for planning instruction to meet curriculum goals, including the incorporation of learning theory, subject matter, curriculum development, and student development: Behavioral objectives—affective, cognitive, and psychomotor

5. A—Feedback: Subject Category II. Instruction and Assessment: Planning Instruction: Techniques for planning instruction to meet curriculum goals, including the incorporation of learning theory, subject matter, curriculum development, and student development: Learner objectives and outcomes

6. C—Feedback: Subject Category II. Instruction and Assessment: Planning Instruction: Techniques for planning instruction to meet curriculum goals, including the incorporation of learning theory, subject matter, curriculum development, and student development: Learner objectives and outcomes

7. B—Feedback: Subject Category II. Instruction and Assessment: Planning Instruction: Techniques for planning instruction to meet curriculum goals, including the incorporation of learning theory, subject matter, curriculum development, and student development: Behavioral objectives—affective, cognitive, and psychomotor

8. C—Feedback: Subject Category II. Instruction and Assessment: Planning Instruction: Techniques for planning instruction to meet curriculum goals, including the incorporation of learning theory, subject matter, curriculum development, and student development: Behavioral objectives—affective, cognitive, and psychomotor

9. D—Feedback: Subject Category II. Instruction and Assessment: Instructional Strategies: Major categories, advantages, and appropriate uses of instructional strategies: Direct instruction

10. A—Feedback: Subject Category II. Instruction and Assessment: Planning Instruction: Techniques for creating effective bridges between curriculum goals and students' experiences: Activating students' prior knowledge and Building new skills on those previously acquired

11. D—Feedback: Subject Category II. Instruction and Assessment: Instructional Strategies: Major categories, advantages, and appropriate uses of instructional strategies: Questioning

12. C—Feedback: Subject Category II. Instruction and Assessment: Instructional Strategies: Major categories, advantages, and appropriate uses of instructional strategies: Direct instruction

13. B—Feedback: Subject Category II. Instruction and Assessment: Instructional Strategies: Principles, techniques, and methods associated with major instructional strategies: Student-centered models

14. A—Feedback: Subject Category II. Instruction and Assessment: Instructional Strategies: Major categories, advantages, and appropriate uses of instructional strategies: Discovery learning

15. D—Feedback: Subject Category II. Instruction and Assessment: Instructional Strategies: Principles, techniques, and methods associated with major instructional strategies: Student-centered models

16. B—Feedback: Subject Category II. Instruction and Assessment: Instructional Strategies: Methods for enhancing student learning through the use of a variety of resources and materials: Computers, Internet resources, Web pages, email

17. A—Feedback: Subject Category II. Instruction and Assessment: Instructional Strategies: Methods for enhancing student learning through the use of a variety of resources and materials: Computers, Internet resources, Web pages, email

18. B—Feedback: Subject Category II. Instruction and Assessment: Instructional Strategies: Methods for enhancing student learning through the use of a variety of resources and materials: Computers, Internet resources, Web pages, email

19. B—Feedback: Subject Category II. Instruction and Assessment: Instructional Strategies: Major categories, advantages, and appropriate uses of instructional strategies: Direct instruction

20. D—Feedback: Subject Category II. Instruction and Assessment: Planning Instruction: Techniques for planning instruction to meet curriculum goals, including the incorporation of learning theory, subject matter, curriculum development, and student development: Behavioral objectives—affective, cognitive, and psychomotor

21. A—Feedback: Subject Category II. Instruction and Assessment: Instructional Strategies: Methods for enhancing student learning through the use of a variety of resources and materials: Computers, Internet resources, Web pages, email

22. D—Feedback: Subject Category IV. Profession and Community: The Larger Community: Factors in the students' environment outside of school (family circumstances, community environments, health, and economic conditions) that may influence students' life and learning

23. D—Feedback: Subject Category III. Communication Techniques: Types of questions that can stimulate discussion in different ways for different purposes: Stimulating curiosity and Encouraging divergent thinking

24. D—Feedback: Subject Category III. Communication Techniques: Types of questions that can stimulate discussion in different ways for different purposes: Encouraging divergent thinking

25. A—Feedback: Subject Category IV. Profession and the Community: The Reflective Practitioner: Types of resources available for professional development and learning: Professional literature

26. A—Feedback: Subject Category II. Instruction and Assessment: Instructional Strategies: Principles, techniques, and methods associated with major instructional strategies: Direct instruction: Mastery learning

27. C—Feedback: Subject Category II. Instruction and Assessment: Instructional Strategies: Principles, techniques, and methods associated with major instructional strategies: Direct instruction: David Ausubel's "Advance Organizers"

28. D—Feedback: Subject Category II. Instruction and Assessment: Planning Instruction: Techniques for creating effective bridges between curriculum goals and students' experiences: Transitions

All Subject Categories are as listed in the ETS Principles of Learning and Teaching, *Tests at a Glance*, located at *ftp://ftp.ets.org/pub/tandl/0522.pdf*.

CHAPTER 13

Motivation, Teaching, and Learning

1. According to Maslow's hierarchy of motives, which of the following needs must be satisfied before a person can attain esteem? (Text Hint: See page 416)

   a. Safety

   b. Cognitive

   c. Self-actualization

   d. Aesthetic

2. The cognitive perspective on motivation emphasizes which of the following? (Text Hint: See page 417)

   a. The student's capacity for personal growth

   b. The teacher's ability to influence the student's behavior

   c. The nature of the environment in which learning takes place

   d. The student's internal motivation to achieve

3. Which of the following factors would most likely increase intrinsic motivation to learn as a student progresses through the elementary to high school years? (Text Hint: See page 419)

   a. Increased emphasis on the importance of getting good grades

   b. Increased boredom as assignments become more tedious

   c. Increased sense of being challenged at a level consistent with ability

   d. Increased feelings of isolation due to teachers' behaviors toward students

4. Geraldo usually does well in history class, but did poorly on a recent test. He believes that his poor score was due to lack of sufficient studying. After all, he had a term paper due that same day in science class, and had spent most of that week writing the paper rather than studying for the test. This view best represents a combination of which of the following causal attributions? (Text Hint: See page 423)

   a. External-Stable-Uncontrollable

   b. External-Unstable-Controllable

   c. Internal-Stable-Uncontrollable

   d. Internal-Unstable-Controllable

5. When faced with a difficult task, Marvin focuses on his abilities, or lack thereof. He tends to feel overwhelmed by his own inadequacies and therefore has difficulty meeting the challenge. Marvin can best be described as which of the following? (Text Hint: See page 425)

   a. Performance-oriented

   b. Helpless-oriented

   c. Mastery-oriented

   d. Goal-oriented

6. Mario is an eighth grade student whose older brother just dropped out of high school. Which of the following goals will most likely help Mario improve his self-efficacy and sense of achievement? (Text Hint: See page 426)

    a. I want to graduate from high school.

    b. I want to go to college someday.

    c. I want to be a doctor or a lawyer when I grow up.

    d. I want to get an A in science this semester.

7. Which of the following scenarios best depicts a student with "failure syndrome"? (Text Hint: See page 437)

    a. Freddie tries to answer questions, but frequently answers incorrectly.

    b. Doug enjoys class discussions, but often gets distracted by noise outside the classroom.

    c. Maya slumps in her chair when the teacher is looking for someone to solve a problem at the chalkboard.

    d. Andrea dislikes physical education class because other kids make fun of her.

8. Mr. Thetu is trying to reach uninterested or alienated students and motivate them. Which of the following should he not do? (Text Hint: See page 439)

    a. Work on developing a positive relationship

    b. Make school more extrinsically interesting

    c. Teach them strategies for making academic work more enjoyable

    d. Consider a mentor

9. Mr. Qintero has noticed that some of his best students possess the belief that they are able to learn class material, and they believe that they will be able to perform well in their school activities. Which of the following best describes these students? (Text Hint: See page 426)

    a. These students lack attributions

    b. These students are just very intelligent

    c. These students have a high sense of self-efficacy

    d. These students are completely extrinsically motivated

10. Patty usually does well on math tests; however, on the last unit test Patti did poorly. She believes that her poor score was due to the teacher's asking difficult questions. She does not think that the teacher asked fair questions. Patty thinks that since the teacher is biased while giving math exams she may not get a good grade in math class this year. This view best represents a combination of which of the following causal attributions? (Text Hint: See page 423)

    a. External-Stable-Uncontrollable

    b. External-Unstable-Controllable

    c. Internal-Stable-Uncontrollable

    d. Internal-Unstable-Controllable

11. Henrietta knows that the success of her math group is dependent on which students, she, the team captain, picks to be on her math team. She wants to win the math group competition so she is determined to pick the students that she knows are good in math and will do well. She knows that this is going to cause some problems since her friends who are in this class will expect to be on Henrietta's team. However, Henrietta wants to win and therefore is only concerned with what she has to do in order to attain that goal. Henrietta can best be described as which of the following? (Text Hint: See page 425)

    a. Performance-oriented

    b. Helpless-oriented

    c. Mastery-oriented

    d. Goal-oriented

12. Ms. Argoal wants to improve students' self-efficacy in her class. Which of the following would not be recommended for Ms. Argoal to do? (Text Hint: See page 426)

    a. Teach specific strategies.

    b. Guide students in setting goals.

    c. Consider mastery.

    d. Use only extrinsic motivation.

    e. Provide students with support.

13. Trey's teacher notices that he exhibits a pattern of having low expectations for success and a tendency to give up at the first sign of difficulty. Trey does not put forth enough effort, often beginning tasks halfheartedly and then giving up quickly when he encounters a challenge. He also exhibits low efficacy and has problems with his attributions. Trey is exhibiting _____. (Text Hint: See page 437)

    a. a need for affiliation

    b. a performance orientation

    c. the failure syndrome

    d. a social motive

14. The school year began just last week, but Mrs. Rundra already knows that this school year will be challenging. She has a large amount of students who are low achievers with low ability who have difficulty keeping up and have developed low-achieving expectations, students with failure syndrome, and students obsessed with protecting their self-worth by avoiding failure. All of the students described in this scenario can best be classified as being _____. (Text Hint: See page 437)

    a. discouraged students

    b. students who are lacking a need for affiliation

    c. students who are having trouble with their social contexts

    d. students who are having trouble with their social relationships

15. Mr. Lobos is discussing Jessica's motivation with her parents at their scheduled parent-teacher conference. Her parents want to know how they can positively affect their child's motivation and achievement. Mr. Lobos tells them that they need to know enough about Jessica to know the right amount of challenge and the right amount of support. He also tells them that providing a positive climate will help to motivate Jessica to internalize her parents' values and goals. In addition, Mr. Lobos tells Jessica's parents that _____. (Text Hint: See page 432)

    a. their demographic factors are really the only ones that will be of more importance

    b. their close monitoring of her behavior and use of strict punishment is an asset

    c. it is important to model motivated achievement behavior, such as persistence and hard work

    d. they should never exhibit any signs of failure in the home so that Jessica does not imitate that behavior

16. Amber is the most popular girl in her class. She is always surrounded by many friends and dates regularly. Amber likes all of the attention; in fact over the summers when her parents send her to spend time with her relatives in another city, Amber feels like something is drastically missing from her life. Although, she loves her relatives, she does not receive the peer attention that she so craves. In fact, she can hardly wait to be back with her friends. Usually as soon as she arrives in town she throws a party where she will embellish about her summer trip in order to maintain her friends approval. Amber is displaying _____. (Text Hint: See page 417)

    a. a strong need for affiliation

    b. a helpless orientation

    c. the failure syndrome

    d. an internal, unstable, and uncontrollable attribute

17. Mrs. Pfeist has read research that has found that students who feel they have supportive, caring teachers are more strongly motivated to engage in academic work than students with unsupportive, uncaring teachers. Mrs. Pfeist would like to ensure that her ninth graders know that she cares. Which of the following is correct about teachers who care? (Text Hint: See page 433)

    a. Teaches, even if students are not paying attention, so that they will know to pay attention next time

    b. Forgets students' names often because it is not as important as getting them to listen

    c. Makes an effort to make class interesting; teaches in a special way

    d. Does not try to help students so that they will get it on their own

18. Erica's mother is very independent, creative, and seems to live according to the beat of a different drummer. Although she has a few close friends, she is able to get along with many different types of people. Which term best describes Erica's mother? (Text Hint: See page 416)

    a. Democratic

    b. Self-actualized

    c. Extrinsically motivated

    d. Solution-oriented

19. Critics of Maslow's hierarchy of needs assert which of the following? (Text Hint: See page 417)

    a. Self-actualization is impossible to attain.

    b. Students cannot satisfy their cognitive needs without first satisfying their love and belongingness needs.

    c. Safety needs should come first in the sequence, followed by physiological needs.

    d. It is not necessary to satisfy individual needs in the order specified by Maslow.

20. All of the following statements help to explain the decline in intrinsic motivation in the middle and high school years EXCEPT? (Text Hint: See page 422)

    a. Many teachers are more controlling just at the time when adolescents are seeking more autonomy.

    b. Educators believe that it is important for children to develop greater extrinsic motivation as they grow older.

    c. The teacher-student relationship becomes more impersonal at a time when students are seeking independence from their parents and need more support from other adults.

    d. The increased emphasis on grades and competitive comparisons at this time fuels adolescents' natural self-consciousness.

21. Derek is working on a word problem that involves a new algebra concept. Although he doesn't immediately understand how to solve the problem, he pays close attention to the teacher's explanation and tries to relate the new problem to similar homework he finished the night before. What type of achievement orientation does Derek exhibit? (Text Hint: See page 424)

    a. Solution orientation

    b. Helpless orientation

    c. Mastery orientation

    d. Performance orientation

22. At the beginning of the school year, Latoya created a list. At the top of the list she wrote, "I want to finish reading a 100-page chapter book by the end of the month." What type of self-regulatory behavior is Latoya engaging in? (Text Hint: See page 428)

    a. Goal setting

    b. Self-monitoring

    c. Extrinsic motivation

    d. Peer modeling

Answer Key

1. A—Feedback: Subject Category I. Students as Learners: Student Motivation and the Learning Environment: Theoretical foundations about human motivation and behavior: Abraham Maslow

2. D—Feedback: Subject Category I. Students as Learners: Student Motivation and the Learning Environment: Theoretical foundations about human motivation and behavior

3. C—Feedback: Subject Category I. Students as Learners: Student Motivation and the Learning Environment: Factors and situations that are likely to promote or diminish students' motivation to learn: how to help students become self-motivated

4. D—Feedback: Subject Category I. Students as Learners: Student Motivation and the Learning Environment: Important terms that relate to motivation and behavior: Attribution

5. B—Feedback: Subject Category I. Students as Learners: Student Motivation and the Learning Environment: Important terms that relate to motivation and behavior: Learned helplessness

6. D—Feedback: Subject Category I. Students as Learners: Student Motivation and the Learning Environment: How knowledge of human motivation and behavior should influence strategies for organizing and supporting individual and group work in the classroom

7. C—Feedback: Subject Category I. Students as Learners: Student Motivation and the Learning Environment: Important terms that relate to motivation and behavior: Failure syndrome

8. B—Feedback: Subject Category I. Students as Learners: Student Motivation and the Learning Environment: Factors and situations that are likely to promote or diminish students' motivation to learn: how to help students become self-motivated

9. C—Feedback: Subject Category I. Students as Learners: Student Motivation and the Learning Environment: How knowledge of human motivation and behavior should influence strategies for organizing and supporting individual and group work in the classroom

10. A—Feedback: Subject Category I. Students as Learners: Student Motivation and the Learning Environment: Important terms that relate to motivation and behavior: Attribution

11. A—Feedback: Subject Category I. Students as Learners: Student Motivation and the Learning Environment: Important terms that relate to motivation and behavior

12. D—Feedback: Subject Category I. Students as Learners: Student Motivation and the Learning Environment: How knowledge of human motivation and behavior should influence strategies for organizing and supporting individual and group work in the classroom

13. C—Feedback: Subject Category I. Students as Learners: Student Motivation and the Learning Environment: Important terms that relate to motivation and behavior: Failure syndrome

14. A—Feedback: Subject Category I. Students as Learners: Student Motivation and the Learning Environment: How knowledge of human motivation and behavior should influence strategies for organizing and supporting individual and group work in the classroom

15. C—Feedback: Subject Category I. Students as Learners: Student Motivation and the Learning Environment: Principles of effective management and strategies to promote positive relationships, cooperation, and purposeful learning: Communicating with parents and caregivers

16. A—Feedback: Subject Category I. Students as Learners: Student Motivation and the Learning Environment: Important terms that relate to motivation and behavior: Affiliation

17. C—Feedback: Subject Category I. Students as Learners: Student Motivation and the Learning Environment: How knowledge of human motivation and behavior should influence strategies for organizing and supporting individual and group work in the classroom

18. B—Feedback: Subject Category I. Students as Learners: Student Motivation and the Learning Environment: Important terms that relate to motivation and behavior: Self-actualization

19. D—Feedback: Subject Category I. Students as Learners: Student Motivation and the Learning Environment: Theoretical foundations about human motivation and behavior: Abraham Maslow

20. B—Feedback: Subject Category I. Students as Learners: Student Motivation and the Learning Environment: Factors and situations that are likely to promote or diminish students' motivation to learn: how to help students become self-motivated

21. C—Feedback: Subject Category I. Students as Learners: Student Motivation and the Learning Environment: Important terms that relate to motivation and behavior: Mastery orientation

22. A—Feedback: Subject Category I. Students as Learners: Student Motivation and the Learning Environment: Important terms that relate to motivation and behavior: Goal setting

All Subject Categories are as listed in the ETS Principles of Learning and Teaching, *Tests at a Glance*, located at *ftp://ftp.ets.org/pub/tandl/0522.pdf*.

CHAPTER 14

Managing the Classroom

1. In the current view of classroom management, the teacher is best viewed as which of the following? (Text Hint: See page 448)

    a. Guide

    b. Leader

    c. Director

    d. Dictator

2. Classroom management principles sometimes are applied differently in elementary and secondary schools because _____. (Text Hint: See page 449)

    a. teachers are trained differently

    b. of the differing school structures

    c. of different administrative organization

    d. they are not applied differently across elementary and secondary schools

3. Mr. Gonzalez is having difficulty keeping students on task. Which of the following strategies will most likely increase academic learning time in the classroom? (Text Hint: See page 452)

    a. Remember that a good sense of humor is important.

    b. Hold students accountable for their work done during class.

    c. Allow ample time for transition from one activity to the next.

    d. Interrupt class presentations when distracted by student misbehavior.

4. A teacher wants to have a class discussion on current events in which all 23 of her students can participate equally. Which of the following seating arrangements would be most suitable for this event? (Text Hint: See page 456)

    a. Cluster style

    b. Face-to-face style

    c. Off-set style

    d. Seminar style

5. Students will most likely become self-reliant in classrooms that are managed with which strategy? (Text Hint: See page 459)

    a. Authoritarian

    b. Authoritative

    c. Permissive

    d. Punitive

6. Jerome has started his first day student teaching and finds that his cooperating teacher is consistently aware of what is happening in the classroom, monitors students' behavior on a regular basis, and responds to misbehavior before it escalates. How would you describe Jerome's cooperating teacher? (Text Hint: See page 459)

   a. With-it

   b. Omnipotent

   c. Punitive

   d. None of the above

7. Which of the following are recommended strategies for increasing academic learning time? (Text Hint: See page 452)

   a. Flip-flopping from one topic to another

   b. Maximizing transition time between activities

   c. Avoiding dwelling on a topic once the point has been made

   d. Responding to distractions

8. Rules and procedures should be _____ and _____. (Text Hint: See page 462)

   a. firm and punitive

   b. flexible and subjective

   c. reasonable and necessary

   d. set in stone

9. When getting students to share and assume responsibility in the classroom, teachers should do what? (Text Hint: See page 463)

   a. Involve students in the planning and implementation of classroom initiatives.

   b. Accept reasonable excuses infrequently.

   c. Emphasize teacher control.

   d. Have students develop the classroom management plan.

10. Ms. Ryan offers students praise whenever they show that they are on task. Ms. Ryan is using what management strategy? (Text Hint: See page 464)

    a. Shaping

    b. Controlling the student's behavior

    c. Reinforcement

    d. Prompting

11. Mrs. Alvarez had been having difficulty getting Tyrone to work in cooperative learning groups. So she had started just putting him at the same table working among other students. When he did this reliably without getting into trouble, she asked him to simply share the materials with students at the same table. Now he can work in cooperative groups without getting into trouble. What is the name for the strategy Mrs. Alvarez employed? (Text Hint: See page 464)

    a. Shaping

    b. Controlling the student's behavior

    c. Reinforcement

    d. Prompting

12. For communicating with parents of students, all of the following strategies are recommended EXCEPT which one? (Text Hint: See page 465)

    a. Be an active listener.

    b. Use a manipulative mode of communication.

    c. Make eye contact.

    d. Use "I" messages.

13. Which of the following is the best strategy for developing active listening skills? (Text Hint: See page 468)

    a. Practice paraphrasing other people's comments.

    b. Practice criticizing people with different points of view.

    c. Practice offering advice to people who need it.

    d. Practice interrupting politely.

14. Of the following modes of communication, which most accurately depicts one that is manipulative? (Text Hint: See page 466)

    a. Making demands in a hostile tone.

    b. Allowing others to have their way while keeping your own feelings to yourself.

    c. Trying to make someone else feel sorry for you.

    d. Stating your opinion directly and without apology.

15. Linus is really upset with Janice. So Linus confronts Janice and shares his displeasure and says he doesn't want her to take his book anymore without asking. In turn, he promises not to exclude her from working on his team. Which mode of communication is Linus using? (Text Hint: See page 466)

    a. Aggressive style

    b. Manipulative style

    c. Passive style

    d. Assertive style

16. Mrs. Henley makes sure to intermittently restate what students have to say when they come to her with a concern. She feels this is the most effective way to show students that their concerns are important to her as well. Mrs. Henley is using what listening skill? (Text Hint: See page 469)

    a. Paraphrasing

    b. Using "I" messages

    c. "You" messages

    d. Synthesizing

17. What are the three C's of classroom management? (Text Hint: See page 479)

    a. Caring community, calmness, and consideration

    b. Control, constructive conduct rules, and civic values

    c. Cooperative community, constructive conflict resolution, and civic values

    d. Cooperation, community, and civic duty

18. Mr. Johnson wants to get the school year off to a good start. What can he do to make good use of the first weeks of school? (Text Hint: See page 451)

    a. He should remain at his desk so that students don't feel over-controlled.

    b. He should give students games and puzzles and avoid "real" assignments.

    c. He should avoid talking about rules and procedures so that students develop a positive attitude about the class.

    d. He should give students opportunities to experience success with content activities.

19. Mrs. Quincy teaches middle school science. Her classroom includes an aquarium with fish, a terrarium with an iguana, and a cage with a hamster. The desks are arranged in groups of four so that students can discuss science experiments and work together. Three different centers are set up around the perimeter of the classroom, each focused on a different area of science. Which of the following best describes Mrs. Quincy's approach to classroom arrangement? (Text Hint: See page 454)

    a. She knows that arranging an engaging, interactive, and well-organized classroom will contribute to positive student behaviors and overall learning.

    b. She is wasting her time with classroom decorations and should focus more on seatwork.

    c. She is providing students with a chaotic and distracting classroom environment.

    d. She is creating an impersonal classroom environment.

20. COMP, Second Step, and Skills for Life are examples of classroom management programs that emphasize _____? (Text Hint: See page 480)

    a. punishment and negative reinforcement of inappropriate behavior

    b. conflict-resolution skills, anger management, and empathy

    c. eliminating all conflicts

    d. teacher-directed, authoritarian classroom environments

21. To reduce bullying in schools, teachers should do all of the following EXCEPT _____. (Text Hint: See Ch 14, page 476)

    a. form friendship groups for students who are victims of bullies

    b. hold regular class meetings to discuss bullying among students

    c. develop a school program to "catch students being good"

    d. provide swift and aggressive punishment to bullies

Answer Key

1. A—Feedback: Subject Category I. Students as Learners: Student Motivation and the Learning Environment: Principles of effective management and strategies to promote positive relationships, cooperation, and purposeful learning

2. B—Feedback: Subject Category I. Students as Learners: Student Motivation and the Learning Environment: Principles of effective management and strategies to promote positive relationships, cooperation, and purposeful learning

3. B—Feedback: Subject Category II. Instruction and Assessment: Planning Instruction: Techniques for creating effective bridges between curriculum goals and students' experiences: Independent practice, including homework

4. D—Feedback: Subject Category I. Students as Learners: Student Motivation and the Learning Environment: Principles of effective management and strategies to promote positive relationships, cooperation, and purposeful learning: Arranging classroom space

5. C—Feedback: Subject Category I. Students as Learners: Student Motivation and the Learning Environment: Principles of effective management and strategies to promote positive relationships, cooperation, and purposeful learning

6. A—Feedback: Subject Category I. Students as Learners: Student Motivation and the Learning Environment: Principles of effective management and strategies to promote positive relationships, cooperation, and purposeful learning: Responding to student misbehavior

7. C—Feedback: Subject Category I. Students as Learners: Student Motivation and the Learning Environment: Principles of effective management and strategies to promote positive relationships, cooperation, and purposeful learning: Pacing and the structure of the lesson

8. C—Feedback: Subject Category I. Students as Learners: Student Motivation and the Learning Environment: Principles of effective management and strategies to promote positive relationships, cooperation, and purposeful learning: Establishing classroom rules, punishments, and rewards

9. A—Feedback: Subject Category I. Students as Learners: Student Motivation and the Learning Environment: Principles of effective management and strategies to promote positive relationships, cooperation, and purposeful learning: Establishing classroom rules, punishments, and rewards

10. C—Feedback: Subject Category I. Students as Learners: Student Motivation and the Learning Environment: Principles of effective management and strategies to promote positive relationships, cooperation, and purposeful learning: Giving timely feedback

11. A—Feedback: Subject Category I. Students as Learners: Student Motivation and the Learning Environment: Principles of effective management and strategies to promote positive relationships, cooperation, and purposeful learning: How knowledge of human emotion and behavior should influence strategies for organizing and supporting individual and group work in the classroom

12. B—Feedback: Subject Category I. Students as Learners: Student Motivation and the Learning Environment: Principles of effective management and strategies to promote positive relationships, cooperation, and purposeful learning: Communicating with parents and caregivers

13. A—Feedback: Subject Category III. Communication Techniques: Basic, effective verbal and nonverbal communication techniques

14. C—Feedback: Subject Category III. Communication Techniques: Basic, effective verbal and nonverbal communication techniques

15. D—Feedback: Subject Category III. Communication Techniques: Basic, effective verbal and nonverbal communication techniques

16. A—Feedback: Subject Category III. Communication Techniques: Basic, effective verbal and nonverbal communication techniques

17. C—Feedback: Subject Category I. Students as Learners: Student Motivation and the Learning Environment: Principles of effective management and strategies to promote positive relationships, cooperation, and purposeful learning

18. D—Feedback: Subject Category I. Students as Learners: Student Motivation and the Learning Environment: Principles of effective management and strategies to promote positive relationships, cooperation, and purposeful learning

19. A—Feedback: Subject Category I. Students as Learners: Student Motivation and the Learning Environment: Principles of effective management and strategies to promote positive relationships, cooperation, and purposeful learning: Arranging classroom space

20. B—Feedback: Subject Category I. Students as Learners: Student Motivation and the Learning Environment: Principles of effective management and strategies to promote positive relationships, cooperation, and purposeful learning: Modeling conflict resolution, problem solving, and anger management

21. D—Feedback: Subject Category I. Students as Learners: Student Motivation and the Learning Environment: Principles of effective management and strategies to promote positive relationships, cooperation, and purposeful learning: Providing positive guidance

All Subject Categories are as listed in the ETS Principles of Learning and Teaching, *Tests at a Glance*, located at *ftp://ftp.ets.org/pub/tandl/0522.pdf.*

CHAPTER 15
Standardized Tests and Teaching

1. A standardized test is least appropriate in which of the following situations? (Text Hint: See page 488)
   a. Selecting students for entrance to a particular college.
   b. Determining whether a group of students have met their teacher's objectives.
   c. Comparing the students in one classroom to those in another.
   d. Evaluating the quality of a new educational program.

2. The extent to which a test yields the same performance when a student is given the test on two different occasions is called _____. (Text Hint: See page 492)
   a. alternate forms reliability
   b. split-half reliability
   c. test-retest reliability
   d. concurrent validity

3. Which form of validity refers to the extent to which a test measures the student's knowledge of a particular subject? (Text Hint: See page 491)
   a. Predictive validity
   b. Construct validity
   c. Concurrent validity
   d. Content validity

4. Sometimes Maya gets very high scores on intelligence tests. Sometimes her scores are very low. And, from time to time, she gets an average score for someone in her age group. In Maya's case, the tests are best described as which of the following? (Text Hint: See page 491)|
   a. Both reliable and valid
   b. Reliable, but not valid
   c. Not reliable, but valid
   d. Neither reliable nor valid

5. What do supporters of state-mandated achievement tests argue? (Text Hint: See page 496)
   a. That such tests are one of the best ways to hold schools and teachers accountable for students' learning.
   b. That such tests should include essay items.
   c. That such tests are not reliable.
   d. That such tests do not match the age-appropriate curriculum.

6. Which of the following reasons is offered to explain the poor academic performance of American students, as compared to students of other countries? (Text Hint: See page 499)

    a. Standardized tests taken by American students include more open-ended items than do such tests taken by students of other countries

    b. Inadequate time spent on schoolwork

    c. American students spend more time doing homework than do students of other countries

    d. American schools have smaller class sizes than do schools in countries of comparison

7. Which of the following is a measure of central tendency? (Text Hint: See page 503)

    a. Mean

    b. Sample size

    c. Standard deviation

    d. Range

8. Suppose 1000 students take a particular exam. Their scores follow a normal distribution and range from 20 to 75. Of the following values, which would most likely be the mean? (Text Hint: See page 505)

    a. 33

    b. 40

    c. 49

    d. 54

9. A group of students received the following scores on a quiz: 44, 40, 40, 36, 35, 33, 33, 33, and 30. What is the mean? (Text Hint: See page 503)

    a. 33

    b. 35

    c. 36

    d. 37

10. A group of students received the following scores on a quiz: 44, 40, 40, 36, 35, 33, 33, 33, and 30. What is the standard deviation? (Text Hint: See page 504)

    a. 3.34

    b. 4.47

    c. 5.23

    d. 6.11

11. A person who gets the second-highest score of ten people taking an exam would be assigned which percentile rank score? (Text Hint: See page 506)

    a. 90%

    b. 85%

    c. 80%

    d. 75%

12. In a normal distribution, approximately what percent of scores fall between the mean and two standard deviations above the mean? (Text Hint: See page 505)

    a. 34%

    b. 48%

    c. 68%

    d. 95%

13. In a normal distribution, 99 percent of the scores fall between which two values? (Text Hint: See page 505)

    a. One standard deviation below the mean and the mean

    b. One standard deviation below the mean and one standard deviation above the mean

    c. Two standard deviations below the mean and two standard deviations above the mean

    d. Three standard deviations below the mean and three standard deviations above the mean

14. A z-score is an example of which of the following? (Text Hint: See page 507)

    a. Standard score

    b. Stanine

    c. Grade equivalent

    d. Percentile rank

15. A group of students received the following scores on a quiz: 44, 40, 40, 36, 35, 33, 33, 33, and 30. What is the mode? (Text Hint: See page 503)

    a. 33

    b. 35

    c. 36

    d. 37

16. Mrs. Brewtu is aware of the controversy surrounding standardized testing. In order to ensure that her students' scores are reflective of their performance, she _____. (Text Hint: See page 510)

    a. gives them extra time to finish the standardized tests

    b. lets them take the tests a few times before they are to be scored

    c. gives them a high-stakes test to determine whether or not they should take other tests

    d. gives her students alternative assessments so she can determine how the standardized test scores compare

17. Mr. Capadro wants all of his tenth grade students to do well on the upcoming standardized test. Because more than 70% of Mr. Capadro's students are minorities, what should Mr. Capadro be most aware of? (Text Hint: See page 511)

    a. The controversy of the potential for cultural bias in standardized tests may require him to give his students alternative assessments.

    b. The controversy of the potential for cultural bias in standardized tests may require him to give them extra time to finish the standardized tests.

    c. The controversy of the potential for cultural bias in standardized tests may require him to let them take the tests a few times before they are to be scored.

    d. The controversy of the potential for cultural bias in standardized tests may require him to give them a high-stakes test to determine whether or not they should take other tests.

18. Mrs. Dorafill wants to use standardized test scores from the end of the previous year in planning her students' instruction for the next year. How can Mrs. Dorafill use standardized test scores from the end of the previous year to plan for the next coming school year? (Text Hint: See page 509)

    a. By using them to develop a very low or very high expectation for individual students

    b. By using them to provide her with an indication of a student's general ability

    c. By using them to develop a very low or very high expectation for the entire class

    d. By using them as the single indicator when grouping students

19. Ms. Lili just received her class's test scores in the form of standard scores. What type of scores could Ms. Lili expect to see on her class's results? (Text Hint: See page 507)

    a. A z-score

    b. A t-score

    c. Stanine score

    d. Grade-equivalent score

    e. All of the above scores are standard scores

20. Mr. Jensen was told by his principal that the scores of all of the students in his class formed a normal distribution. Knowing this information, what should Mr. Jensen expect with regard to his students' scores? (Text Hint: See page 505)

    a. That most of the scores were above the mean.

    b. That most of the scores were below the mean.

    c. That most of the scores clustered around the mean.

    d. That his students' scores were not on a bell-shaped curve.

21. All of the following are facets of the federal *No Child Left Behind* act EXCEPT _____. (Text Hint: See page 498)

    a. by 2005–2006, teachers who are not considered "highly qualified" will receive a reduction in pay or a warning of dismissal

    b. separate objectives are to be proposed for students who are economically disadvantaged, students from ethnic minority groups, students with disabilities, and students with limited English proficiency

    c. by 2005–2006, states will be required to give all students annual standardized tests in grades 3 through 8

    d. schools that are labeled as "underperforming" must be closed if they do not show improvement after five years

22. Mrs. Williams learns that Jerome scored in the 88th percentile for reading comprehension while Terrence scored in the 81st percentile. She concludes that Jerome is a better reader than Terrence. Mrs. Williams is most likely _____. (Text Hint: See page 508)

    a. using test scores to place students in reading groups

    b. biased

    c. a test scoring expert

    d. overinterpreting test scores

23. Mrs. Walker wishes to supplement standardized testing with alternative assessments that emphasize real-world problem solving. Which type of assessment will meet Mrs. Walker's needs? (Text Hint: See page 512)

    a. IQ tests

    b. Portfolio assessment

    c. Short-answer exams

    d. True-false exams

24. In recent years, schools, teachers, and students have felt greater pressure to perform well on state-mandated standardized tests. Potentially serious consequences can result for low-performing schools, teachers, and students. For this reason, many teachers _____. (Text hint: See Ch 15, page 495)

    a. incorporate state objectives into their classroom planning and instruction

    b. generally spend more time teaching the subjects tested

    c. are feeling pressured to teach a narrower curriculum and lower-level thinking skills

    d. All of the above

25. Intelligence tests and career placement tests are examples of _____. B (Text hint: See Ch 15, page 493)
    a. achievement tests
    b. aptitude tests
    c. high-stakes tests
    d. norm-referenced tests

Answer Key

1. B—Feedback: Subject Category II. Instruction and Assessment: Assessment Strategies: Measurement theory and assessment-related issues: Uses of assessments

2. C—Feedback: Subject Category II. Instruction and Assessment: Assessment Strategies: Measurement theory and assessment-related issues: Characteristics of assessments: Reliability

3. D—Feedback: Subject Category II. Instruction and Assessment: Assessment Strategies: Measurement theory and assessment-related issues: Characteristics of assessments: Validity

4. D—Feedback: Subject Category II. Instruction and Assessment: Assessment Strategies: Measurement theory and assessment-related issues: Characteristics of assessments: Validity and Reliability

5. A—Feedback: Subject Category II. Instruction and Assessment: Assessment Strategies: Measurement theory and assessment-related issues: Types of assessments: Achievement tests

6. B—Feedback: Subject Category II. Instruction and Assessment: Assessment Strategies: Measurement theory and assessment-related issues: Interpreting and communicating results of assessments

7. A—Feedback: Subject Category II. Instruction and Assessment: Assessment Strategies: Measurement theory and assessment-related issues: Scoring assessments: Reporting assessment results

8. C—Feedback: Subject Category II. Instruction and Assessment: Assessment Strategies: Measurement theory and assessment-related issues: Characteristics of assessments: Mean

9. C—Feedback: Subject Category II. Instruction and Assessment: Assessment Strategies: Measurement theory and assessment-related issues: Characteristics of assessments: Mean

10. B—Feedback: Subject Category II. Instruction and Assessment: Assessment Strategies: Measurement theory and assessment-related issues: Scoring assessments: Reporting assessment results: Standard deviation

11. C—Feedback: Subject Category II. Instruction and Assessment: Assessment Strategies: Measurement theory and assessment-related issues: Scoring assessments: Percentile rank

12. B—Feedback: Subject Category II. Instruction and Assessment: Assessment Strategies: Measurement theory and assessment-related issues: Scoring assessments: Reporting assessment results: Standard deviation

13. D—Feedback: Subject Category II. Instruction and Assessment: Assessment Strategies: Measurement theory and assessment-related issues: Scoring assessments: Reporting assessment results: Standard deviation

14. A—Feedback: Subject Category II. Instruction and Assessment: Assessment Strategies: Measurement theory and assessment-related issues: Scoring assessments: Reporting assessment results: Standard score

15. A—Feedback: Subject Category II. Instruction and Assessment: Assessment Strategies: Measurement theory and assessment-related issues: Characteristics of assessments: Mode

16. D—Feedback: Subject Category II. Instruction and Assessment: Assessment Strategies: Measurement theory and assessment-related issues: Types of assessments: Alternative assessments

17. A—Feedback: Subject Category II. Instruction and Assessment: Assessment Strategies: Measurement theory and assessment-related issues: Understanding measurement theory and assessment-related issues

18. B—Feedback: Subject Category II. Instruction and Assessment: Assessment Strategies: Measurement theory and assessment-related issues: Uses of assessments

19. E—Feedback: Subject Category II. Instruction and Assessment: Assessment Strategies: Measurement theory and assessment-related issues: Scoring assessments: Reporting assessment results

20. C—Feedback: Subject Category II. Instruction and Assessment: Assessment Strategies: Measurement theory and assessment-related issues: Scoring assessments: Normal distribution

21. A—Feedback: Subject Category II. Instruction and Assessment: Assessment Strategies: Measurement theory and assessment-related issues: Types of assessments: Standardized tests

22. D—Feedback: Subject Category II. Instruction and Assessment: Assessment Strategies: Measurement theory and assessment-related issues: Interpreting and communicating results of assessments

23. B—Feedback: Subject Category II. Instruction and Assessment: Assessment Strategies: Measurement theory and assessment-related issues: Types of assessments: Portfolios

24. D—Feedback: Subject Category II. Instruction and Assessment: Planning Instruction: Techniques for planning instruction to meet curriculum goals, including the incorporation of learning theory, subject matter, curriculum development, and student development: National and state learning standards

25. B—Feedback: Subject Category II. Instruction and Assessment: Assessment Strategies: Measurement theory and assessment-related issues: Types of assessments: Aptitude tests

All Subject Categories are as listed in the ETS Principles of Learning and Teaching, *Tests at a Glance*, located at *ftp://ftp.ets.org/pub/tandl/0522.pdf*.

CHAPTER 16

Classroom Assessment

1. Research suggests that teachers spend about how much of their professional time dealing with matters of assessment? (Text Hint: See page 520)
   a. 5–10%
   b. 10–20%
   c. 20–30%
   d. 30–50%

2. Of the following activities, which is the best example of pre-instruction assessment? (Text Hint: See page 520)
   a. Look over students' prior grades in the subject of interest.
   b. Ask students to clarify answers given during class.
   c. Monitor students' progress toward reaching learning targets.
   d. Report assessment results for school-level analysis.

3. Which of the following is the best example of formative assessment? (Text Hint: See page 522)
   a. Observe students' nonverbal behavior to learn about their abilities and interests.
   b. Describe the extent to which students have achieved instructional goals and objectives.
   c. Communicate students' strengths and weaknesses to parents.
   d. Identify difficulties that students are experiencing and offer advice.

4. Which of the following questions is the best example of a thinking-based item designed to assess students' abilities to evaluate? (Text Hint: See page 522)
   a. Give one example of a situation that demonstrates Newton's first law of motion.
   b. Identify one weakness in the argument that deforestation will enhance the greenhouse effect.
   c. Were dinosaurs warm-blooded?
   d. Why do birds fly?

5. The extent to which an assessment is a reasonable sample of what actually occurs in the classroom is referred to as which of the following? (Text Hint: See page 525)
   a. Content-related evidence
   b. Pluralistic assessment
   c. Instructional validity
   d. Item discrimination

6. Reliability refers to the extent to which a test does which of the following? (Text Hint: See page 525)
   a. Provides all students an equal opportunity to succeed
   b. Provides equivalent scores for a diverse group of individuals
   c. Produces a consistent, reproducible measure of performance
   d. Measures what it is intended to measure

7. When writing multiple choice test items for an exam, all of the following strategies are recommended EXCEPT which one? (Text Hint: See page 530)

   a. Make sure that alternatives are grammatically correct.

   b. Use the exact wording as it appears in the textbook.

   c. Make every effort to write the stem as a question.

   d. Include as much of the item as possible in the stem.

8. An item is considered poor if its item discrimination index falls in which of the following ranges? (Text Hint: See page 533)

   a. 0 to .19

   b. 0.2 to .39

   c. 0.4 to .69

   d. 0.70 to 1.0

9. Which of the following are good examples of constructed-response items? (Text Hint: See page 533)

   a. True-false questions

   b. Matching items

   c. Multiple-choice items

   d. Essay items

10. Choose the most effective way to score essay questions from the following scenarios: _____. (Text Hint: See page 534)

    a. Ms. Elijah outlines a good example of an acceptable response before reading students' essays

    b. Mr. Miles always reads through each student's complete essays before moving onto the next student's responses

    c. When Mr. Quan encounters an irrelevant or incorrect response, he puts them off to the side to deal with at a later time

    d. Mrs. Clooney does not reread essays because she feels the initial response is always the correct interpretation of a student's answer

11. Which of the following item formats is an example of a performance assessment? (Text Hint: See page 538)

    a. Multiple choice

    b. Matching

    c. True/false

    d. Essay

12. A best-work portfolio accomplishes which of the following goals? (Text Hint: See page 544)

    a. Shows the student's growth during a given school year

    b. Shows the student's growth over a period of several years

    c. Shows a collection of the student's most outstanding work

    d. Shows the student's most outstanding piece of work

13. Which of the following describes a major benefit of using portfolios as tools for assessment? (Text Hint: See page 545)

    a. Opportunity to evaluate students' improvement

    b. Simplicity of establishing criteria and assigning grades

    c. Ease of comparing one student's work with another student's work

    d. Ability to treat skills in isolated contexts

14. In Candace's third period algebra course, her teacher uses grading to evaluate students in need of remedial work before moving on to the next skill. Which purpose of grading does this meet? (Text Hint: See page 545)

    a. Administrative

    b. Informational

    c. Motivational

    d. Guidance

15. When grading students, Mr. Lopez consistently compares students' scores with that of their peers. This is a good example of which standard of comparison? (Text Hint: See page 547)

    a. Norm-referenced grading

    b. Criteria-referenced grading

    c. Standards-based grading

    d. None of the above

16. When reporting students' scores to parents through report cards, checklists of skills and objectives are mainly used in _____. (Text Hint: See page 549)

    a. high schools

    b. junior high schools

    c. upper elementary grades

    d. kindergartens and elementary schools

17. Mr. Woodward utilized electronic portfolios in his literature class. What are examples of materials he might have students include in the portfolio? (Text Hint: See page 552)

    a. Critical writing samples

    b. Unit test scores

    c. PowerPoint presentations

    d. All of the above

18. Aurbach's Cirady Profile, HyperStudio, and FileMaker Pro are all examples of _____. (Text Hint: See page 552)

    a. portfolios

    b. performance-based assessments

    c. electronic portfolios

    d. electronic record-keeping tools

19. Ms. Hall is using a program on the Internet to input and monitor data about her students' academic progress. Ms. Hall is using a _____. (Text Hint: See page 554)

    a. web-based assessment

    b. portfolio assessment

    c. performance assessment

    d. summative assessment

20. Mr. Kouta developed a rating scale for evaluating his students' history dioramas. This rating scale is called _____. (Text Hint: See page 540)

    a. a checklist

    b. an answer key

    c. performance criteria

    d. a scoring rubric

21. Which of the following statements best describes current views about assessment? (Text Hint: See page 520)

    a. Assessment should be integrated throughout the instructional process.

    b. Assessment should be implemented at the conclusion of a particular lesson or unit of study.

    c. Assessment should only be implemented by teachers who are specially trained in the areas of traditional and alternative assessments.

    d. None of the above.

22. The majority of Mr. Robinson's students are from low socioeconomic backgrounds and have little experience with the world beyond their neighborhoods. He is concerned about fairness in standardized testing. Mr. Robinson feels that performance assessment should be used during and after instruction to supplement standardized testing. This type of assessment is _____. (Text Hint: See page 526)

    a. formative assessment

    b. objective assessment

    c. pluralistic assessment

    d. traditional assessment

23. Mr. Riggles created a multiple-choice and essay quiz for his students after they finished reading *Roll of Thunder, Hear My Cry*. The exam tested students on the main characters, plot, setting, and climax of the book. This type of assessment is an example of a(n) _____. (Text hint: See page 523)

    a. informal assessment

    b. summative assessment

    c. formative assessment

    d. standardized assessment

Answer Key

1. C—Feedback: Subject Category II. Instruction and Assessment: Assessment Strategies: Measurement theory and assessment-related issues: Understanding measurement theory and assessment-related issues

2. A—Feedback: Subject Category II. Instruction and Assessment: Assessment Strategies: Measurement theory and assessment-related issues: Types of assessments

3. D—Feedback: Subject Category II. Instruction and Assessment: Assessment Strategies: Measurement theory and assessment-related issues: Uses of assessments: Formative evaluation

4. B—Feedback: Subject Category III. Communication Techniques: Types of questions that can stimulate discussion in different ways for different purposes: Helping students articulate their ideas and thinking processes

5. C—Feedback: Subject Category II. Instruction and Assessment: Assessment Strategies: Measurement theory and assessment-related issues: Characteristics of assessments: Validity

6. C—Feedback: Subject Category II. Instruction and Assessment: Assessment Strategies: Measurement theory and assessment-related issues: Characteristics of assessments: Reliability

7. B—Feedback: Subject Category II. Instruction and Assessment: Assessment Strategies: Measurement theory and assessment-related issues: Types of assessments

8. A—Feedback: Subject Category II. Instruction and Assessment: Assessment Strategies: Measurement theory and assessment-related issues: Characteristics of assessments

9. D—Feedback: Subject Category II. Instruction and Assessment: Assessment Strategies: Measurement theory and assessment-related issues: Types of assessments: Essays written to prompts

10. A—Feedback: Subject Category II. Instruction and Assessment: Assessment Strategies: Measurement theory and assessment-related issues: Scoring assessments: Rubrics

11. D—Feedback: Subject Category II. Instruction and Assessment: Assessment Strategies: Measurement theory and assessment-related issues: Types of assessments: Performance assessments

12. C—Feedback: Subject Category II. Instruction and Assessment: Assessment Strategies: Measurement theory and assessment-related issues: Types of assessments: Portfolios

13. A—Feedback: Subject Category II. Instruction and Assessment: Assessment Strategies: Measurement theory and assessment-related issues: Types of assessments: Portfolios

14. D—Feedback: Subject Category II. Instruction and Assessment: Assessment Strategies: Measurement theory and assessment-related issues: Uses of assessments: Diagnostic evaluation

15. A—Feedback: Subject Category II. Instruction and Assessment: Assessment Strategies: Measurement theory and assessment-related issues: Characteristics of assessments: Norm-referenced

16. D—Feedback: Subject Category II. Instruction and Assessment: Assessment Strategies: Measurement theory and assessment-related issues: Scoring assessments: Reporting assessment results

17. D—Feedback: Subject Category II. Instruction and Assessment: Assessment Strategies: Measurement theory and assessment-related issues: Types of assessments: Portfolios

18. C—Feedback: Subject Category II. Instruction and Assessment: Assessment Strategies: Measurement theory and assessment-related issues: Types of assessments: Portfolios

19. A—Feedback: Subject Category II. Instruction and Assessment: Assessment Strategies: Measurement theory and assessment-related issues: Types of assessments: Web-based assessment

20. D—Feedback: Subject Category II. Instruction and Assessment: Assessment Strategies: Measurement theory and assessment-related issues: Scoring assessments: Rubrics

21. A—Feedback: Subject Category II. Instruction and Assessment: Assessment Strategies: Measurement theory and assessment-related issues: Understanding measurement theory and assessment-related issues

22. C—Feedback: Subject Category II. Instruction and Assessment: Assessment Strategies: Measurement theory and assessment-related issues: Types of assessments: Performance assessments

23. B—Feedback: Subject Category II. Instruction and Assessment: Assessment Strategies: Measurement theory and assessment-related issues: Uses of assessments: Summative evaluation

All Subject Categories are as listed in the ETS Principles of Learning and Teaching, *Tests at a Glance*, located at *ftp://ftp.ets.org/pub/tandl/0522.pdf*.

Part III

Content Practice Quizzes by PRAXIS II™ Subject Category

I. Students as Learners

a. Student Development and the Learning Process

1. Theoretical foundations about how learning occurs: how students construct knowledge, acquire skills, and develop habits of mind

1. Who was the first individual to use the term "gifted" to describe students who scored exceptionally high on intelligence tests? (Text Hint: See page 6)[1]
   a. Mamie Clark
   b. William James
   c. John Dewey
   d. Leta Hollingsworth

2. An individual who takes a constructivist approach to teaching would most likely encourage students to do which of the following? (Text Hint: See page 8)
   a. Solve math problems.
   b. Collaborate with others.
   c. Memorize information.
   d. Assemble puzzles.

3. Which of the following researchers, during the late 1880s, argued for the importance of observing teaching and learning in the classrooms for improving education? (Text Hint: See page 8)
   a. John Dewey
   b. William James
   c. E. L. Thorndike
   d. Leta Hollingsworth

4. _____ occurs when a child incorporates new knowledge into existing knowledge. (Text Hint: See page 39)
   a. Assimilation
   b. Accommodation
   c. Equilibration
   d. Lateralization

5. Choose the best example of seriation from the following examples. (Text Hint: See page 45)
   a. Lorna lines her blocks up in a straight row.
   b. Billy lines his blocks by color.
   c. Jermaine lines his blocks from biggest to smallest.
   d. Troy chews on his blocks.

---

[1] All text hint references are to *Educational Psychology*, 2/e, Classroom Update, by John. W. Santrock.

6. The teacher notices Shawn cannot solve a problem on his own, but can when he is given either adult or peer guidance. This guidance is called _____. (Text Hint: See page 51)

    a. assisted performance

    b. the zone of proximal development

    c. preoperational thinking

    d. lateralization

7. Which one of the following is the best example of scaffolding? (Text Hint: See page 52)

    a. Mr. Christiansen takes every opportunity to nurture students' individual strengths.

    b. Mrs. Jackson has students write their term papers on an area of each student's interests.

    c. Ms. Alicia always provides a detailed lesson on the Civil War before giving students their term paper assignments.

    d. Mr. Thompson demonstrates how to write the letter "z" in cursive at the blackboard before having students do so.

8. Vygotsky's stage in the development of speech characterized by silent "self-talk" is called _____. (Text Hint: See page 52)

    a. private speech

    b. personal speech

    c. egocentric speech

    d. social speech

9. The link between the home and the school is an example of a _____. (Text Hint: See page 68)

    a. microsystem

    b. mesosystem

    c. exosystem

    d. macrosystem

    e. chronosystem

10. The school board passes a new rule that limits the number of students allowed in each classroom in order to enhance teacher-student relationships. This is an example of which environmental system? (Text Hint: See page 69)

    a. microsystem

    b. mesosystem

    c. exosystem

    d. macrosystem

    e. chronosystem

11. Which of the following provides the best example of the macrosystem, as described in Bronfenbrenner's ecological theory? (Text Hint: See page 70)

    a. Students interact directly with their teacher.

    b. A parent attends a parent-teacher conference without the student.

    c. Local government approves increased funding for public school libraries.

    d. Society progresses toward acceptability of females serving in more administrative roles in the schools.

12. According to William Stern's 1912 definition of intelligence quotient (IQ), a person would have an IQ greater than 100 under which of the following conditions? (Text Hint: See page 107)

    a. A person's chronological age is greater than his or her own mental age.

    b. A person's mental age is greater than his or her own chronological age.

    c. A person earns average scores on an intelligence test, as compared to other individuals of the same chronological age.

    d. A person earns a higher than average score on an intelligence test, as compared to other individuals of the same chronological age.

13. William Stern's (1912) intelligence quotient is defined as which of the following? (Text Hint: See page 107)

    a. A person's chronological age divided by the person's mental age, multiplied by 100

    b. A person's mental age divided by the person's chronological age, multiplied by 100

    c. A person's mental age divided by a standard value for their age, multiplied by 100

    d. A person's mental age divided by the average mental age for other people of the same chronological age, multiplied by 100

14. Which of the following individuals proposed that there are eight types of intelligence and developed Project Spectrum to apply this information to classroom teaching? (Text Hint: See page 111)

    a. Robert Sternberg

    b. William Stern

    c. Alfred Binet

    d. Howard Gardner

15. Which of the following descriptions of students reveals the greatest level of "analytical" intelligence, as proposed by Robert Sternberg? (Text Hint: See page 110)

    a. Carlos has won numerous awards for his ability to play the piano.

    b. Mika is a champion tennis player.

    c. Anna won the science fair for designing an irrigation system.

    d. Kara earned a perfect score on her midterm history exam.

16. A psychologist who wants to emphasize the importance of nature in the nature-nurture debate would cite which of the following factors as being most influential in an individual's intelligence? (Text Hint: See page 117)

    a. The individual attended preschool.

    b. The individual enjoys reading books.

    c. The individual does well in school.

    d. The individual's parents have high IQs.

17. Learning is primarily the result of _____. (Text Hint: See page 210)

    a. development

    b. experience

    c. innate abilities

    d. socialization

18. All of the following questions reflect a cognitive information processing approach, except which one? (Text Hint: See page 246)
    a. How do children get information into memory, store it, and retrieve it?
    b. How can teachers help children improve their memory and study strategies?
    c. How do environmental factors influence the age at which a child learns to crawl?
    d. What are the best strategies for helping children become better problem solvers?

19. Which of the following scenarios best demonstrates automaticity? (Text Hint: See page 247)
    a. Margie knows that 3 times 4 equals 12 without thinking about it.
    b. Jordan counts the number of apples in a basket.
    c. Kara practices how to print the alphabet.
    d. Harry uses his fingers to add 5 plus 4.

20. Which of the following scenarios presents the best example of encoding? (Text Hint: See page 247)
    a. Tamara is writing a letter.
    b. Brian is practicing how to count.
    c. Joan remembers her first day of school.
    d. Julie is listening to music.

21. Which of the following scenarios best depicts elaboration? (Text Hint: See page 252)
    a. Jose memorized a list of spelling words for a spelling bee.
    b. Kate and Sue brainstormed ideas for a poster.
    c. Taylor practiced writing the numbers and alphabet.
    d. John thought about his vegetable garden when his class studied botany.

22. Which of the following examples best illustrates chunking? (Text Hint: See page 254)
    a. Georgia thinks of personal examples when learning about new concepts in science.
    b. Jodi classifies animals based on common features and differences.
    c. Adam uses symbols to represent words that he has difficulty spelling.
    d. Harold and Mohammed work together when designing a telescope.

23. Which of the following statements best describes the nature of declarative memory? (Text Hint: See page 259)
    a. Karen applies knowledge to perform a certain task.
    b. Scott recognizes a famous person.
    c. Natasha is able to provide specific factual information about an event.
    d. Ivan recalls a specific event from his or her past.

24. According to the decay theory, which of the following is the cause of forgetting? (Text Hint: See page 263)
    a. Lack of schema
    b. Disintegration of memory traces
    c. Lack of initial encoding
    d. Interference by new information

25. Mr. Abraham is having a guest speaker come into his first grade class to give his students a lesson on space travel. The guest speaker is very humorous and presented attention-grabbing devices and pictures. Immediately upon the speaker's leaving, Mr. Abraham discusses the presentation with his class. He is puzzled to discover that although the students enjoyed the presentation, they did not seem to know the subject matter of the presentation. Most students could not recall what the guest speaker had actually said. They did, however, remember all of the unusual items that the guest speaker brought with her. In this scenario, why did Mr. Abraham's class have trouble recalling the subject matter of the presentation? (Text Hint: See page 249)

    a. Because the students lacked short-term memory

    b. Because the students' attention was drawn away from the lesson by the interesting objects the speaker brought in to the class

    c. Because the students do not have memory traces

    d. Because the students experienced the decay theory

26. Susan is excited about returning to school after summer vacation. Her first day of middle school ended great, and once Susan is at home she begins to recall that day's events. Susan's memory of the day's events is called_____. (Text Hint: See page 259)

    a. procedural knowledge

    b. chunking

    c. episodic memory

    d. semantic memory

27. Brian, an eleventh grader, is taking his French exam. He prepared for this exam and he knows the information; however, while taking the exam Brian is having trouble recalling the information because the teacher did not provide a word bank from which to choose the answer. Brian's forgetting is most likely due to _____. (Text Hint: See page 263)

    a. cue-dependent forgetting

    b. interference theory

    c. decay theory

    d. sensory register

28. Todd and Kimberly are seated opposite one another getting ready to begin a game of Scrabble. Todd is 10 years old and Kimberly is 15 years old. Their camp counselor says to Kimberly, "Now Kimberly, go easy on Todd, remember he is younger than you and there are differences in memory ability between the two of you." However, much to Kimberly and the camp counselor's surprise, Todd beats Kimberly at every game he plays with her. In fact, Todd has competed in Scrabble matches and has received awards and trophies. Todd's winning all of the matches against Kimberly was most likely because _____. (Text Hint: See page 266)

    a. Todd's intelligence was greater than Kimberly's.

    b. Todd was probably cheating and Kimberly did not notice.

    c. Todd was just lucky and Kimberly was not.

    d. Todd was an expert in Scrabble and Kimberly was a beginner.

29. Quinn tells his teacher that someone in the class took his pencil while he was working with his reading group. He says that several children have explanations for what happened to his pencil and he would like his teacher to hear them all. Although several of the children claim they saw what happened, they all have different versions of the event. Nathan says that Ron took the pencil just like he took Nathan's eraser yesterday. Keri tells the teacher that it was Ron who took the pencil because he was sitting next to Quinn's desk at the time. Finally, Cecilia says that it was Teresa who took the pencil and then gave it to Ron in exchange for his multicolored pen. The students' various stories of what happened to Ron's pencil are best accounted for by _____. (Text Hint: See page 260)

    a. schema theories

    b. network theories

    c. encoding specificity principle

    d. expertise

30. Experts do all of the following EXCEPT _____. (Text Hint: See page 266)

    a. approach new situations with the same strategies

    b. detect meaningful patterns of information

    c. retrieve key aspects of their knowledge with little effort

    d. acquire extensive knowledge that is organized in a manner that shows a deep understanding of the subject

31. Jake has difficulty in determining which information is central to understanding a concept and which details are peripheral. This is an example of the _____ stage of expertise. (Text Hint: See page 268)

    a. retrieval

    b. encoded

    c. metacognitive

    d. acclimation

32. The three types of memory that vary according to their time frames include all of the following EXCEPT _____. (Text Hint: See page 255)

    a. sensory memory

    b. semantic memory

    c. short-term memory

    d. long-term memory

33. Mrs. Moran's geometry class is learning how to prove theorems. Mrs. Moran instructs them on this concept and then will test her students in the same setting in which the concept was learned. In Mrs. Moran's class, what type of transfer are her students involved in? (Text Hint: See page 305)

    a. Near

    b. Far

    c. Low-road

    d. High-road

34. Mr. Vista always encourages his students to think about how they can apply information that they have already learned to a new context. What type of transfer is Mr. Vista encouraging his students to do? (Text Hint: See page 306)

    a. Forward-rearing transfer

    b. Backward-rearing transfer

    c. Near transfer

    d. Far transfer

35. Constructivism emphasizes that individuals learn best when they _____. (Text Hint: See page 314)
    a. work in collaborative groups
    b. actively put together knowledge and understanding
    c. learn effective strategies for retrieving information
    d. solve-real world problems

36. Unlike Piaget's model of child development, Vygotsky's model emphasizes the importance of social interactions in shaping children's knowledge. (Text Hint: See page 314)
    a. True
    b. False

37. Situated cognition is best described as _____. (Text Hint: See page 316)
    a. thinking that is located in social and physical contexts
    b. a technique for changing the level of support over the course of a teaching session
    c. a social constructivist program that encourages reflection and discussion through using adults as role models, children teaching children, and online computer consultation
    d. the importance of gleaning knowledge from different contexts

38. Three of the following teachers are using scaffolding to help their students learn. Which one is *NOT* a good example of scaffolding? (Text Hint: See page 316)
    a. Ms. Lilly gives her class some hints about how to solve an especially difficult algebra problem.
    b. Mrs. Branson teaches a golf swing by gently guiding each student through the correct movement a few times.
    c. Ms. Niles gives John a structure to follow when he writes his first poem.
    d. Mr. Johnson takes his students to the computer lab.

39. Cognitive apprenticeship is a tool that involves _____. (Text Hint: See page 317)
    a. an expert stretching and supporting a novice's understanding and use of a culture's skills
    b. a technique for changing the level of support over the course of a teaching session
    c. a social constructivist program that encourages reflection and discussion through using adults as role models, children teaching children, and online computer consultation
    d. thinking that is located in social and physical contexts

2. Human development in the physical, social, emotional, moral, and cognitive domains

1. Which of the following is an example of a biological process that might be studied by an educational psychologist? (Text Hint: See page 35)
    a. The development of social relationships
    b. The changes in children's motor skills
    c. The changes in children's ability to think logically
    d. The influence of parental nurturing on children's tendency to be aggressive

2. During the period of development known as "middle and late childhood," a child typically does which of the following? (Text Hint: See page 35)
    a. Masters the fundamental skills of writing
    b. Prefers to spend time with parents than with peers
    c. Makes important career decisions
    d. Learns to identify letters of the alphabet

3. Myelination of areas in the brain related to hand-eye coordination is typically completed during which stage of an individual's life? (Text Hint: See page 37)

   a. Infancy

   b. Early childhood

   c. Adolescence

   d. Young adulthood

4. Patricia demonstrates object permanence when her rattle is taken and hidden under a blanket and she _____. (Text Hint: See page 40)

   a. looks to find something new to play with

   b. lifts the blanket to look for the rattle

   c. begins to play with her mother

   d. cries hysterically

5. The preoperational stage, as described by Piaget, includes individuals in which of the following age groups? (Text Hint: See page 40)

   a. Birth to 2 years

   b. 2 to 7 years

   c. 7 to 11 years

   d. 11 years through adulthood

6. According to Piaget, a child is *first* able to understand that sequences or procedures are reversible when the child reaches which of the following stages? (Text Hint: See page 43)

   a. Sensorimotor stage

   b. Preoperational stage

   c. Concrete operational stage

   d. Formal operational stage

7. Tracy examines the possibilities of working with Sam. He is very good at working with computers, so he may be a good partner for helping to complete the research project. However, Tracy also knows that Sam is chronically irresponsible and may neglect the project. Tracy decides to test the waters by talking to other students who have worked with Sam as well as asking Sam a few questions about his ideas about carrying out the project to determine his likelihood of helping out. Which stage of Piaget's theory do you think Tracy is at? (Text Hint: See page 46)

   a. Sensorimotor

   b. Preoperational

   c. Concrete Operational

   d. Formal Operational

8. The following emphases are central to Vygotsky's theory. (Text Hint: See page 51)

   a. Zone of proximal development

   b. Sociocultural influences

   c. Language

   d. All the above

9. Which of the following represents Vygotsky's view of the origin of cognitive development? (Text Hint: See page 51)

    a. Intelligence

    b. Genetics

    c. Social interactions

    d. Self-regulated behavior

10. Kylie's parents are so proud because Kylie has just said her first word. Having only this information, how old would you guess Kylie is? (Text Hint: See page 62)

    a. 3–6 months

    b. 10–13 months

    c. 18–24 months

    d. at least 36 months

11. Critics of Piaget assert all of the following EXCEPT _____. (Text Hint: See page 49)

    a. children's cognitive development does not occur in synchronous stages

    b. children at one cognitive stage can be trained to reason at a higher cognitive stage

    c. children go through cognitive stages at the same rate

    d. culture and education exert strong influences on children's cognitive development

12. Effective teachers who work with formal operational thinkers do all of the following EXCEPT _____. (Text Hint: See page 48)

    a. realize that many adolescents are not full-fledged formal operational thinkers

    b. present a problem that has one, clear approach to solving it

    c. propose a problem and invite students to form hypotheses about how to solve it

    d. develop projects and investigations for students to carry out

13. Which of the following provides the best example of the microsystem, as described in Bronfenbrenner's ecological theory? (Text Hint: See page 68)

    a. Students interact directly with their teacher.

    b. A parent attends a parent-teacher conference without the student.

    c. Local government approves increased funding for public school libraries.

    d. Society progresses toward acceptability of females serving in more administrative roles in the schools.

14. Which of the following is the final stage of development, as proposed by Erikson? (Text Hint: See page 72)

    a. Autonomy versus shame and doubt

    b. Trust versus mistrust

    c. Integrity versus despair

    d. Identity versus identity confusion

15. According to Erikson's life-span development theory, at approximately what age does a person undergo the stage of autonomy versus shame and doubt? (Text Hint: See page 71)

    a. The first year

    b. The second year

    c. Age 6 to puberty

    d. Adolescence

16. On the basis of Erikson's life-span development theory, which of the following strategies would best enable a teacher to stimulate identity exploration in adolescents? (Text Hint: See page 73)

    a. Encourage individuals to express their views freely.

    b. Structure activities around success rather than failure.

    c. Provide opportunities for fantasy play.

    d. Evaluate students' opinions carefully and critically

17. Which of the following statements best describes a student with identity diffusion? (Text Hint: See page 92)

    a. The student has explored career paths and made a commitment toward a goal.

    b. The student has accepted someone else's idea for a career path and made a commitment toward that goal.

    c. The student has not explored career paths and lacks a goal.

    d. The student has explored career paths but has made no commitments toward any path.

18. Alina, a high school student, loves to work with computers. She is also very active in student government. She would like to pursue a career that involves interacting with people. She is considering careers in computer programming and computer sales, as well as careers in politics and law. She hopes to make a final decision by the end of this school year. Which of the following labels best describes Alina's identity status? (Text Hint: See page 92)

    a. Identity diffusion

    b. Identity moratorium

    c. Identity achievement

    d. Identity foreclosure

19. A high school student who feels it is wrong to cheat because if he gets caught he will be sent to the office is revealing which level of Kohlberg's moral reasoning? (Text Hint: See page 95)

    a. Preconventional

    b. Conventional

    c. Postconventional

20. An individual in the conventional level of Kohlberg's theory would turn to which of the following when making a moral decision? (Text Hint: See page 96)

    a. Family expectations

    b. Potential punishment involved

    c. Individual values

    d. Personal needs and desires

21. An individual in the postconventional level of Kohlberg's theory would turn to which of the following when making a moral decision? (Text Hint: See page 96)

    a. Family expectations

    b. Potential punishment involved

    c. Individual values

    d. Personal needs and desires

22. Kohlberg's second level of morality, reflecting an internalization of standards created by other people in society, is called _____. (Text Hint: See page 96)
    a. preconventional
    b. conventional
    c. midconventional
    d. postconventional

23. Individuals who evaded the draft due to fear for their lives would be considered _____; while those who did so out of principles of peace would be _____. (Text Hint: See page 95)
    a. preconventional; postconventional
    b. conventional; preconventional
    c. postconventional; conventional
    d. conventional; postconventional

24. Kohlberg and Gilligan have proposed theories of moral development. Kohlberg's focuses on _____; Gilligan's focuses on _____. (Text Hint: See page 97)
    a. justice; care
    b. care; justice
    c. rightness; wrongness
    d. relationships; abstract reasoning

25. Rolanda generally responds to new experiences negatively, is impulsive, and is sometimes aggressive. How would you characterize Rolanda's temperament? (Text Hint: See page 127)
    a. easy
    b. difficult
    c. slow-to-warm-up

26. Which of the following would be the best example of a slow-to-warm-up child? (Text Hint: See page 127)
    a. Lily is fairly accommodating but is often not interested in doing things.
    b. Reece is a happy child who gets along with acquaintances of the family, but can be hesitant around complete strangers.
    c. Peter is aggressive and usually rejects new people in his life

27. Imagine a teacher who prefers that her classroom is quiet and controlled. How would this teacher most likely label her bodily-kinesthetic and extroverted students? (Text Hint: See pages 127–128)
    a. Temperamental
    b. Easy
    c. Slow-to-warmup
    d. Difficult

Answer Key

1. Theoretical foundations about how learning occurs: how students construct knowledge, acquire skills, and develop habits of mind

1. D—Feedback: Subject Category I. Students as Learners: Student Development and the Learning Process: Theoretical foundations about how learning occurs—how students construct knowledge, acquire skills, and develop habits of mind: Examples of important theorists

2. B—Feedback: Subject Category I. Students as Learners: Student Development and the Learning Process: Theoretical foundations about how learning occurs—how students construct knowledge, acquire skills, and develop habits of mind: Important terms that relate to learning theory: Constructivism

3. B—Feedback: Subject Category I. Students as Learners: Student Development and the Learning Process: Theoretical foundations about how learning occurs—how students construct knowledge, acquire skills, and develop habits of mind: Examples of important theorists

4. A—Feedback: Subject Category I. Students as Learners: Student Development and the Learning Process: Important terms that relate to learning theory

5. C—Feedback: Subject Category I. Students as Learners: Student Development and the Learning Process: Theoretical foundations about how learning occurs—how students construct knowledge, acquire skills, and develop habits of mind: Important terms that relate to learning theory: Seriation

6. A—Feedback: Subject Category I. Students as Learners: Student Development and the Learning Process: Important terms that relate to learning theory

7. D—Feedback: Subject Category I. Students as Learners: Student Development and the Learning Process: Important terms that relate to learning theory

8. A—Feedback: Subject Category I. Students as Learners: Student Development and the Learning Process: Important terms that relate to learning theory

9. B—Feedback: Subject Category I. Students as Learners: Student development and the Learning Process: Important terms that relate to learning theory: Mesosystem

10. C—Feedback: Subject Category I. Students as Learners: Student development and the Learning Process: Important terms that relate to learning theory: Exosystem

11. D—Feedback: Subject Category I. Students as Learners: Student development and the Learning Process: Important terms that relate to learning theory: Macrosystem

12. B—Feedback: Subject Category I. Students as Learners: Student Development and the Learning Process: Theoretical foundations about how learning occurs: Important terms that relate to learning theory: Intelligence

13. B—Feedback: Subject Category I. Students as Learners: Student Development and the Learning Process: Theoretical foundations about how learning occurs: Important terms that relate to learning theory: Intelligence

14. D—Feedback: Subject Category I. Students as Learners: Student Development and the Learning Process: Theoretical foundations about how learning occurs: Examples of important theorists: Howard Gardner

15. D—Feedback: Subject Category I. Students as Learners: Student Development and the Learning Process: Theoretical foundations about how learning occurs: Examples of important theorists: Robert Sternberg

16. D—Feedback: Subject Category I. Students as Learners: Student development and the Learning Process: Theoretical foundations about how learning occurs: how students construct knowledge, acquire skills, and develop habits of mind

17. B—Feedback: Subject Category I. Students as Learners: Student Development and the Learning Process: Theoretical foundations about how learning occurs—how students construct knowledge, acquire skills, and develop habits of mind: Important terms that relate to learning theory: Learning

18. C—Feedback: Subject Category I. Students as Learners: Student development and the Learning Process: Theoretical foundations about how learning occurs: how students construct knowledge, acquire skills, and develop habits of mind

19. A—Feedback: Subject Category I. Students as Learners: Student Development and the Learning Process: Important terms that relate to learning theory

20. D—Feedback: Subject Category I. Students as Learners: Student Development and the Learning Process: Important terms that relate to learning theory

21. D—Feedback: Subject Category I. Students as Learners: Student Development and the Learning Process: Important terms that relate to learning theory

22. B—Feedback: Subject Category I. Students as Learners: Student Development and the Learning Process: Important terms that relate to learning theory

23. C—Feedback: Subject Category I. Students as Learners: Student Development and the Learning Process: Important terms that relate to learning theory: Memory

24. B—Feedback: Subject Category I. Students as Learners: Student Development and the Learning Process: Important terms that relate to learning theory: Memory

25. B—Feedback: Subject Category I. Students as Learners: Student Development and the Learning Process: Important terms that relate to learning theory: Memory

26. C—Feedback: Subject Category I. Students as Learners: Student Development and the Learning Process: Important terms that relate to learning theory: Memory

27. A—Feedback: Subject Category I. Students as Learners: Student Development and the Learning Process: Important terms that relate to learning theory: Memory

28. D—Feedback: Subject Category I. Students as Learners: Student development and the Learning Process: Important terms that relate to learning theory: Expert and novice knowledge

29. A—Feedback: Subject Category I. Students as Learners: Student development and the Learning Process: Important terms that relate to learning theory: Schemata

30. A—Feedback: Subject Category I. Students as Learners: Student Development and the Learning Process: Theoretical foundations about how learning occurs—how students construct knowledge, acquire skills, and develop habits of mind: Important terms that relate to learning theory: Learning

31. D—Feedback: Subject Category I. Students as Learners: Student development and the Learning Process: Important terms that relate to learning theory: Acclimation

32. B—Feedback: Subject Category I. Students as Learners: Student Development and the Learning Process: Important terms that relate to learning theory: Memory

33. A—Feedback: Subject Category I. Students as Learners: Student Development and the Learning Process: Important terms that relate to learning theory: Transfer

34. B—Feedback: Subject Category I. Students as Learners: Student Development and the Learning Process: Important terms that relate to learning theory: Transfer

35. B—Feedback: Subject Category I. Students as Learners: Student Development and the Learning Process: Theoretical foundations about how learning occurs—how students construct knowledge, acquire skills, and develop habits of mind: Important terms that relate to learning theory: Constructivism

36. A—Feedback: Subject Category I. Students as Learners: Theoretical foundations about how learning occurs: how students construct knowledge, acquire skills, and develop habits of mind: Examples of important theorists: Lev Vygotsky

37. A—Feedback: Subject Category I. Students as Learners: Important terms that relate to learning theory: Situated cognition

38. D—Feedback: Subject Category I. Students as Learners: Important terms that relate to learning theory: Scaffolding

39. A—Feedback: Subject Category I. Students as Learners: Important terms that relate to learning theory: Cognitive apprenticeship

2. Human development in the physical, social, emotional, moral, and cognitive domains

1. B—Feedback: Subject Category I. Students as Learners: Student Development and the Learning Process: Human development in the physical, social, emotional, moral, and cognitive domains: Impact of students' physical, social, emotional, moral, and cognitive development on their learning and how to address these factors when making decisions

2. A—Feedback: Subject Category I. Students as Learners: Student Development and the Learning Process: Human development in the physical, social, emotional, moral, and cognitive domains: Major progressions in each developmental domain and the ranges of individual variation within each domain

3. B—Feedback: Subject Category I. Students as Learners: Student Development and the Learning Process: Human development in the physical, social, emotional, moral, and cognitive domains: Major progressions in each developmental domain and the ranges of individual variation within each domain

4. B—Feedback: Subject Category I. Students as Learners: Student Development and the Learning Process: Human development in the physical, social, emotional, moral, and cognitive domains: Major progressions in each developmental domain and the ranges of individual variation within each domain

5. B—Feedback: Subject Category I. Students as Learners: Student Development and the Learning Process: Human development in the physical, social, emotional, moral, and cognitive domains: Contributions of important theorists: Jean Piaget

6. C—Feedback: Subject Category I. Students as Learners: Student Development and the Learning Process: Human development in the physical, social, emotional, moral, and cognitive domains: Contributions of important theorists: Jean Piaget

7. D—Feedback: Subject Category I. Students as Learners: Student Development and the Learning Process: Human development in the physical, social, emotional, moral, and cognitive domains: Contributions of important theorists: Jean Piaget

8. D—Feedback: Subject Category I. Students as Learners: Student Development and the Learning Process: Human development in the physical, social, emotional, moral, and cognitive domains: Contributions of important theorists: Lev Vygotsky

9. C—Feedback: Subject Category I. Students as Learners: Student Development and the Learning Process: Human development in the physical, social, emotional, moral, and cognitive domains: Contributions of important theorists: Lev Vygotsky

10. B—Feedback: Subject Category I. Students as Learners: Student Development and the Learning Process: Human development in the physical, social, emotional, moral, and cognitive domains: Major progressions in each developmental domain and the ranges of individual variation within each domain

11. C—Feedback: Subject Category I. Students as Learners: Student Development and the Learning Process: Human development in the physical, social, emotional, moral, and cognitive domains: Contributions of important theorists

12. B—Feedback: Subject Category I. Students as Learners: Student Development and the Learning Process: Human development in the physical, social, emotional, moral, and cognitive domains: Impact of students' physical, social, emotional, moral, and cognitive development on their learning and how to address these factors when making decisions

13. A—Feedback: Subject Category I. Students as Learners: Student Development and the Learning Process: Human development in the physical, social, emotional, moral, and cognitive domains: Contributions of Bronfenbrenner

14. C—Feedback: Subject Category I. Students as Learners: Student Development and the Learning Process: Human development in the physical, social, emotional, moral, and cognitive domains: Major progressions in each developmental domain and the ranges of individual variation within each domain

15. B—Feedback: Subject Category I. Students as Learners: Student Development and the Learning Process: Human development in the physical, social, emotional, moral, and cognitive domains: Major progressions in each developmental domain and the ranges of individual variation within each domain

16. A—Feedback: Subject Category I. Students as Learners: Student development and the Learning Process: Human development in the physical, social, emotional, moral, and cognitive domains: The impact of students' physical, social, emotional, moral, and cognitive development on their learning and how to address these factors when making instructional decisions

17. C—Feedback: Subject Category I. Students as Learners: Student Development and the Learning Process: Human development in the physical, social, emotional, moral, and cognitive domains: Major progressions in each developmental domain and the ranges of individual variation within each domain

18. B—Feedback: Subject Category I. Students as Learners: Student Development and the Learning Process: Human development in the physical, social, emotional, moral, and cognitive domains: Major progressions in each developmental domain and the ranges of individual variation within each domain

19. A—Feedback: Subject Category I. Students as Learners: Student development and the Learning Process: Human development in the physical, social, emotional, moral, and cognitive domains: Theoretical contributions of important theorists: Lawrence Kohlberg

20. A—Feedback: Subject Category I. Students as Learners: Student development and the Learning Process: Human development in the physical, social, emotional, moral, and cognitive domains: Theoretical contributions of important theorists: Lawrence Kohlberg

21. C—Feedback: Subject Category I. Students as Learners: Student development and the Learning Process: Human development in the physical, social, emotional, moral, and cognitive domains: Theoretical contributions of important theorists: Lawrence Kohlberg

22. B—Feedback: Subject Category I. Students as Learners: Student development and the Learning Process: Human development in the physical, social, emotional, moral, and cognitive domains: Theoretical contributions of important theorists: Lawrence Kohlberg

23. A—Feedback: Subject Category I. Students as Learners: Student development and the Learning Process: Human development in the physical, social, emotional, moral, and cognitive domains: Theoretical contributions of important theorists: Lawrence Kohlberg

24. A—Feedback: Subject Category I. Students as Learners: Student development and the Learning Process: Human development in the physical, social, emotional, moral, and cognitive domains: Theoretical Contributions of important theorists: Lawrence Kohlberg and Carol Gilligan

25. B—Feedback: Subject Category I. Students as Learners: Student Development and the Learning Process: Impact of students' physical, social, emotional, moral, and cognitive development on their learning and how to address these factors when making decisions

26. A—Feedback: Subject Category I. Students as Learners: Student Development and the Learning Process: Impact of students' physical, social, emotional, moral, and cognitive development on their learning and how to address these factors when making decisions

27. D—Feedback: Subject Category I. Students as Learners: Student Development and the Learning Process: Impact of students' physical, social, emotional, moral, and cognitive development on their learning and how to address these factors when making decisions

All Subject Categories are as listed in the ETS Principles of Learning and Teaching, *Tests at a Glance*, located at ftp://ftp.ets.org/pub/tandl/0522.pdf.

b. Students as Diverse Learners

1. Differences in the ways students learn and perform

1. Effective teachers tend to display which of the following traits? (Text Hint: See page 9)
   a. They do not allow students to ask questions about political issues.
   b. They are knowledgeable about people from different cultural backgrounds.
   c. They discourage students from discussing ethnic issues.
   d. They encourage students to work alone.

2. Researchers have found that in some ethnic groups, aspects of the authoritarian parenting style may be associated with _____. (Text Hint: See page 75)
   a. pro-social behaviors
   b. identity diffusion
   c. positive child outcomes, such as high academic achievement
   d. enhanced language development

3. All of the following skills are included in Howard Gardner's eight types of intelligence except which one? (Text Hint: See page 111)
   a. Sensory skills
   b. Movement skills
   c. Verbal skills
   d. Intrapersonal skills

4. Which of Gardner's intelligences is involved in an activity calling for self-reflection and setting life goals? (Text Hint: See page 111)
   a. Verbal skills
   b. Interpersonal skills
   c. Intrapersonal skills
   d. Naturalist skills

5. Which of the following would be the best example of an impulsive student? (Text Hint: See page 124)
   a. Lamar actively sets his own learning goals.
   b. Rhonda performs poorly in school yet is good at problem-solving when it is in an area of her interest.
   c. Jonathan is an above-average student who has a knack for quickly and accurately coming up with the answers.
   d. Sheila resolves problems in interpersonal relationships through thoughtful introspection.

6. Which of the following would be the best example of a surface style learner? (Text Hint: See page 124)
   a. Uses systematic reasoning and logic when making decisions
   b. Enjoys working in small groups rather than working alone
   c. Evaluates and criticizes other people's points of view
   d. Relies on intuition when solving problems

7. Which of the following is the most accurate way to conceptualize learning and thinking styles? (Text Hint: See page 125)

   a. They are heavily dependent on intelligence.

   b. They may be dependent on the content domain.

   c. They are reliably consistent across content domains.

   d. You've either got them or you don't.

8. A student who is emotionally stable would most accurately be described as which of the following? (Text Hint: See page 127)

   a. Careful, organized, and disciplined

   b. Sociable, fun-loving, and affectionate

   c. Calm, secure, and self-satisfied

   d. Imaginative, interested in variety, and independent

9. Research suggests that people in all cultures have a tendency to do all of the following except which one? (Text Hint: See page 135)

   a. Believe that what happens in other cultures is unnatural and incorrect

   b. Behave in ways that favor their own cultural group

   c. Prefer to associate with individuals from different cultural groups

   d. Feel proud of their own cultural group

10. Which of the following strategies would be most appropriate in helping an individualist teacher interact effectively with students from a collectivist culture? (Text Hint: See page 136)

    a. Emphasize cooperation rather than competition.

    b. Encourage students to work independently rather than in groups.

    c. Avoid becoming friendly with students or parents.

    d. Boast about one's own accomplishments frequently.

11. Which of the following statements best represents a sexist attitude? (Text Hint: See page 156)

    a. In a recent study of eighth graders, boys scored higher on science tests than girls.

    b. Since women do poorly in math, they should not become engineers.

    c. Boys are more active than girls and therefore are more likely to fidget.

    d. Hormonal changes of puberty lead to increased body fat for girls.

12. Ms. Williams is reading over her students' names as listed on her attendance record. Although she has not met any of her future students because the school year will not officially begin until the following day, Ms. Williams is already classifying some of her students as being more intelligent, less competent, or more responsible on the basis of their ethnic names. What is Ms. Williams engaging in? (Text Hint: See Ch 5, page 142)

    a. Creating a hierarchy based on genders

    b. Creating ineffective teaching strategies

    c. Preparing for a collectivist teaching year

    d. Creating stereotypes based on ethnicity

13. Mrs. Guenero is careful of the behaviors that she exhibits in her class because she believes that gender development occurs through observation and imitation of gender behavior. She is also aware of the reinforcement and punishment that she gives her students for gender behavior. (Text Hint: See page 154)

    a. Psychoanalytic theory of gender

    b. Cognitive developmental theory of gender

    c. Gender schema theory

    d. Social learning theory

14. Susan and Jerry's teacher has noticed that Susan, like most other female students in her class, enjoys establishing connections and negotiating when she is engaged in talking relationships; whereas Jerry, like most other male students in the class, prefers talk that gives information. This is because _____is usually preferred by females more than by males and _____ is usually preferred by males more than by females. (Text Hint: See page 159)

    a. sexism; gender stereotypes

    b. rapport talk; report talk

    c. report talk; rapport talk

    d. prejudice; discrimination

15. Thirteen-year old Diane is feminine and nurturing yet assertive and commanding. Diane is demonstrating the concept of_____. (Text Hint: See page 160)

    a. androgyny

    b. gender stereotypes

    c. discrimination

    d. prejudice

16. Although boys are more physically aggressive than girls, girls are more likely to engage in verbally aggressive behavior such as _____. (Text Hint: See pages 159)

    a. relational aggression

    b. rapport talk

    c. report talk

    d. gender bias

17. Gender-role critics believe that parents should raise their children to be competent individuals, not masculine, feminine, or androgynous. This view is known as _____. (Text Hint: See page 162)

    a. gender denial

    b. sex-typing

    c. gender equity

    d. gender-role transcendence

2. Areas of exceptionality in students' learning

1. Of children with disabilities, approximately what percent are considered mentally retarded? (Text Hint: See page 175)

    a. 6%

    b. 11%

    c. 18%

    d. 23%

2. A student with epilepsy will most likely display which of the following behaviors? (Text Hint: See page 177)

   a. Staring and/or convulsions

   b. Complaining of nasal congestion and earaches

   c. Difficulty learning to spell

   d. Shaking and unclear speech

3. A student whose speech is hoarse, harsh, or too loud has which of the following disorders? (Text Hint: See page 181)

   a. Voice disorder

   b. Language disorder

   c. Fluency disorder

   d. Articulation disorder

4. Hannah has difficulty working independently. When asked to sit in her seat for long periods of time, she frequently gets up to sharpen her pencil, look out the window, or flip through books on the bookshelf. She does poorly on repetitive tasks such as math drills. And she rarely completes her homework. Hannah most likely has which of the following conditions? (Text Hint: See page 186)

   a. Mental retardation

   b. Attention deficit/hyperactivity disorder

   c. Down's syndrome

   d. Dyslexia

5. Maria keeps rubbing her eyes during the teacher's lesson, which takes place through the use of an overhead. She also holds books close to her face when she reads and she has even complained to her parents that sometimes things on a page appear to be moving around. Maria has a _____. (Text Hint: See page 176)

   a. receptive disorder

   b. expressive disorder

   c. visual impairment

   d. attention deficit/hyperactivity disorder

6. Joey is once again not following directions. The teacher notices that Joey usually has no problems following directions if he turns one ear toward her or if he asks several times to have the directions repeated. Joey most likely has one of these conditions. (Text Hint: See page 176)

   a. Visual impairment

   b. Hearing impairment

   c. Articulation problem

   d. Mental retardation

7. A child in your class is identified as being mentally retarded. In addition to having low intelligence, the child also will likely exhibit _____. (Text Hint: See page 178)

   a. deficits in adapting to everyday life

   b. deficits with regard to social responsibility

   c. deficits in skills such as toileting, feeding, and self-control

   d. deficits with regard to peer interaction

   e. all of the above are correct

8. Erin has problems pronouncing sounds correctly and as a result, she avoids communicating with her peers and is often embarrassed by having to discuss anything with the teacher. Erin's parents have begun to take her to a speech therapist and Erin's speech is slowly improving. Erin is most likely to have_____. (Text Hint: See page 181)

   a. autism

   b. visual impairment

   c. articulation disorder

   d. voice disorder

   e. fluency disorder

9. Tera finds it difficult to communicate with her peers and her teacher. She easily understands what they are saying to her but when she tries to communicate her response and express her thoughts, she finds it very difficult. Tera is most likely to have _____. (Text Hint: See page 181)

   a. expressive language disorder

   b. articulation disorder

   c. receptive language disorder

   d. voice disorder

   e. fluency disorder

10. Mrs. Chiden has just been informed that she will have several students in her class next school year with learning disabilities. Mrs. Chiden can expect these students to all _____. (Text Hint: See page 182)

   a. have normal intelligence or above

   b. have difficulty in at least one academic area and usually several

   c. have no other diagnosed problem or disorder that can be attributing as the cause of the disability.

   d. all of the above are correct

11. Rodney is on anticonvulsant medication. However, he still has episodes in which he loses consciousness, becomes rigid, shakes, and moves jerkily. This episode can last a few minutes. Rodney most likely has _____. (Text Hint: See page 177)

   a. mental retardation

   b. autism

   c. attention deficit/hyperactivity disorder

   d. epilepsy

12. Most of the students who have been diagnosed with a learning disability have which type of disability? (Text Hint: See page 175)

   a. Emotional disturbances

   b. Autism

   c. Hearing impairments

   d. Speech and language impairments

13. To control their behavior, 85–90 percent of children with ADHD _____. (Text Hint: See page 187)

   a. are placed in classes that emphasize rigorous physical activity

   b. are placed in environments with limited structure

   c. are taking stimulation medication such as Ritalin

   d. are placed in special education classes

14. Which of the following statements is true about students with ADHD? (Text Hint: See page 187)

    a. Most physicians refuse to prescribe medication for children with milder forms of ADHD.

    b. The number of children diagnosed and treated for ADHD has increased substantially, by some estimates doubling in the 1990s.

    c. Girls are diagnosed with ADHD equally as often as boys.

    d. Although signs of ADHD are often present in the preschool years, their classification doesn't take place until the middle school years.

3. Legislation and institutional responsibilities relating to exceptional students

1. Ms. Meyers is a regular classroom teacher who has just begun working with children with special needs. Her principal has advised that she be familiarized with the Individuals with Disabilities Education Act (IDEA), since she will now be interacting with parents whose children have special needs and she will have to create individualized education plans (IEP). Which of the following is not true and therefore not one of the items that Ms. Meyers will be learning about regarding IDEA's specific provisions that relate to the parents of a child with a disability? (Text Hint: See page 191)

    a. Schools are required to send notices to parents of proposed actions.

    b. Parents are not allowed to attend meetings regarding the child's individualized education plans (IEP).

    c. Parents are allowed to attend meetings regarding the child's placement.

    d. Parents have the right to appeal school decisions to an impartial evaluator.

2. In 1975, Congress passed the Education for All Handicapped Children Act. What does this law require? (Text Hint: See page 191)

    a. All students with disabilities receive homebound instruction.

    b. All students with disabilities receive life skills training.

    c. All students with disabilities be placed in separate, special education classes.

    d. All students with disabilities be given a free, appropriate public education.

3. The overrepresentation of minorities in special education programs has led to concern among education leaders. The U.S. Office of Education cites all of these as concerns EXCEPT _____.(Text Hint: See page 193)

    a. students may be underserved or receive services that do not meet their needs

    b. students may be misclassified or inappropriately labeled

    c. special education classes are overcrowded

    d. placement in special education classes may be a form of discrimination

4. Children with disabilities can be placed in a variety of settings. Which of the following is considered a least restrictive environment? (Text hint: See page 192)

    a. Regular classroom with supplementary instruction

    b. Part of time spent in a resource room

    c. Special schools

    d. Homebound instruction

5. Lauren is a hearing-impaired student who is receiving instruction in a regular second-grade classroom. This approach to educating students with disabilities is called _____. (Text hint: See page 192)

    a. collaborative consultation

    b. inclusion

    c. special education

    d. interactive teaming

4. Approaches for accommodating various learning styles, intelligences, or exceptionalities, including:

1. Which of the following best describes a criticism of tracking? (Text Hint: See page 121)
   a. Slower students in each track "hold back" the progress of the class.
   b. Better students in each track set the pace at which topics are covered.
   c. Students in the low-track group are stigmatized.
   d. A small percentage of students in each track are destined to fail.

2. An enrichment program is a standard option for teaching which of the following groups of children? (Text Hint: See page 202)
   a. Children with attention deficit/hyperactivity disorder
   b. Children with autism
   c. Children who are gifted
   d. Children who are mentally retarded

3. Mrs. Barone is using technology in her classroom to help children with disabilities function in the classroom environment. The technology she is using consists of various services and devices that include communication aids, alternative computer keyboards, and adaptive services. What type of technology is Mrs. Barone using? (Text Hint: See page 198)
   a. Assistive technology
   b. Instructional technology
   c. Regular education technology
   d. Receptive technology

4. Hugo has been identified as being gifted. What are the program options available for educating children who are gifted? (Text Hint: See page 202)
   a. Special classes
   b. Acceleration and enrichment programs in the regular classroom setting
   c. Enrichment programs in the regular classroom setting
   d. Mentor and apprenticeship programs in or out of the regular classroom setting or work-study programs in the community
   e. All of the above are correct

5. Process of second language acquisition and strategies to support the learning of students

1. Critics of bilingual education have voiced concern that bilingual education fails to do which of the following? (Text Hint: See page 143)
   a. Enhance students' self-esteem.
   b. Increase the likelihood of academic success.
   c. Prepare students for the workplace.
   d. Show respect for students' family and community

2. Mrs. Perez is a teacher at Springfield Elementary School. She teaches academic subjects to immigrant children in their native languages, while gradually adding English instruction. What type of teacher is Mrs. Perez? (Text Hint: See page 143)

   a. A bilingual education teacher

   b. A special education teacher

   c. A regular classroom teacher

   d. A resource education teacher

3. Hugo and Javier are brothers whose parents moved to the U.S. from a Latin American country a few years ago. Hugo is fourteen and Javier is six. Although both boys can speak and write the English language, Hugo made faster progress than Javier initially. However, Hugo has more difficulty pronouncing the English accent and he scores significantly lower than his brother on tests of grammar. What is likely to account for the differences in language acquisition of these two brothers? (Text Hint: See page 144)

   a. Javier is more motivated than Hugo and therefore learned the language better.

   b. Javier probably got more individual attention because he is the younger one.

   c. Hugo is older than Javier and although he can become competent at a second language, it is a more difficult task than that of learning it as a child like his brother.

   d. Hugo probably has a lower IQ than Javier and thus cannot be as competent as his brother at learning a second language.

6. How students' learning is influenced by individual experiences, talents, and prior learning, as well as language, culture, family, and community values

1. Which of the following is the best example of an argument for environmental influences on language? (Text Hint: See page 57)

   a. Humans are prewired to learn language.

   b. Even if parents do not speak to children, children still demonstrate language acquisition.

   c. Parents' reinforcement of children's linguistic attempts helps them to fine-tune their use of language

   d. Children have an inborn propensity to figure language out all on their own.

2. Children are most likely to have high self-esteem and get along well with their peers when raised with which of the following styles of parenting? (Text Hint: See page 74)

   a. Indulgent

   b. Neglectful

   c. Authoritarian

   d. Authoritative

3. Researchers who study peer relations among children have noted that "popular" children typically display which of the following characteristics? (Text Hint: See page 81)

   a. They listen carefully.

   b. They are conceited.

   c. They engage in delinquent behavior.

   d. They are aggressive.

4. Of the following activities, which is most "developmentally appropriate" for school children between 5 and 8 years of age? (Text Hint: See page 84)

   a. Highly structured activity

   b. Reading silently while sitting at a desk

   c. Teacher-directed lesson

   d. Pursuit of student-selected project

5. The current controversy about early childhood education is largely comprised of three groups: advocates of a constructivist approach, advocates of an instructivist approach, and _____. (Text Hint: See page 86)

   a. advocates of programs that emphasize children's intellectual development

   b. advocates of home-based programs

   c. advocates of culture-based curriculum

   d. advocates of authoritarian instruction

6. The NAEYC states that standards in early childhood education are useful when they _____. (Text Hint: See page 86)

   a. guide disciplinary consequences for children

   b. are developed by local governments

   c. emphasize developmentally appropriate content

   d. are used to rank and place children

7. Mr. Denosting wants to empower his students. Which of the following would he need to begin doing in his classroom? (Text Hint: See page 146)

   a. Better representing minorities and cultural groups

   b. Giving students the opportunity to learn about the struggles of different ethnic groups

   c. Helping white and students of color develop multiple perspectives within their curricula

   d. All of the above are correct

8. Ms. Rogers asks her students to write down their family histories so that she may include parts of each of the student's family's past in the class's history lesson. Ms. Rogers is engaging in _____ education. (Text Hint: See page 147)

   a. minority

   b. culturally-relevant

   c. issues-centered

   d. moral

9. Parents in impoverished communities _____. (Text Hint: See pages 136, 137)

   a. typically exhibit indulgent parenting styles

   b. are less involved in their children's school activities

   c. are equally likely to read to their children as their counterparts in economically advantaged communities

   d. rarely give their children access to TV

10. Mr. Sanders is concerned about one of his students. The student, Mateo, has serious and persistent problems concerning his relationships with other students; he displays aggression and is often out of control. Mateo displays signs of depression that can last up to several weeks, and he experiences fears that are often school related and interfere with his learning. Mateo is most likely to be suffering from _____. (Text Hint: See page 188)

    a. mental retardation

    b. attention deficit/hyperactivity disorder

    c. emotional and behavioral disorders

    d. sensory disorders

11. As students in U.S. schools have become more ethnically diverse in recent decades, teacher demographics _____. (Text Hint: See page 229)

    a. have changed to reflect their students' ethnic backgrounds

    b. are about 50 percent African-American

    c. are primarily comprised of African-American and Latino males

    d. are overwhelmingly non-Latino White females

12. Enrique is learning to read; his teacher understands the contribution of the social context in helping children to reach. Being that Enrique is Hispanic, his teacher wants to be informed about how much emphasis the culture places on reading, and the extent to which his parents have exposed him to books before he entered formal schooling. Enrique's teacher wants to give him and all of the other students the opportunity to discuss what they have read with the class. Enrique's teacher is using_____ to reading. (Text Hint: See page 345)

    a. a cognitive approach

    b. a social constructivist approach

    c. the whole language approach

    d. the interactive approach

Answer Key

1. Differences in the ways students learn and perform

1. B—B Feedback: Subject Category I. Students as Learners: Students as Diverse Learners: Differences in the ways students learn and perform: Cultural expectations and styles

2. C—Feedback: Subject Category I. Students as Learners: Students as Diverse Learners: Differences in the ways students learn and perform: Cultural expectations and styles

3. A—Feedback: Subject Category I. Students as Learners: Students as Diverse Learners: Differences in the ways students learn and perform: Multiple intelligences

4. C—Feedback: Subject Category I. Students as Learners: Students as Diverse Learners: Differences in the ways students learn and perform: Multiple intelligences

5. C—Feedback: Subject Category I. Students as Learners: Students as Diverse Learners: Differences in the ways students learn and perform: Learning styles

6. D—Feedback: Subject Category I. Students as Learners: Students as Diverse Learners: Differences in the ways students learn and perform: Learning styles

7. B—Feedback: Subject Category I. Students as Learners: Students as Diverse Learners: Differences in the ways students learn and perform: Learning styles

8. C—Feedback: Subject Category I. Students as Learners: Students as Diverse Learners: Differences in the ways students learn and perform: Learning styles

9. C—Feedback: Subject Category I. Students as Learners: Students as Diverse Learners: Differences in the ways students learn and perform: Cultural expectations and styles

10. A—Feedback: Subject Category I. Students as Learners: Students as Diverse Learners: Differences in the ways students learn and perform: Cultural expectations and styles

11. B—Feedback: Subject Category I. Students as Learners: Students as Diverse Learners: Differences in the ways students learn and perform: Gender differences

12. D—Feedback: Subject Category I. Students as Learners: Students as Diverse Learners: Differences in the ways students learn and perform: Cultural expectations and styles

13. D—Feedback: Subject Category I. Students as Learners: Students as Diverse Learners: Differences in the ways students learn and perform: Gender differences

14. B—Feedback: Subject Category I. Students as Learners: Students as Diverse Learners: Differences in the ways students learn and perform: Gender differences

15. A—Feedback: Subject Category I. Students as Learners: Students as Diverse Learners: Differences in the ways students learn and perform: Gender differences

16. A—Feedback: Subject Category I. Students as Learners: Students as Diverse Learners: Differences in the ways students learn and perform: Gender differences

17. D—Feedback: Subject Category I. Students as Learners: Students as Diverse Learners: Differences in the ways students learn and perform: Gender differences

2. Areas of exceptionality in students' learning

1. B—Feedback: Subject Category I. Students as Learners: Students as Diverse Learners: Areas of exceptionality in students' learning: Functional and mental retardation

2. A—Feedback: Subject Category I. Students as Learners: Students as Diverse Learners: Areas of exceptionality in students' learning: Special physical or sensory challenges

3. A—Feedback: Subject Category I. Students as Learners: Students as Diverse Learners: Areas of exceptionality in students' learning: Special physical or sensory challenges

4. B—Feedback: Subject Category I. Students as Learners: Students as Diverse Learners: Areas of exceptionality in students' learning: ADHD

5. C—Feedback: Subject Category I. Students as Learners: Students as Diverse Learners: Areas of exceptionality in students' learning: Special physical or sensory challenges

6. B—Feedback: Subject Category I. Students as Learners: Students as Diverse Learners: Areas of exceptionality in students' learning: Special physical or sensory challenges

7. E—Feedback: Subject Category I. Students as Learners: Students as Diverse Learners: Areas of exceptionality in students' learning: Functional and mental retardation

8. C—Feedback: Subject Category I. Students as Learners: Students as Diverse Learners: Areas of exceptionality in students' learning: Special physical or sensory challenges

9. A—Feedback: Subject Category I. Students as Learners: Students as Diverse Learners: Areas of exceptionality in students' learning: Special physical or sensory challenges

10. D—Feedback: Subject Category I. Students as Learners: Students as Diverse Learners: Areas of exceptionality in students' learning: Learning disabilities

11. D—Feedback: Subject Category I. Students as Learners: Students as Diverse Learners: Areas of exceptionality in students' learning: Special physical or sensory challenges

12. D—Feedback: Subject Category I. Students as Learners: Students as Diverse Learners: Areas of exceptionality in students' learning: Learning disabilities

13. C—Feedback: Subject Category I. Students as Learners: Students as Diverse Learners: Areas of exceptionality in students' learning: ADHD

14. B—Feedback: Subject Category I. Students as Learners: Students as Diverse Learners: Areas of exceptionality in students' learning: ADHD

3. Legislation and institutional responsibilities relating to exceptional students

1. B—Feedback: Subject Category I. Students as Learners: Students as Diverse Learners: Legislation and institutional responsibilities relating to exceptional students: Americans with Disabilities Act (ADA), Individuals with Disabilities Education Act (IDEA); Section 504 Protections for Students

2. D—Feedback: Subject Category I. Students as Learners: Students as Diverse Learners: Legislation and institutional responsibilities relating to exceptional students: Americans with Disabilities Act (ADA)

3. C—Feedback: Subject Category I. Students as Learners: Students as Diverse Learners: Legislation and institutional responsibilities relating to exceptional students

4. A—Feedback: Subject Category I. Students as Learners: Students as Diverse Learners: Legislation and institutional responsibilities relating to exceptional students: Least restrictive environment

5. B—Feedback: Subject Category I. Students as Learners: Students as Diverse Learners: Legislation and institutional responsibilities relating to exceptional students: Inclusion

4. Approaches for accommodating various learning styles, intelligences, or exceptionalities, including:

1. C—Feedback: Subject Category Students as Learners: Students as Diverse Learners: Approaches for accommodating various learning styles, intelligences, or exceptionalities: Differentiated instruction

2. C—Feedback: Subject Category I. Students as Diverse Learners: Approaches for accommodating various learning styles, intelligences, or exceptionalities: Differentiated instruction

3. A—Feedback: Subject Category I. Students as Learners: Students as Diverse Learners: Approaches for accommodating various learning styles, intelligences, or exceptionalities: Differentiated instruction and Testing modifications

4. E—Feedback: Subject Category I. Students as Diverse Learners: Approaches for accommodating various learning styles, intelligences, or exceptionalities: Differentiated instruction

5. Process of second language acquisition and strategies to support the learning of students

1. C—Feedback: Subject Category I. Students as Learners: Students as Diverse Learners: Process of second language acquisition and strategies to support the learning of students

2. A—Feedback: Subject Category I. Students as Learners: Students as Diverse Learners: Process of second language acquisition and strategies to support the learning of students

3. C—Feedback: Subject Category I. Students as Learners: Students as Diverse Learners: Process of second language acquisition and strategies to support the learning of students

6. How students' learning is influenced by individual experiences, talents, and prior learning, as well as language, culture, family, and community values

1. C—Feedback: Subject Category I. Students as Learners: Students as Diverse Learners: Understanding of influences of individual experiences, talents, and prior learning, as well as language, culture, family, and community values on students' learning: Linguistic patterns and differences

2. D—Feedback: Subject Category I. Students as Learners: Students as Diverse Learners: How students' learning is influenced by individual experiences, talents, and prior learning, as well as language, culture, family, and community values: Family backgrounds

3. A—Feedback: Subject Category I. Students as Learners: Students as Diverse Learners: How students' learning is influenced by individual experiences, talents, and prior learning, as well as language, culture, family, and community values

4. D—Feedback: Subject Category I. Students as Learners: Students as Diverse Learners: How students' learning is influenced by individual experiences, talents, and prior learning, as well as language, culture, family, and community values: Age-appropriate knowledge and behavior

5. A—Feedback: Subject Category I. Students as Learners: Students as Diverse Learners: How students' learning is influenced by individual experiences, talents, and prior learning, as well as language, culture, family, and community values: Age-appropriate knowledge and behavior

6. C—Feedback: Subject Category I. Students as Learners: Students as Diverse Learners: How students' learning is influenced by individual experiences, talents, and prior learning, as well as language, culture, family, and community values: Age-appropriate knowledge and behavior

7. D—Feedback: Subject Category I. Students as Learners: Students as Diverse Learners: Understanding of influences of individual experiences, talents, and prior learning, as well as language, culture, family, and community values on students' learning: Multicultural backgrounds and the student culture at the school

8. B—Feedback: Subject Category I. Students as Learners: Students as Diverse Learners: How students' learning is influenced by individual experiences, talents, and prior learning, as well as language, culture, family, and community values: Family backgrounds

9. B—Feedback: Subject Category I. Students as Learners: Students as Diverse Learners: How students' learning is influenced by individual experiences, talents, and prior learning, as well as language, culture, family, and community values: Family backgrounds

10. C—Feedback: Subject Category I. Students as Learners: Students as Diverse Learners: Understanding of influences of individual experiences, talents, and prior learning, as well as language, culture, family, and community values on students' learning: Social and emotional issues

11. D—Feedback: Subject Category I. Students as Learners: Students as Diverse Learners: How students' learning is influenced by individual experiences, talents, and prior learning, as well as language, culture, family, and community values: Multicultural backgrounds

12. B—Feedback: Subject Category I. Students as Learners: Students as Diverse Learners: How students' learning is influenced by individual experiences, talents, and prior learning, as well as language, culture, family, and community values: Multicultural backgrounds and Family backgrounds

All Subject Categories are as listed in the ETS Principles of Learning and Teaching, *Tests at a Glance*, located at *ftp://ftp.ets.org/pub/tandl/0522.pdf*.

c. Student Motivation and the Learning Environment

1. Theoretical foundations about human motivation and behavior

1. Which of the following best represents the social cognitive perspective? (Text Hint: See page 226)
   a. The environment causes behaviors.
   b. The environment and behaviors have a reciprocal relationship.
   c. Behavior is the result of cognitive factors, behavioral factors, and environmental factors.
   d. There is no relationship between the environment, behavior, and personal consequences

2. According to Bandura, what is the concept of self-efficacy? (Text Hint: See page 226)
   a. The belief that one can master a situation and produce positive outcomes.
   b. The belief that one can change the outcome of a situation by providing external consequences.
   c. The belief that one can regulate learning by becoming more aware of how it is that we acquire knowledge.
   d. Occurs when a person observes and imitates someone else's behavior.

3. According to Maslow's hierarchy of motives, which of the following needs must be satisfied before a person can attain esteem? (Text Hint: See page 416)
   a. Safety
   b. Cognitive
   c. Self-actualization
   d. Aesthetic

4. The cognitive perspective on motivation emphasizes which of the following? (Text Hint: See page 417)
   a. The student's capacity for personal growth
   b. The teacher's ability to influence the student's behavior
   c. The nature of the environment in which learning takes place
   d. The student's internal motivation to achieve

5. Critics of Maslow's hierarchy of needs assert which of the following? (Text Hint: See page 417)
   a. Self-actualization is impossible to attain.
   b. Students cannot satisfy their cognitive needs without first satisfying their love and belongingness needs.
   c. Safety needs should come first in the sequence, followed by physiological needs.
   d. It is not necessary to satisfy individual needs in the order specified by Maslow.

2. Important terms that relate to motivation and behavior

1. Which of the following is the best example of classical conditioning? (Text Hint: See page 212)
   a. Harold gets hungry each morning about one half hour before lunchtime.
   b. Susan likes to chew gum during class because it helps her to relax.
   c. Isaac cries when he arrives at the doctor's office because he usually gets shots near the end of each visit.
   d. Andrea takes the long way home after school because she likes to avoid a busy intersection.

2. Mr. Roberts, having to step out of the class for a moment, tells Melody to watch the class. Melody begins to get teased by her classmates for being a goody-goody and the teacher's pet. When Mr. Roberts returns, Melody tells him that she does not ever want to be left in charge of the class again. In this situation, Melody was_____. (Text Hint: See page 216)

   a. positively reinforced by her classmates

   b. negatively reinforced by her classmates

   c. punished by her classmates

   d. punished by the teacher

3. Which of the following scenarios best depicts "extinction"? (Text Hint: See page 216)

   a. Ivan used to bring his lunch to school every day because his mother always praised him for doing so. Now that she has stopped praising him, he often forgets.

   b. Ruby used to get very nervous when she played her violin in public. She recently started practicing relaxation techniques prior to each performance, and now she usually feels calm.

   c. Heather forgot to take off her muddy shoes at the door until recently, when her mother posted a sign in the hallway.

   d. Dennis runs to the door when he hears a truck pull into the driveway because he knows that his father opens the door within moments of when Dennis hears the sound of his father's car.

4. Which of the following scenarios best depicts a punishment? (Text Hint: See page 216)

   a. A student answers a question correctly. The teacher compliments the student. The student continues to raise her hand to answer questions.

   b. A student answers a question correctly. The teacher stops criticizing the student for not paying attention. The student continues to raise her hand to answer questions.

   c. A student answers a question incorrectly. The teacher criticizes the student for not paying attention. The student begins to pay attention and starts answering questions correctly.

   d. A student answers a question incorrectly. The teacher stops asking the student to answer questions. The student starts paying attention during class.

5. Ms. Santos is explaining geometric angles, when she sees Stanley poke his pencil in Sharon's arm. Sharon winces but does not say anything. Ms. Santos immediately tells Stanley that he has lost 10 minutes of recess. In this scenario, Ms. Santos used a _____. (Text Hint: See page 216)

   a. positive reinforcer

   b. negative reinforcer

   c. punishment

   d. none of the above are correct

6. Mr. Elliot is walking around the learning centers in the room helping his students with their activity. Jack tells Mr. Elliot that Jan is not doing her part of the work, in fact she is distracting them by telling them jokes. Mr. Elliot privately asks Jan to get to work and stop telling jokes or she will have to go back to her seat and work independently. Jan does not cause further problems in her group. In this example, Mr. Elliot used_____, and it was _____. (Text Hint: See page 216)

   a. punishment, ineffective

   b. negative reinforcer, effective

   c. punishment, effective

   d. negative reinforcer, ineffective

7. Mr. Bristol hands his eighth graders an agenda that tells them the due dates for all their assignments are exactly one month apart. What type of reinforcement schedule did Mr. Bristol put his eighth graders on? (Text Hint: See page 220)

   a. Fixed ratio

   b. Fixed interval

   c. Variable ratio

   d. Variable interval

8. Every half hour or so, a teacher compliments a certain student for staying in his seat and working quietly, unless the student fails to do so. This teacher is using which of the following schedules of reinforcement? (Text Hint: See page 220)

   a. Fixed-interval

   b. Fixed-ratio

   c. Variable-interval

   d. Variable-ratio

9. Kyle's third grade class is watching a presentation by local college students on how to improve reading and writing skills. Kyle is excited about learning how to improve his reading and writing skills. However, even though he paid close attention to the presentation, and he remembers all the tips that were shown and demonstrated, Kyle does not think that he has the skill that the presenters have. In fact, he thinks that these tips are not ones that he would be able to apply. According to observational learning theory, which of the following processes is Kyle having difficulty with? (Text Hint: See page 228)

   a. Attention

   b. Retention

   c. Production

   d. Motivation

10. Mr. Rojas says "what great behavior Daniel is showing, he is standing quietly in line the way he is supposed to be." Soon, all of the third graders in Mr. Rojas class are standing in line quietly like Daniel. Why did all of the third grade students imitate Daniel's behavior? (Text Hint: See page 229)

    a. Because they were classically conditioned to do so.

    b. Because they watched Daniel, a model, be positively reinforced for doing so and thought they would be positively reinforced if they copied Daniel's behavior.

    c. Because Daniel was negatively reinforced by the teacher and they wanted to be negatively reinforced as well.

    d. Because they watched Daniel, a model, be punished for doing so and thought they would be punished if they did not copy Daniel's behavior.

11. Ally just received an A on her spelling test. Her teacher, Mrs. Succo, compliments her on her achievement. Ally continues to do well on her spelling tests. This scenario best depicts a _____. (Text Hint: See page 216)

    a. positive reinforcer

    b. negative reinforcer

    c. punishment

    d. none of the above are correct

12. Marchand is a first grader in Mr. Tobia's class whose homework would sometimes end up in the wrong bin. Mr. Tobia has decided to always ensure that he reinforces Marchand for putting his homework in the bin labeled "Today's homework" and not in the other bins that Mr. Tobias has in the classroom. Marchand has been placing his homework in the right bin every day. In this scenario, what is Mr. Tobia's intention? (Text Hint: See page 216)

    a. To use generalization on Marchand

    b. To use discrimination on Marchand

    c. To use extinction on Marchand

    d. To use punishment on Marchand

13. Mr. Mijuet had been consistently praising Talan for contributing comments in the class discussions. However, Mr. Mijuet has noticed that Talan has become disruptive and that his comments are frequently not pertinent to the discussion that the class is having. Mr. Mijuet decides to ignore Talan's inappropriate comments and behavior during class discussions and give him attention and praise only when his comments are relevant. Talan's contributions to the class discussion are no longer inappropriate. In this scenario, Mr. Mijuet is using _____ (Text Hint: See page 216)

    a. shaping

    b. prompts

    c. Premack Principle

    d. extinction

14. Tanya is working on a book report that is due the next day in school. She is talking to herself saying, "This is a little confusing, but I think I can do it. If I keep working, I know I'll get it done." This is an example of _____. (Text Hint: See page 234)

    a. observational learning

    b. social cognitive approaches to learning

    c. the Premack Principle

    d. a self-instructional method

15. Geraldo usually does well in history class, but did poorly on a recent test. He believes that his poor score was due to lack of sufficient studying. After all, he had a term paper due that same day in science class, and had spent most that week writing the paper rather than studying for the test. This view best represents a combination of which of the following causal attributions? (Text Hint: See page 423)

    a. External-Stable-Uncontrollable

    b. External-Unstable-Controllable

    c. Internal-Stable-Uncontrollable

    d. Internal-Unstable-Controllable

16. When faced with a difficult task, Marvin focuses on his abilities, or lack thereof. He tends to feel overwhelmed by his own inadequacies and therefore has difficulty meeting the challenge. Marvin can best be described as which of the following? (Hint: See page 425)

    a. Performance-oriented

    b. Helpless-oriented

    c. Mastery-oriented

    d. Goal-oriented

17. Which of the following scenarios best depicts a student with "failure syndrome"? (Text Hint: See page 437)

    a. Freddie tries to answer questions, but frequently answers incorrectly.

    b. Doug enjoys class discussions, but often gets distracted by noise outside the classroom.

    c. Maya slumps in her chair when the teacher is looking for someone to solve a problem at the chalkboard.

    d. Andrea dislikes physical education class because other kids make fun of her

18. Patty usually does well on math tests; however, on the last unit test Patti did poorly. She believes that her poor score was due to the teacher's asking difficult questions. She does not think that the teacher asked fair questions. Patty thinks that since the teacher is biased while giving math exams she may not get a good grade in math class this year. This view best represents a combination of which of the following causal attributions? (Text Hint: See page 423)

    a. External-Stable-Uncontrollable

    b. External-Unstable-Controllable

    c. Internal-Stable-Uncontrollable

    d. Internal-Unstable-Controllable

19. Henrietta knows that the success of her math group is dependent on which students, she, the team captain, picks to be on her math team. She wants to win the math group competition so she is determined to pick the students that she knows are good in math and will do well. She knows that this is going to cause some problems since her friends who are in this class will expect to be on Henrietta's team. However, Henrietta wants to win and therefore is only concerned with what she has to do in order to attain that goal. Henrietta can best be described as which of the following? (Text Hint: See page 425)

    a. Performance-oriented

    b. Helpless-oriented

    c. Mastery-oriented

    d. Goal-oriented

20. Trey's teacher notices that he exhibits a pattern of having low expectations for success and a tendency to give up at the first sign of difficulty. Trey does not put forth enough effort, often beginning tasks halfheartedly and then giving up quickly when he encounters a challenge. He also exhibits low efficacy and has problems with his attributions. Trey is exhibiting _____. (Text Hint: See page 437)

    a. a need for affiliation

    b. a performance orientation

    c. the failure syndrome

    d. a social motive

21. Amber is the most popular girl in her class. She is always surrounded by many friends and dates regularly. Amber likes all of the attention; in fact over the summers when her parents send her to spend time with her relatives in another city, Amber feels like something is drastically missing from her life. Although, she loves her relatives, she does not receive the peer attention that she so craves. In fact, she can hardly wait to be back with her friends. Usually, as soon as she arrives in town, she throws a party where she will embellish about her summer trip in order to maintain her friends approval. Amber is displaying _____. (Text Hint: See page 417)

    a. a strong need for affiliation

    b. a helpless orientation

    c. the failure syndrome

    d. an internal, unstable, and uncontrollable attribute

22. Erica's mother is very independent, creative, and seems to live according to the beat of a different drummer. Although she has a few close friends, she is able to get along with many different types of people. Which term best describes Erica's mother? (Text Hint: See page 416)
    a. Democratic
    b. Self-actualized
    c. Extrinsically motivated
    d. Solution-oriented

23. Derek is working on a word problem that involves a new algebra concept. Although he doesn't immediately understand how to solve the problem, he pays close attention to the teacher's explanation and tries to relate the new problem to similar homework he finished the night before. What type of achievement orientation does Derek exhibit? (Text Hint: See page 424)
    a. Solution orientation
    b. Helpless orientation
    c. Mastery orientation
    d. Performance orientation

24. At the beginning of the school year, Latoya created a list. At the top of the list she wrote, "I want to finish reading a 100-page chapter book by the end of the month." What type of self-regulatory behavior is Latoya engaging in? (Text Hint: See page 428)
    a. Goal setting
    b. Self-monitoring
    c. Extrinsic motivation
    d. Peer modeling

3. How knowledge of human motivation and behavior should influence strategies for organizing and supporting individual and group work in the classroom

1. Ms. Alvarez has been teaching for 20 years. She has learned that it is best to structure her class so that students complete the projects and activities that they really do not like first; only after completing these "disliked" activities can they engage in the projects and activities that they do like. This is an example of _____ (Text Hint: See page 219)
    a. negative reinforcement
    b. time-out
    c. Premack Principle
    d. punishment

2. The first step in self-regulated learning is _____. (Text Hint: See page 236)
    a. goal-setting and strategic planning
    b. monitoring outcomes and refining strategies
    c. putting a plan into action and monitoring the plan self-evaluation and self-monitoring

3. Mrs. Renir tells her second graders that once they complete their reading assignment, they may go and play on the computers. In this scenario, Mrs. Renir is using _____. (Text Hint: See page 219)
    a. extinction
    b. generalization
    c. Premack Principle
    d. a schedule of reinforcement

4. Winston is very anxious when it comes to taking tests. He usually performs poorly on tests because of his anxiety and not his lack of knowledge. Winston's teacher has decided to have Winston associate relaxation with taking tests. She has Winston imagine a relaxing situation and think of it a few days before the test, the morning of the test, right before taking the test, and finally while he is taking his test. In this example, Winston's teacher is using which of the following _____. (Text Hint: See page 214)

   a. generalization

   b. systematic desensitization

   c. discrimination

   d. negative reinforcement

5. Which of the following is NOT true of peer tutoring? (Text Hint: See page 319)

   a. Using students of different grade levels to serve as mentors for students.

   b. Alternating the tutor and tutee roles between students.

   c. Delegating the responsibility of testing to tutors.

   d. Communicating to parents your use of peer tutoring in the classroom.

6. Mr. Weiss takes time at the beginning of the school year to put students into groups to help students become better listeners, get used to contributing to a team product, and get experience with handling problem situations. Mr. Weiss is attempting to use _____. (Text Hint: See page 326)

   a. team-building skills

   b. scaffolding

   c. cognitive apprenticeship

   d. a collaborative school

7. Mario is an eighth grade student whose older brother just dropped out of high school. Which of the following goals will most likely help Mario improve his self-efficacy and sense of achievement? (Text Hint: See page 426)

   a. I want to graduate from high school.

   b. I want to go to college someday.

   c. I want to be a doctor or a lawyer when I grow up.

   d. I want to get an A in science this semester.

8. Mr. Qintero has noticed that some of his best students possess the belief that they are able to learn class material, and they believe that they will be able to perform well in their school activities. Which of the following best describes these students? (Text Hint: See page 426)

   a. These students lack attributions.

   b. These students are just very intelligent.

   c. These students have a high sense of self-efficacy.

   d. These students are completely extrinsically motivated.

9. The school year began just last week, but Mrs. Rundra already knows that this school year will be challenging. She has a large amount of students who are low achievers with low ability who have difficulty keeping up and have developed low-achieving expectations, students with failure syndrome, and students obsessed with protecting their self-worth by avoiding failure. All of the students described in this scenario can best be classified as being _____. (Text Hint: See page 437)

   a. discouraged students

   b. students who are lacking a need for affiliation

   c. students who are having trouble with their social contexts

   d. students who are having trouble with their social relationships

10. Mrs. Pfeist has read research that has found that students who feel they have supportive, caring teachers are more strongly motivated to engage in academic work than students with unsupportive, uncaring teachers. Mrs. Pfeist would like to ensure that her ninth graders know that she cares. Which of the following is correct about teachers who care? (Text Hint: See page 433)

   a. Teaches even if students are not paying attention so that they will know to pay attention next time

   b. Forgets students' names often because it is not as important as getting them to listen

   c. Makes an effort to make class interesting; teaches in a special way

   d. Does not try to help students so that they will get it on their own

4. Factors and situations that are likely to promote or diminish students' motivation to learn, and how to help students to become self-motivated

1. Which of the following actions by teachers would most likely increase the self-esteem of an elementary school child? (Text Hint: See page 91)

   a. Complimenting the student for being polite toward others

   b. Criticizing the student for making a mistake on a homework assignment

   c. Punishing the student for interrupting somebody else

   d. Showing little interest in the student's work

2. Which of the following factors would most likely increase intrinsic motivation to learn as a student progresses through the elementary to high school years? (Text Hint: See page 419)

   a. Increased emphasis on the importance of getting good grades

   b. Increased boredom as assignments become more tedious

   c. Increased sense of being challenged at a level consistent with ability

   d. Increased feelings of isolation due to teachers' behaviors toward students

3. Mr. Thetu is trying to reach uninterested or alienated students and motivate them. Which of the following should he not do? (Text Hint: See page 439)

   a. Work on developing a positive relationship

   b. Make school more extrinsically interesting

   c. Teach them strategies for making academic work more enjoyable

   d. Consider a mentor

4. All of the following statements help to explain the decline in intrinsic motivation in the middle and high school years EXCEPT _____. (Text Hint: See page 422)

   a. many teachers are more controlling just at the time when adolescents are seeking more autonomy

   b. educators believe that it is important for children to develop greater extrinsic motivation as they grow older

   c. the teacher-student relationship becomes more impersonal at a time when students are seeking independence from their parents and need more support from other adults

   d. the increased emphasis on grades and competitive comparisons at this time fuels adolescents' natural self-consciousness

5. Principles of effective classroom management and strategies to promote positive relationships, cooperation, and purposeful learning

1. All of the following traits are characteristics of "worst" teachers EXCEPT _____. (Text Hint: See page 13)

   a. having a dull/boring class

   b. making unclear or confusing explanations

   c. treating students like adults

   d. lacking control

2. Effective teachers typically exhibit _____. (Text Hint: See page 8)

   a. rigidity in their teaching methods

   b. solid professional knowledge and skills

   c. predictability in their lesson plans and curriculum

   d. control over every aspect of the classroom

3. Dillon agrees to stop pushing at the drinking fountain. His teacher agrees to let him be first at the drinking fountain Friday if he does not push his peers all week. This is an example of _____. (Text Hint: See page 221)

   a. contracting

   b. prompting

   c. a schedule of reinforcement

   d. extinction

4. Group rewards are essential for the effective use of cooperative learning. Which of the following is (are) good examples of group rewards? (Text Hint: See page 322)

   a. Ms. Jackson recognizes winning teams in the class newsletter.

   b. Mr. Randall writes individual notes home to praise each student.

   c. Mr. Wallace takes the time to praise each student individually after class.

   d. Mrs. Chen raises each student's unit grade with an improved test score.

5. Mr. Lobos is discussing Jessica's motivation with her parents at their scheduled parent-teacher conference. Her parents want to know how they can positively affect their child's motivation and achievement. Mr. Lobos tells them that they need to know enough about Jessica to know the right amount of challenge and the right amount of support. He also tells them that providing a positive climate will help to motivate Jessica to internalize her parents' values and goals. In addition, Mr. Lobos tells Jessica's parents that _____. (Text Hint: See page 432)

   a. their demographic factors are really the only ones that will be of more importance

   b. their close monitoring of her behavior and use of strict punishment is an asset

   c. it is important to model motivated achievement behavior, such as persistence and hard work

   d. they should never exhibit any signs of failure in the home so that Jessica does not imitate that behavior

6. In the current view of classroom management, the teacher is best viewed as which of the following? (Text Hint: See page 448)

   a. Guide

   b. Leader

   c. Director

   d. Dictator

7. Classroom management principles sometimes are applied differently in elementary and secondary schools because _____. (Text Hint: See page 449)

    a. teachers are trained differently

    b. of the differing school structures

    c. of different administrative organization

    d. They are not applied differently across elementary and secondary schools.

8. A teacher wants to have a class discussion on current events in which all 23 of her students can participate equally. Which of the following seating arrangements would be most suitable for this event? (Text Hint: See page 456)

    a. Cluster style

    b. Face-to-face style

    c. Off-set style

    d. Seminar style

9. Students will most likely become self-reliant in classrooms that are managed with which strategy? (Text Hint: See page 459)

    a. Authoritarian

    b. Authoritative

    c. Permissive

    d. Punitive

10. Jerome has started his first day student teaching and finds that his cooperating teacher is consistently aware of what is happening in the classroom, monitors students' behavior on a regular basis, and responds to misbehavior before it escalates. How would you describe Jerome's cooperating teacher? (Text Hint: See page 459)

    a. With-it

    b. Omnipotent

    c. Punitive

    d. None of the above

11. Which of the following are recommended strategies for increasing academic learning time? (Text Hint: See page 452)

    a. Flip-flopping from one topic to another

    b. Maximizing transition time between activities

    c. Avoiding dwelling on a topic once the point has been made

    d. Responding to distractions

12. Rules and procedures should be _____. (Text Hint: See page 462)

    a. firm and punitive

    b. flexible and subjective

    c. reasonable and necessary

    d. set in stone

13. When getting students to share and assume responsibility in the classroom, teachers should do what? (Text Hint: See page 463)

    a. Involve students in the planning and implementation of classroom initiatives

    b. Accept reasonable excuses infrequently

    c. Emphasize teacher control

    d. Have students develop the classroom management plan

14. Ms. Ryan offers students praise whenever they show that they are on task. Ms. Ryan is using what management strategy? (Text Hint: See page 464)
    a. Shaping
    b. Controlling the student's behavior
    c. Reinforcement
    d. Prompting

15. Mrs. Alvarez had been having difficulty getting Tyrone to work in cooperative learning groups. So she had started just putting him at the same table working among other students. When he did this reliably without getting into trouble, she asked him to simply share the materials with students at the same table. Now he can work in cooperative groups without getting into trouble. What is the name for the strategy Mrs. Alvarez employed? (Text Hint: See page 464)
    a. Shaping
    b. Controlling the student's behavior
    c. Reinforcement
    d. Prompting

16. For communicating with parents of students, all of the following strategies are recommended EXCEPT which one? (Text Hint: See page 465)
    a. Be an active listener.
    b. Use a manipulative mode of communication.
    c. Make eye contact.
    d. Use "I" messages.

17. What are the three C's of classroom management? (Text Hint: See page 479)
    a. Caring community, calmness, and consideration
    b. Control, constructive conduct rules, and civic values
    c. Cooperative community, constructive conflict resolution, and civic values
    d. Cooperation, community, and civic duty

18. Mr. Johnson wants to get the school year off to a good start. What can he do to make good use of the first weeks of school? (Text Hint: See page 451)
    a. He should remain at his desk so that students don't feel over-controlled.
    b. He should give students games and puzzles and avoid "real" assignments.
    c. He should avoid talking about rules and procedures so that students develop a positive attitude about the class.
    d. He should establish daily procedures and routines and give students opportunities to experience success.

19. Mrs. Quincy teaches middle school science. Her classroom includes an aquarium with fish, a terrarium with an iguana, and a cage with a hamster. The desks are arranged in groups of four so that students can discuss science experiments and work together. Three different centers are set up around the perimeter of the classroom, each focused on a different area of science. Which of the following best describes Mrs. Quincy's approach to classroom arrangement? (Text Hint: See page 454)
    a. She knows that arranging an engaging, interactive, and well-organized classroom will contribute to positive student behaviors and overall learning.
    b. She is wasting her time with classroom decorations and should focus more on seatwork.
    c. She is providing students with a chaotic and distracting classroom environment.
    d. She is creating an impersonal classroom environment.

20. COMP, Second Step, and Skills for Life are examples of classroom management programs that emphasize _____. (Text Hint: See page 480)

    a. punishment and negative reinforcement of inappropriate behavior

    b. conflict-resolution skills, anger management, and empathy

    c. eliminating conflicts

    d. teacher-directed, authoritarian classroom environments

21. To reduce bullying in schools, teachers should do all of the following EXCEPT _____. (Text Hint: See page 476)

    a. form friendship groups for students who are victims of bullies

    b. hold regular class meetings to discuss bullying among students

    c. develop a school program to "catch students being good"

    d. provide swift and aggressive punishment to bullies

Answer Key

1. Theoretical foundations about human motivation and behavior

1. C—Feedback: Subject Category I. Students as Learners: Student Motivation and the Learning Environment: Theoretical foundations about human motivation and behavior

2. A—Feedback: Subject Category I. Students as Learners: Student Motivation and the Learning Environment: Theoretical foundations about human motivation and behavior: Albert Bandura

3. A—Feedback: Subject Category I. Students as Learners: Student Motivation and the Learning Environment: Theoretical foundations about human motivation and behavior: Abraham Maslow

4. D—Feedback: Subject Category I. Students as Learners: Student Motivation and the Learning Environment: Theoretical foundations about human motivation and behavior

5. D—Feedback: Subject Category I. Students as Learners: Student Motivation and the Learning Environment: Theoretical foundations about human motivation and behavior: Abraham Maslow

2. Important terms that relate to motivation and behavior

1. C—Feedback: Subject Category I. Students as Learners: Student motivation and the learning environment: Important terms that relate to motivation and behavior: Classical conditioning

2. C—Feedback: Subject Category I. Students as Learners: Student Motivation and the Learning Environment: Important terms that relate to motivation and behavior: Punishment

3. A—Feedback: Subject Category I. Students as Learners: Student Motivation and the Learning Environment: Important terms that relate to motivation and behavior: Extinction

4. C—Feedback: Subject Category I. Students as Learners: Student Motivation and the Learning Environment: Important terms that relate to motivation and behavior: Punishment

5. C—Feedback: Subject Category I. Students as Learners: Student Motivation and the Learning Environment: Important terms that relate to motivation and behavior: Punishment

6. B—Feedback: Subject Category I. Students as Learners: Student Motivation and the Learning Environment: Important terms that relate to motivation and behavior: Negative reinforce

7. B—Feedback: Subject Category I. Students as Learners: Student Motivation and the Learning Environment: Important terms that relate to motivation and behavior: Schedules of reinforcement

8. C—Feedback: Subject Category I. Students as Learners: Student Motivation and the Learning Environment: Important terms that relate to motivation and behavior: Schedules of reinforcement

9. C—Feedback: Subject Category I. Students as Learners: Student Motivation and the Learning Environment: Important terms that relate to motivation and behavior: Production

10. B—Feedback: Subject Category I. Students as Learners: Student Motivation and the Learning Environment: Important terms that relate to motivation and behavior: Positive reinforcement

11. A—Feedback: Subject Category I. Students as Learners: Student Motivation and the Learning Environment: Important terms that relate to motivation and behavior: Positive reinforcement

12. B—Feedback: Subject Category I. Students as Learners: Student Motivation and the Learning Environment: Important terms that relate to motivation and behavior: Discrimination

13. D—Feedback: Subject Category I. Students as Learners: Student Motivation and the Learning Environment: Important terms that relate to motivation and behavior: Extinction

14. D—Feedback: Subject Category I. Students as Learners: Student Motivation and the Learning Environment: Important terms that relate to motivation and behavior: Self-efficacy

15. D—Feedback: Subject Category I. Students as Learners: Student Motivation and the Learning Environment: Important terms that relate to motivation and behavior: Attribution

16. B—Feedback: Subject Category I. Students as Learners: Student Motivation and the Learning Environment: Important terms that relate to motivation and behavior: Learned helplessness

17. C—Feedback: Subject Category I. Students as Learners: Student Motivation and the Learning Environment: Important terms that relate to motivation and behavior: Failure syndrome

18. A—Feedback: Subject Category I. Students as Learners: Student Motivation and the Learning Environment: Important terms that relate to motivation and behavior: Attribution

19. A—Feedback: Subject Category I. Students as Learners: Student Motivation and the Learning Environment: Important terms that relate to motivation and behavior

20. C—Feedback: Subject Category I. Students as Learners: Student Motivation and the Learning Environment: Important terms that relate to motivation and behavior: Failure syndrome

21. A—Feedback: Subject Category I. Students as Learners: Student Motivation and the Learning Environment: Important terms that relate to motivation and behavior: Affiliation

22. B—Feedback: Subject Category I. Students as Learners: Student Motivation and the Learning Environment: Important terms that relate to motivation and behavior: Self-actualization

23. C—Feedback: Subject Category I. Students as Learners: Student Motivation and the Learning Environment: Important terms that relate to motivation and behavior: Mastery orientation

24. A—Feedback: Subject Category I. Students as Learners: Student Motivation and the Learning Environment: Important terms that relate to motivation and behavior: Goal setting

3. How knowledge of human motivation and behavior should influence strategies for organizing and supporting individual and group work in the classroom

1. C—Feedback: Subject Category I. Students as Learners: Student Motivation and the Learning Environment: How knowledge of human motivation and behavior should influence strategies for organizing and supporting individual and group work in the classroom

2. A—Feedback: Subject Category I. Students as Learners: Student Motivation and the Learning Environment: How knowledge of human motivation and behavior should influence strategies for organizing and supporting individual and group work in the classroom

3. C—Feedback: Subject Category I. Students as Learners: Student Motivation and the Learning Environment: How knowledge of human motivation and behavior should influence strategies for organizing and supporting individual and group work in the classroom

4. B—Feedback: Subject Category I. Students as Learners: Student Motivation and the Learning Environment: How knowledge of human motivation and behavior should influence strategies for organizing and supporting individual and group work in the classroom

5. C—Feedback: Subject Category I. Students as Learners: Student Motivation and the Learning Environment: How knowledge of human motivation and behavior should influence strategies for organizing and supporting individual and group work in the classroom

6. A—Feedback: Subject Category I. Students as Learners: Student Motivation and the Learning Environment: How knowledge of human motivation and behavior should influence strategies for organizing and supporting individual and group work in the classroom

7. D—Feedback: Subject Category I. Students as Learners: Student Motivation and the Learning Environment: How knowledge of human motivation and behavior should influence strategies for organizing and supporting individual and group work in the classroom

8. C—Feedback: Subject Category I. Students as Learners: Student Motivation and the Learning Environment: How knowledge of human motivation and behavior should influence strategies for organizing and supporting individual and group work in the classroom

9. A—Feedback: Subject Category I. Students as Learners: Student Motivation and the Learning Environment: How knowledge of human motivation and behavior should influence strategies for organizing and supporting individual and group work in the classroom

10. C—Feedback: Subject Category I. Students as Learners: Student Motivation and the Learning Environment: How knowledge of human motivation and behavior should influence strategies for organizing and supporting individual and group work in the classroom

4. Factors and situations that are likely to promote or diminish students' motivation to learn, and how to help students to become self-motivated

1. A—Feedback: Subject Category I. Students as Learners: Student Motivation and the Learning Environment: Factors and situations that are likely to promote or diminish students' motivation to learn; how to help students become self-motivated

2. C—Feedback: Subject Category I. Students as Learners: Student Motivation and the Learning Environment: Factors and situations that are likely to promote or diminish students' motivation to learn; how to help students become self-motivated

3. B—Feedback: Subject Category I. Students as Learners: Student Motivation and the Learning Environment: Factors and situations that are likely to promote or diminish students' motivation to learn; how to help students become self-motivated

4. B—Feedback: Subject Category I. Students as Learners: Student Motivation and the Learning Environment: Factors and situations that are likely to promote or diminish students' motivation to learn; how to help students become self-motivated

5. Principles of effective classroom management and strategies to promote positive relationships, cooperation, and purposeful learning

1. C—Feedback: Subject Category I. Students as Learners: Student Motivation and the Learning Environment: Principles of effective management and strategies to promote positive relationships, cooperation, and purposeful learning

2. B—Feedback: Subject Category I. Students as Learners: Student Motivation and the Learning Environment: Principles of effective management and strategies to promote positive relationships, cooperation, and purposeful learning

3. A—Feedback: Subject Category I. Students as Learners: Student Motivation and the Learning Environment: Principles of effective classroom management and strategies to promote positive relationships, cooperation, and purposeful learning: Responding to student misbehavior

4. A—Feedback: Subject Category I. Students as Learners: Student Motivation and the Learning Environment: Principles of effective management and strategies to promote positive relationships, cooperation, and purposeful learning: Establishing classroom rules, punishments, and rewards

5. C—Feedback: Subject Category I. Students as Learners: Student Motivation and the Learning Environment: Principles of effective management and strategies to promote positive relationships, cooperation, and purposeful learning: Communicating with parents and caregivers

6. A—Feedback: Subject Category I. Students as Learners: Student Motivation and the Learning Environment: Principles of effective management and strategies to promote positive relationships, cooperation, and purposeful learning

7. B—Feedback: Subject Category I. Students as Learners: Student Motivation and the Learning Environment: Principles of effective management and strategies to promote positive relationships, cooperation, and purposeful learning

8. D—Feedback: Subject Category I. Students as Learners: Student Motivation and the Learning Environment: Principles of effective management and strategies to promote positive relationships, cooperation, and purposeful learning: Arranging classroom space

9. B—Feedback: Subject Category I. Students as Learners: Student Motivation and the Learning Environment: Principles of effective management and strategies to promote positive relationships, cooperation, and purposeful learning

10. A—Feedback: Subject Category I. Students as Learners: Student Motivation and the Learning Environment: Principles of effective classroom management and strategies to promote positive relationships, cooperation, and purposeful learning: Responding to student misbehavior

11. C—Feedback: Subject Category I. Students as Learners: Student Motivation and the Learning Environment: Principles of effective management and strategies to promote positive relationships, cooperation, and purposeful learning: Pacing and the structure of the lesson

12. C—Feedback: Subject Category I. Students as Learners: Student Motivation and the Learning Environment: Principles of effective management and strategies to promote positive relationships, cooperation, and purposeful learning: Establishing classroom rules, punishments, and rewards

13. A—Feedback: Subject Category I. Students as Learners: Student Motivation and the Learning Environment: Principles of effective management and strategies to promote positive relationships, cooperation, and purposeful learning: Establishing classroom rules, punishments, and rewards

14. C—Feedback: Subject Category I. Students as Learners: Student Motivation and the Learning Environment: Principles of effective management and strategies to promote positive relationships, cooperation, and purposeful learning: Giving timely feedback

15. A—Feedback: Subject Category I. Students as Learners: Student Motivation and the Learning Environment: Principles of effective management and strategies to promote positive relationships, cooperation, and purposeful learning: How knowledge of human emotion and behavior should influence strategies for organizing and supporting individual and group work in the classroom

16. B—Feedback: Subject Category I. Students as Learners: Student Motivation and the Learning Environment: Principles of effective management and strategies to promote positive relationships, cooperation, and purposeful learning: Communicating with parents and caregivers

17. C—Feedback: Subject Category I. Students as Learners: Student Motivation and the Learning Environment: Principles of effective management and strategies to promote positive relationships, cooperation, and purposeful learning

18. D—Feedback: Subject Category I. Students as Learners: Student Motivation and the Learning Environment: Principles of effective management and strategies to promote positive relationships, cooperation, and purposeful learning

19. A—Feedback: Subject Category I. Students as Learners: Student Motivation and the Learning Environment: Principles of effective management and strategies to promote positive relationships, cooperation, and purposeful learning: Arranging classroom space

20. B—Feedback: Subject Category I. Students as Learners: Student Motivation and the Learning Environment: Principles of effective management and strategies to promote positive relationships, cooperation, and purposeful learning: Modeling conflict resolution, problem solving, and anger management

21. D—Feedback: Subject Category I. Students as Learners: Student Motivation and the Learning Environment: Principles of effective management and strategies to promote positive relationships, cooperation, and purposeful learning: Providing positive guidance

All Subject Categories are as listed in the ETS Principles of Learning and Teaching, *Tests at a Glance*, located at *ftp://ftp.ets.org/pub/tandl/0522.pdf*.

II. Instruction and Assessment

a. Instructional Strategies

1. Major cognitive processes associated with student learning

1. Which of the following teachers is using a teacher strategy that is recommended for students from impoverished backgrounds? (Text Hint: See page 140)
   a. Mrs. Rall is a disciplinarian; she thinks restricting freedom creates a good working environment.
   b. Mr. Mesing disregards motivation as a priority; he thinks it does not effectively impact achievement.
   c. Mr. Amista teaches to improve thinking skills.
   d. Ms. Rysra looks for ways to bring in guest speakers from non-impoverished backgrounds.

2. Multiple-choice questions assess a student's ability to _____. (Text Hint: See page 263)
   a. recognize the correct answer
   b. recall the correct answer
   c. construct the correct answer
   d. explain the correct answer

3. Mr. Tyrell wants his tenth grade students to learn a list of Spanish verbs and their conjugations by the following week. He tells them to make sure that they memorize the list by the exam day. According to Mr. Tyrell's instructions, what process are students most likely to use to remember the list of verbs and their conjugations? (Text Hint: See page 251)
   a. Organization
   b. Rehearsal
   c. Elaboration
   d. Attention

4. Mrs. Kily's ninth grade science class is learning the difference between the states of matter: solid, gas, and liquid. She tells them to imagine the molecules in these states of matter as Ping-Pong balls. Therefore she tells them to envision a solid as a group of Ping-Pong balls lumped together in a mass, a gas as all of those Ping-Pong balls moving very fast over an area, and a liquid as those ping pong balls moving but slower than they did as a gas. Mrs. Kily is helping her students remember by _____. (Text Hint: See page 253)
   a. metacognition
   b. serial positioning effect
   c. construction of images
   d. mnemonics

5. Rehearsal is a strategy best used when students need to _____. (Text Hint: See page 251)
   a. generate examples of a concept
   b. encode information for long-term memory
   c. remember a list of items for a brief period of time
   d. organize information

6. Which of the following scenarios presents the best example of prototype matching? (Text Hint: See page 285)

    a. Tyler is deciding whether an item is a member of a category by comparing it with the most typical item(s) of the category.

    b. Brianna is naming all of the non-examples of a concept.

    c. Joseph is writing all of the examples of a concept on the board.

    d. Jana is listening to the teacher list all of the defining features of a concept.

7. Which of the following scenarios best depicts a student or students thinking critically? (Text Hint: See page 288)

    a. Abdul memorized a list of spelling words for a spelling bee.

    b. Felix and Sue are thinking reflectively and productively, as well as evaluating the evidence.

    c. Gabriel and Todd are brainstorming ideas for the class play.

    d. Martin is trying to think of all of the examples of the concept "vegetable."

8. Which of the following examples best illustrates problem solving? (Text Hint: See page 298)

    a. Athena thinks of personal examples when learning about new concepts in geometry.

    b. Isabella classifies animals based on common features.

    c. Cheryl uses made-up symbols to represent words that she is memorizing.

    d. Mona and Asha work together to find an appropriate way to attain a goal.

9. A type of formal reasoning that involves four parts, with the relation of the last two parts being the same as the relation of the first two parts is called _____. (Text Hint: See page 287)

    a. an analogy

    b. deductive reasoning

    c. inductive reasoning

    d. critical thinking

10. Swen is not excited about having to read another Shakespearean play. He has already read two of Shakespeare's plays and he concluded from reading those two plays that he dislikes the general nature of Shakespeare's plays. Swen is engaging in _____. (Text Hint: See page 287)

    a. inductive reasoning

    b. deductive reasoning

    c. critical thinking

    d. decision making

11. Alex and Brian are engaging in a detective game in which they must gather and sort through all of the clues in order to determine who has committed a crime. Alex and Brian are engaging in _____ when playing this detective game. (Text Hint: See page 287)

    a. inductive reasoning

    b. deductive reasoning

    c. critical thinking

    d. decision making

12. Uma is trying to decide whether next year she should take calculus, which is considered an advanced mathematics class for her grade level, or algebra II, which is the regular mathematics for her grade level. In making this decision, Uma is weighing the costs and the benefits of this decision by creating a plus and minuses list. Uma is using _____. (Text Hint: See page 290)

    a. subgoaling

    b. hypothesis testing

    c. decision making

    d. belief perseverance

13. Mrs. Kombly encourages her students to brainstorm, to be internally motivated, and to be flexible and playful in their thinking. She is also careful that she does not become overcontrolling of her students. Mrs. Kombly is fostering _____ in her classroom. (Text Hint: See page 293)

    a. intelligence

    b. decision making

    c. creativity

    d. problem solving

14. Ronald is very good at being able to think about something in novel and unusual ways and come up with unique solutions to the problem. This means that Ronald is very_____. (Text Hint: See page 293)

    a. good at problem solving

    b. good at analogies

    c. good at thinking critically

    d. creative

15. Ronnie's history teacher has just given an extra credit assignment consisting of a research project. Ronnie decides to assess her current situation, which is that she has some possible ideas for this project. She then sketches out a plan to reduce the difference between her current state and the goal of doing the project. She knows that she must now reduce the number of topic ideas down to one, research that idea by going to the library, and asking her uncle, who is a historian, if he has any books on the topic. What is Ronnie using to solve her problem? (Text Hint: See page 299)

    a. An algorithm

    b. Subgoaling

    c. Means-end analysis

    d. Fixation

16. Which of the following statements about creativity is true? (Text Hint: See page 294)

    a. Creative students are able to generate a single, best way to solve a problem.

    b. Students who are creative in math are also creative in other disciplines such as language arts, science, and the visual arts.

    c. Creative students think about things in novel and unusual ways.

    d. Most highly intelligent students are very creative.

17. Mrs. Daniels' students are building a model of the rainforest in the classroom. They are making trees using twisted, brown paper as well as a variety of tropical flowers and birds. What is Mrs. Daniels fostering in her students? (Text Hint: See page 268)

    a. Concept mapping

    b. Problem based learning

    c. Convergent thinking

    d. Creativity

18. Mr. Berman is moderating a classroom debate about year-round schooling. Students in Group 1 are in favor of year-round schools and Group 2 is opposed to year-round schools. Group 2 is sharing research that refutes the position of Group 1. A Group 2 student is passionately speaking against a point that was made by a Group 1 student. Which statement best describes what is happening in Mr. Berman's classroom? (Text Hint: See page 289)

    a. The students are engaging in a critical thinking activity.

    b. Mr. Berman is in danger of losing control of his classroom.

    c. Students are being encouraged to give a single, correct answer about year-round schooling.

    d. Mr. Berman is pitting students against each other and will ultimately undermine friendships.

19. When students are having fun in the classroom, _____. (Text Hint: See page 296)

    a. they are less likely to absorb and retain information

    b. they are less attentive and less motivated to learn

    c. they are more likely to engage in disruptive and dangerous behavior

    d. they are more likely to consider creative solutions to problems

20. Which of the following assignments is most consistent with the social constructivist approach to writing? (Text Hint: See page 314)

    a. Writing a book report about a novel read aloud during class

    b. Creating an outline to summarize main events studied during history class

    c. Writing a term paper about a topic studied during science class

    d. Writing an essay about a recent significant personal event

21. "Schools for Thought" emphasizes the importance of infusing real-world problems into the curriculum. Which of the following is an example of a real-world problem appropriate for academic content? (Text Hint: See page 331)

    a. How cities can reduce population

    b. The United States' role in reducing world hunger

    c. How to resolve a conflict of opinion

    d. All the above

22. Mr. Azaria is conducting a mock trial in his social studies class to teach students about the judicial branch of government. This activity exemplifies which of the following concepts? (Text Hint: See Ch 10, page 316)

    a. Situated cognition

    b. Scaffolding

    c. Cognitive apprenticeship

    d. Peer tutoring

23. Which of the following is a 4-year, problem-based high school math curriculum that emphasizes solving math problems in context? (Text Hint: See page 357)

    a. Connected mathematics program

    b. Interactive Mathematics Program

    c. Everyday mathematics

    d. Interactive demonstration strategy

24. Ms. Rydell has her students learn about social studies so that they will take what they learned and use it in school and also outside of school. She stresses meaningful learning and thinking critically about values. What approach to social studies is Ms. Rydell taking? (Text Hint: See page 367)

    a. A cognitive approach

    b. A constructivist approach

    c. The traditional approach

    d. The interactive approach

25. Wiring a doll house, making replicas of boats for a regatta, and dropping eggs are examples of _____. (Text Hint: See page 363)

    a. HumBio science curriculum

    b. gender-based science activities

    c. drill and practice

    d. a cognitive, constructivist approach to science

2. Major categories, advantages, and appropriate uses of instructional strategies

1. Current educational reform emphasizes the use of which of the following types of activities or assignments? (Text Hint: See page 8)

    a. Writing reports

    b. Completing worksheets

    c. Working in groups

    d. Using calculators

2. An individual who takes a constructivist approach to teaching would most likely encourage students to do which of the following? (Text Hint: See page 8)

    a. Solve math problems

    b. Collaborate with others

    c. Memorize information

    d. Assemble puzzles

3. Which of the following teachers is exhibiting an individualist teaching strategy? (Text Hint: See page 136)

    a. Mr. Randall stresses cooperation in his classroom, especially in group assignments.

    b. Mrs. Simone thinks that students work best if they work independently rather than in groups.

    c. Mr. Tamishi avoids criticism of students in public; he'd rather express criticism in private.

    d. Ms. Ohara thinks that cultivating long-term relationships with parents and students is very effective.

4. Mrs. Isadora asks to see Toby during recess to discuss his last test performance. "Toby, I want to know why you did not tell me that you were having difficulties," Mrs. Isadora asks. "I thought I knew that stuff. I always think that but then when I take the test I don't do so well," Toby replies. What is likely to be the cause of Toby's problems? (Text Hint: See page 248)

    a. Toby lacks metacognition.

    b. Toby is exceeding the capacity of the sensory register.

    c. Toby is lacking working memory.

    d. Toby is employing organization.

5. Theo is creating a _____, which is a visual representation of a concept that is filled with connections and hierarchical organizations pertinent to each concept. Theo is including examples and non-examples of the concept in order to gain a more sound understanding of the concept. (Text Hint: See page 284)

    a. hypothesis testing

    b. concept map

    c. fixation

    d. prototype matching

6. Mr. Allport has shown his first grade class four different shapes drawn on a large piece of poster board. He has secretly selected one of these shapes and he will now ask his students to develop educated guesses about what concept he has selected. Students begin asking questions related to the different shapes and by eliminating non-examples, they will be able to identify what concept Mr. Allport has chosen. In this scenario, what is Mr. Allport's class taking part in? (Text Hint: See page 284)

    a. Concept mapping

    b. Analogies

    c. Subgoaling

    d. Hypothesis testing

7. Which of the following is an example of social loafing? (Text Hint: See page 322)

    a. Ryan is not doing his work because he knows his group will complete it.

    b. Grant is not feeling well today and is having trouble staying on task.

    c. Miranda's group is disagreeing over which topic to pursue and has reached a stalemate.

    d. Miles is known for his lack of social skills and is not well liked by his peers.

8. When heterogeneous cooperative groups are formed, students of which ability level(s) are most likely to feel left out? (Text Hint: See page 325)

    a. High ability

    b. Medium ability

    c. Low ability

    d. Both low and high ability

9. When working in cooperative groups, the role of the praiser is best described as _____. (Text Hint: See page 327)

    a. thinking about and evaluating the group's progress

    b. equalizing the participation of students in the group

    c. helping with academic content

    d. showing appreciation for each student's contributions

10. Shanice is in charge of writing down ideas the group has and who is responsible for each task. Which group role has she been assigned? (Text Hint: See page 327)

    a. Encourager

    b. Recorder

    c. Materials monitor

    d. Reflector

11. When composing groups of students for small-group work, teachers should _____. (Text Hint: See page 325)

    a. place students with their friends

    b. create groups with diversity in ability, ethnicity, socioeconomic status, and gender

    c. place students of the same ability-level in the same group

    d. separate boys from girls

12. Which of the following conclusions is not true? To develop students' team-building skills, teachers should _____. (Text Hint: See page 326)

    a. help students to become better listeners

    b. give students some practice in contributing to a common product as part of a team

    c. discuss the value of having a group leader and different roles

    d. let teams solve problem situations independently

13. A cognitive approach to reading that emphasizes instruction in strategies, especially metacognitive strategies, is which of the following? (Text Hint: See page 345)

    a. Everyday mathematics

    b. whole language approach

    c. reciprocal teaching

    d. transactional strategy instruction approach

14. Ms. Tesda thinks that the program developed by Stanford University scientists in collaboration with middle school teachers, which integrates the study of ecology, evolution, genetics, physiology, human development, culture, health, and safety is very effective. What program is Ms. Tesda referring to? (Text Hint: See page 362)

    a. transactional strategy instruction approach.

    b. HUMBIO

    c. interactive demonstration strategy

    d. reciprocal teaching

15. Mr. Ortiz will be teaching social studies in an elementary school. How is Mr. Ortiz likely to teach social studies? (Text Hint: See page 364)

    a. As an interdisciplinary course

    b. As a focused single discipline

    c. Integrated across several disciplines

    d. None of the above

16. Which of the following characteristics is most consistent with direct instruction? (Text Hint: See page 383)

    a. It is a student-centered approach.

    b. The classroom environment is typically unstructured.

    c. Academic learning time is kept to a minimum.

    d. The teacher expects students to reach high levels of academic excellence.

17. When using questions in the classroom, all of the following strategies are recommended EXCEPT which one? (Text Hint: See page 386)

    a. Avoiding questions that can be answered with yes or no

    b. Using fact-based questions to lead into thinking-based questions

    c. Allowing plenty of time for students to think about answers

    d. Asking leading questions that suggest the desired answer

18. Advocates for the teacher-centered approach feel that it is the best strategy for teaching _____. (Text Hint: See page 392)

    a. critical thinking

    b. metacognition

    c. basic skills

    d. high school students

19. Ms. Martha has students get into groups for their next activity. She instructs students to work with the paint provided at each table in order to find out how we get green paint. Ms. Martha is using which learner-centered strategy? (Text Hint: See page 397)

    a. Discovery learning

    b. Guided discovery learning

    c. Problem-based learning

    d. Mastery learning

3. Principles, techniques, and methods associated with various instructional strategies

1. Ursula is taking an algebra exam and in order to remember the order in which to perform certain functions on the exam, Ursula aids her memory by writing down the word 'GRUMPY' on her paper. She smiles knowing that this will help her reach the right answers. Ursula is using_____. (Text Hint: See page 264)

   a. the method of loci

   b. rhymes

   c. acronyms

   d. keyword method

2. Mrs. Right wants to ensure that her students remember the information she is presenting in class today. Thus, after she is done with the lesson, she begins a question and answer period in which she asks the students to generate personal examples of the concepts they just learned. What is Mrs. Right using? (Text Hint: See page 252)

   a. Encoding

   b. Elaboration

   c. Retrieval

   d. Chunking

3. If a student has belief perseverance, which of the following would he or she most likely display? (Text Hint: See page 291)

   a. A tendency to search for and use information that supports rather than refutes their ideas.

   b. A tendency to falsely report, after the fact, that he or she accurately predicted an event.

   c. A tendency to have more confidence in judgment and decisions than he or she should based on probability or past occurrence.

   d. A tendency to hold onto a belief even in the face of contradictory evidence.

4. Mrs. Little wants to use the Group Investigation method in her history class. Which of the following would be the best activity to employ? (Text Hint: See page 323)

    a. Group members decide which historical figures they want to study and break up to meet with students from other groups.

    b. Groups decide which historical figure they want to study and delegate responsibilities for initial legwork within the group before getting together to summarize the findings.

    c. Students work together at tables on teacher prepared worksheets.

    d. Each student signs up for a historical figure to research at the library.

5. When a group member is given part of the material to be learned, becomes an expert on that material and then teaches it to others, this is called _____. (Text Hint: See page 323)

    a. reciprocal teaching

    b. jigsaw

    c. student-teams-achievement divisions

    d. group investigation

6. The interactive demonstration strategy helps students to _____. (Text Hint: See page 360)

    a. construct meaningful strategies

    b. integrate ecology, evolution, genetics, physiology, human development, culture, health, and safety

    c. work on everyday problems

    d. overcome misconceptions in science in which the teacher introduces the demonstration, asks students to discuss the demonstration with classmates and predicts its outcome, and then performs the demonstration

7. Mr. Brians is teaching his students to read by emphasizing that they decode and comprehend words. He thinks metacognitive skills as well as general automaticity are important. What approach to teaching reading is Mr. Brians using? (Text Hint: See page 343)

    a. A cognitive approach

    b. A social constructivist approach

    c. The whole language approach

    d. The interactive approach

8. Ty and Amy-Lynn are involved in a book club which will involve peer learning and student-led discussions. In a book club, what is the role of the teacher? (Text Hint: See page 347)

    a. To serve as a guide, but give students responsibility for how the discussions will evolve

    b. To remain completely uninvolved

    c. To be completely in charge of the discussion, topics, and learning

    d. The teacher is not present during book clubs

9. Mrs. Shimm always has her students outline and organize content information prior to beginning their writing. She gives them feedback for their efforts, which is beneficial because it gives the students confidence. What approach to writing is Mrs. Shimm using? (Text Hint: See page 349)

    a. Problem solving

    b. Planning

    c. Revising

    d. Metacognition

10. Ms. Mott's ninth grade science class is taught with an emphasis on discovery and hands-on laboratory investigation; thus her students are helped to construct their own knowledge. What approach to science teaching is Ms. Mott's using? (Text Hint: See page 360)

    a. Cognitive approach

    b. HUMBIO

    c. Social approach

    d. Constructivist approach

11. Sam is excited about returning to school after summer vacation. He will be learning to read. According to research findings presented in your text, what approach is best to teach reading? (Text Hint: See page 342)

    a. Whole language approach is best.

    b. Basic skills and phonetics approach is best.

    c. Both approaches were found to benefit children.

    d. Neither approach was found beneficial.

12. The learner-centered principle described as "the goals of learning" refers to _____. (Text Hint: See page 393)

    a. thinking creatively and critically

    b. making long-term and short-term plans

    c. improving self-esteem and appreciating one's own talents

    d. developing shared construction of important skills

13. Supporters of learner-centered instruction feel it leads to students' _____. (Text Hint: See page 398)

    a. active construction of learning

    b. positive self-esteem

    c. internal motivation

    d. all of the above

14. Which statement best describes an effective teaching strategy for delivering lectures? (Text Hint: See page 385)

    a. Simplify the lecture focus and present a single point of view.

    b. Make the lecture interesting and motivate students' interest in a topic.

    c. Ask students to save their questions until after the conclusion of the lecture.

    d. Avoid using visual aids as they distract students from the lecture focus.

15. _____ involves learning one concept or topic thoroughly before moving on to a more difficult one. (Hint: See page 387)

    a. Mastery learning

    b. Discovery learning

    c. Guided discovery learning

    d. Metacognition

16. _____ is (are) used at the beginning of a lesson to orient students and help them see "the big picture" of what is to come and how information is connected to what they already know. (Text hint: See page 384)

    a. Visual aids

    b. Early assessment

    c. Advance organizers

    d. Essential questions

4. Methods for enhancing student learning through the use of a variety of resources and materials

1. Mr. Johnson utilizes an activity within his social studies class that involves students volunteering in the community. Students are given the option of helping the elderly, working in a hospital, or assisting Habitat for Humanity. This is a good example of _____.(Text Hint: See page 98)

    a. character education

    b. values clarification

    c. cognitive moral education

    d. service learning

2. Mr. Sanchez invites professionals from the local engineering company to serve as after school mentors. These mentors not only provide academic help but also serve as positive role models. This is an example of _____. (Text Hint: See page 231)

    a. positive reinforcement

    b. observational learning

    c. self-regulatory learning

    d. classic conditioning

3. Mr. Anthony frequently invites local writing experts such as journalists and authors to his classroom. He also regularly schedules student-teacher writing conferences to discuss students' writing. Mr. Anthony emphasizes _____. (Text Hint: See page 351)

    a. planning and problem solving in writing

    b. the social context of writing

    c. a cognitive approach to writing

    d. prewriting activities

4. Mr. Stevenson has decided to create a location on the Web in order to post: contact information, students' homework, upcoming field trips, and requests for parental involvement. What has Mr. Stevenson created? (Text Hint: See page 400)

    a. An e-mail address

    b. A Web site

    c. Electronic monitoring

    d. A wireless network

5. What does The Educator's Reference Desk provide? (Text Hint: See page 402)

    a. Provides free information about a wide range of educational topics

    b. Provides online professional development workshops

    c. Provides free access to online encyclopedias

    d. None of the above

6. Which grade level should be able to use keyboards and other common input, discuss common uses of technology in daily life, use technology tools (such as Web tools and scanners), and use telecommunications and online resources? (Text Hint: See page 403)

    a. Prekindergarten–2nd grade

    b. Grades 3–5

    c. Grades 6–8

    d. Grades 9–12

7. Eric wants to conduct research about dolphins on the Web. Which tool should he use to find information on the Internet? (Text Hint: See page 400)

    a. A search engine like Google or Yahoo!

    b. A wireless network

    c. Instant messenger

    d. Email

8. Mrs. Jenkins brought copies of letters written by Revolutionary War soldiers to her social studies classroom. After reading the letters aloud, she asked her students to select one soldier and write a letter back to him. The war letters are examples of _____. (Text Hint: See page 149)

    a. jigsaw classroom materials

    b. state-mandated curriculum

    c. biased materials

    d. primary documents

b. Planning Instruction

1. Techniques for planning instruction to meet curriculum goals, including the incorporation of learning theory, subject matter, curriculum development, and student development

1. Mr. Perez is teaching in the field that seeks to promote civic competence with the goal of helping students make informed and reasoned decisions for the public good as citizens of a culturally diverse, democratic society in an interdependent world. What field is Mr. Perez teaching in? (Text Hint: See page 364)

    a. Mathematics

    b. Social studies

    c. Science

    d. Reading

2. Genevieve in entering high school; she will be enrolled in science classes. How is Genevieve going to be taught science now? (Text Hint: See page 363)

    a. In the sequence: biology, chemistry, and physics.

    b. In the sequence: chemistry, biology, and physics.

    c. In the sequence: physics, chemistry, biology.

    d. None of the above

3. Ms. Alice must set instructional goals for her class, plan activities, prioritize tasks, make time estimates, and create schedules while remaining flexible. How would you characterize Ms. Alice's activity? (Text Hint: See page 377)

    a. Planning

    b. Prioritizing

    c. Creating a lesson plan

    d. Scaffolding

4. Teachers are attending a workshop offering strategies on establishing general content, creating basic curriculum sequence, and ordering and reserving materials. What might an appropriate title for such a workshop be? (Text Hint: See page 379)
   a. Yearly Planning
   b. Term Planning
   c. Unit Planning
   d. Weekly Planning
   e. Daily Planning

5. According to Robert Yinger, which of the following goals is recommended for term planning? (Text Hint: See page 379)
   a. Establishing general content
   b. Detailing of content in three-month segments
   c. Developing a sequence of related and well-organized learning experiences
   d. Laying out activities within the framework of the weekly schedule

6. Which of the following is the best example of a behavioral objective according to Robert Mager? (Text Hint: See page 378)
   a. Students will complete the test with 85 percent accuracy.
   b. Students will correctly employ the "i" before "e" rule with 85 percent accuracy.
   c. Given a 15-item teacher-made test, students will correctly employ the "i" before "e" rule with 85 percent accuracy.
   d. Given a 15-item teacher-made test, students will complete the test with 85 percent accuracy.

7. Which of the following scenarios depicts "application"? (Text Hint: See page 380)
   a. Melinda plants a garden after reading about how to grow plants.
   b. Jerry identifies the assumptions of the theory of the origin of the universe.
   c. Ingrid disagrees with her teacher's interpretation of a story.
   d. Francisco learns about common features of all mammals.

8. Which of the following statements provides the best description of evaluation? (Text Hint: See page 380)
   a. To combine elements to create new information
   b. To break down complex information into smaller parts
   c. To make judgments about ideas or theories
   d. To remember information accurately

9. Which of the following is a category of the affective domain in Bloom's taxonomy? (Text Hint: See page 380)
   a. Application
   b. Valuing
   c. Perception
   d. Comprehension

10. Objectives pertaining to reflex movements, basic fundamental movements, perceptual abilities, physical abilities, skilled movements, and nondiscussive behaviors pertain to which taxonomy? (Text Hint: See page 381)
    a. Cognitive
    b. Affective
    c. Psychomotor

11. Knowledge, comprehension, application, analysis, synthesis, and evaluation are objectives from which of the following domains? (Text Hint: See page 380)

    a. Behavioral domain

    b. Psychomotor domain

    c. Affective domain

    d. Cognitive domain

12. In recent years, schools, teachers, and students have felt greater pressure to perform well on state-mandated standardized tests. Potentially serious consequences can result for low-performing schools and teachers. For this reason, many teachers _____. (Text hint: See page 495)

    a. incorporate state objectives into their classroom planning and instruction

    b. generally spend more time teaching the subjects tested

    c. are feeling pressured to teach a narrower curriculum and lower-level thinking skills

    d. All of the above

13. Mr. Newell's classroom displays pictures of children from around the world and his bookshelves contain a wide range of books and magazines. The majority of his students come from diverse backgrounds and one of Mr. Newell's class rules is that no child may be teased or excluded on the basis of race, ethnicity or gender. Mr. Newell is implementing which kind of classroom curriculum? (Text Hint: See page 149)

    a. Anti-bias curriculum

    b. State curriculum

    c. Emergent curriculum

    d. Subject matter curriculum

2. Techniques for creating effective bridges between curriculum goals and students' experiences

1. To help surface learners think more deeply, teachers can _____. (Text Hint: See page 125)

    a. give assignments that require students to fit information into a larger framework.

    b. set up a system that rewards deep thinking and punishes surface thinking.

    c. ask questions that require memory and recall.

    d. Surface learners are "hardwired" to think in this manner. Nothing can be done to alter this style.

2. On Fridays, sixth grade students spend one hour with kindergarten children. The older students help the younger children with math or reading work. Which of the following terms best describes this example? (Text Hint: See page 319)

    a. The Jigsaw Classroom

    b. Cross-age peer tutoring

    c. Group investigation

    d. Reciprocal teaching

3. Mrs. Treble is using a form of teaching in which she initially explains strategies and then models how to use them in making sense of the text. Then she asks her students to demonstrate the strategies, giving them support as they learn. What teaching strategy is Mrs. Treble using? (Text Hint: See page 346)

    a. Whole language approach

    b. Interactive demonstration strategy

    c. Reciprocal Teaching

    d. HUMBIO

4. Before Mr. Nielson begins his lecture, he reviews the previous day's lesson, discusses its relevance to the day's topic, and provides clear instructions for students' work. Which behavior is Mr. Nielson engaging in? (Text Hint: See page 384)

   a. Orienting

   b. Lecturing

   c. Explaining

   d. Reciting

5. Mr. Gonzalez is having difficulty keeping students on task. Which of the following strategies will most likely increase academic learning time in the classroom? (Text Hint: See page 452)

   a. Remember that a good sense of humor is important.

   b. Hold students accountable for their work done during class.

   c. Allow ample time for transition from one activity to the next.

   d. Interrupt class presentations when distracted by student misbehavior.

6. At the conclusion of a lecture, teachers should _____. (Text Hint: See page 386)

   a. tell students which parts of the lecture will be on the test

   b. select inattentive students to repeat key lecture points

   c. save students' questions until the next day

   d. summarize the main ideas and make connections to future lectures or activities

c. Assessment Strategies

1. Types of assessments

1. What do supporters of state-mandated achievement tests argue? (Text Hint: See page 496)

   a. That such tests are one of the best ways to hold schools and teachers accountable for students' learning.

   b. That such tests should include essay items.

   c. That such tests are not reliable.

   d. That such tests do not match the age-appropriate curriculum.

2. Mrs. Brewtu is aware of the controversy surrounding standardized testing. In order to ensure that her students' scores are reflective of their performance, she _____. (Text Hint: See page 510)

   a. gives them extra time to finish the standardized tests

   b. lets them take the tests a few times before they are to be scored

   c. gives them a high-stakes test to determine whether or not they should take other tests

   d. gives her students alternative assessments so she can determine how the standardized test scores compare

3. All of the following are facets of the federal *No Child Left Behind* act EXCEPT _____. (Hint: See page 498)

   a. by 2005–2006, teachers who are not considered "highly qualified" will receive a reduction in pay or a warning of dismissal

   b. separate objectives are to be proposed for students who are economically disadvantaged, students from ethnic minority groups, students with disabilities, and students with limited English proficiency

   c. by 2005–2006, states will be required to give all students annual standardized tests in grades 3 through 8

   d. schools that are labeled as "under performing" must be closed if they do not show improvement after five years

4. Mrs. Walker wishes to supplement standardized testing with alternative assessments that emphasize real-world problem solving. Which type of assessment will meet Mrs. Walker's needs? (Text Hint: See page 512)

   a. IQ tests

   b. Portfolio assessment

   c. Short-answer exams

   d. True-false exams

5. Of the following activities, which is the best example of pre-instruction assessment? (Text Hint: See page 520)

   a. Look over students' prior grades in the subject of interest.

   b. Ask students to clarify answers given during class.

   c. Monitor students' progress toward reaching learning targets.

   d. Report assessment results for school-level analysis.

6. When writing multiple choice test items for an exam, all of the following strategies are recommended EXCEPT which one? (Text Hint: See page 530)

   a. Make sure that alternatives are grammatically correct.

   b. Use the exact wording as it appears in the textbook.

   c. Make every effort to write the stem as a question.

   d. Include as much of the item as possible in the stem.

7. Which of the following are good examples of constructed-response items? (Text Hint: See page 533)

   a. True-false questions

   b. Matching items

   c. Multiple-choice items

   d. Essay items

8. Which of the following item formats is an example of a performance assessment? (Text Hint: See page 538)

   a. Multiple choice

   b. Matching

   c. True/false

   d. Essay

9. A best-work portfolio accomplishes which of the following goals? (Text Hint: See page 544)

   a. Shows the student's growth during a given school year

   b. Shows the student's growth over a period of several years

   c. Shows a collection of the student's most outstanding work

   d. Shows the student's most outstanding piece of work

10. Which of the following describes a major benefit of using portfolios as tools for assessment? (Text Hint: See page 545)

    a. Opportunity to evaluate students' improvement

    b. Simplicity of establishing criteria and assigning grades

    c. Ease of comparing one student's work with another student's work

    d. Ability to treat skills in isolated contexts

11. Mr. Woodward utilized electronic portfolios in his literature class. What are examples of materials he might have students include in the portfolio? (Text Hint: See page 552)

    a. Critical writing samples

    b. Unit test scores

    c. PowerPoint presentations

    d. All of the above

12. Aurbach's Cirady Profile, HyperStudio, and FileMaker Pro are all examples of _____. (Text Hint: See page 552)

    a. portfolios

    b. performance-based assessments

    c. electronic portfolios

    d. electronic record-keeping tools

13. Ms. Hall is using a program on the Internet to input and monitor data about her students' academic progress. Ms. Hall is using a _____. (Text Hint: See page 554)

    a. web-based assessment

    b. portfolio assessment

    c. performance assessment

    d. summative assessment

14. The majority of Mr. Robinson's students are from low socioeconomic backgrounds and have little experience with the world beyond their neighborhoods. He is concerned about fairness in standardized testing. Mr. Robinson feels that performance assessment should be used during and after instruction to supplement standardized testing. This type of assessment is _____. (Text Hint: See page 526)

    a. formative assessment

    b. objective assessment

    c. pluralistic assessment

    d. traditional assessment

15. Intelligence tests and career placement tests are examples of _____. (Text hint: See page 493)

    a. achievement tests

    b. aptitude tests

    c. high-stakes tests

    d. norm-referenced tests

2. Characteristics of assessments

1. The extent to which a test yields the same performance when a student is given the test on two different occasions is called _____. (Text Hint: See page 492)

    a. alternate forms reliability

    b. split-half reliability

    c. test-retest reliability

    d. concurrent validity

2. Which form of validity refers to the extent to which a test measures the student's knowledge of a particular subject? (Text Hint: See page 491)

   a. Predictive validity

   b. Construct validity

   c. Concurrent validity

   d. Content validity

3. Sometimes Maya gets very high scores on intelligence tests. Sometimes her scores are very low. And, from time to time, she gets an average score for someone in her age group. In Maya's case, the tests are best described as which of the following? (Text Hint: See page 491)|

   a. Both reliable and valid.

   b. Reliable, but not valid.

   c. Not reliable, but valid.

   d. Neither reliable nor valid

4. Suppose 1000 students take a particular exam. Their scores follow a normal distribution and range from 20 to 75. Of the following values, which would most likely be the mean? (Text Hint: See page 505)

   a. 33

   b. 40

   c. 49

   d. 54

5. A group of students received the following scores on a quiz: 44, 40, 40, 36, 35, 33, 33, 33, and 30. What is the mean? (Text Hint: See page 503)

   a. 33

   b. 35

   c. 36

   d. 37

6. A group of students received the following scores on a quiz: 44, 40, 40, 36, 35, 33, 33, 33, and 30. What is the mode? (Text Hint: See page 503)

   a. 33

   b. 35

   c. 36

   d. 37

7. The extent to which an assessment is a reasonable sample of what actually occurs in the classroom is referred to as which of the following? (Text Hint: See page 525)

   a. Content-related evidence

   b. Pluralistic assessment

   c. Instructional validity

   d. Item discrimination

8. Reliability refers to the extent to which a test does which of the following? (Text Hint: See page 525)

   a. Provides all students an equal opportunity to succeed

   b. Provides equivalent scores for a diverse group of individuals

   c. Produces a consistent, reproducible measure of performance

   d. Measures what it is intended to measure

9. An item is considered poor if its item discrimination index falls in which of the following ranges? (Text Hint: See page 533)

    a. 0 to 0.19

    b. 0.2 to 0.39

    c. 0.4 to 0.69

    d. 0.7 to 1.

10. When grading students, Mr. Lopez consistently compares students' scores with that of their peers. This is a good example of which standard of comparison? (Text Hint: See page 547)

    a. Norm-referenced grading

    b. Criteria-referenced grading

    c. Standards-based grading

    d. None of the above

3. Scoring assessments

1. Which is the truest representation of a normal distribution? (Text Hint: See page 107)

    a. Distribution where most scores fall in the middle and some scores fall higher and lower

    b. Distribution of normal people's scores

    c. Distribution where some scores fall in the middle but most fall toward the extremes

    d. There is no "normal" distribution when dealing with the social sciences

2. Which of the following is a measure of central tendency? (Text Hint: See page 503)

    a. Mean

    b. Sample size

    c. Standard deviation

    d. Range

3. A group of students received the following scores on a quiz: 44, 40, 40, 36, 35, 33, 33, 33, and 30. What is the standard deviation? (Text Hint: See Ch 15, page 504)

    a. 3.34

    b. 4.47

    c. 5.23

    d. 6.11

4. A person who gets the second-highest score of ten people taking an exam would be assigned which percentile rank score? (Text Hint: See page 506)

    a. 90%

    b. 85%

    c. 80%

    d. 75%

5. In a normal distribution, approximately what percent of scores fall between the mean and two standard deviations above the mean? (Text Hint: See page 505)

    a. 34%

    b. 48%

    c. 68%

    d. 95%

6. In a normal distribution, 99 percent of the scores fall between which two values? (Text Hint: See page 505)

   a. One standard deviation below the mean and the mean

   b. One standard deviation below the mean and one standard deviation above the mean

   c. Two standard deviations below the mean and two standard deviations above the mean

   d. Three standard deviations below the mean and three standard deviations above the mean

7. A z-score is an example of which of the following? (Text Hint: See page 507)

   a. Standard score

   b. Stanine

   c. Grade equivalent

   d. Percentile rank

8. Ms. Lili just received her class's test scores in the form of standard scores. What type of scores could Ms. Lili expect to see on her class's results? (Text Hint: See page 507)

   a. A z-score

   b. A t-score

   c. Stanine score

   d. Grade-equivalent score

   e. All of the above scores are standard scores

9. Mr. Jensen was told by his principal that the scores of all of the students in his class formed a normal distribution. Knowing this information, what should Mr. Jensen expect with regard to his students' scores? (Text Hint: See page 505)

   a. That most of the scores were above the mean.

   b. That most of the scores were below the mean.

   c. That most of the scores clustered around the mean.

   d. That his students' scores were not on a bell-shaped curve

10. Choose the most effective way to score essay questions from the following scenarios. (Text Hint: See page 534)

    a. Ms. Elijah outlines a good example of an acceptable response before reading students' essays.

    b. Mr. Miles always reads through each student's complete essays before moving onto the next student's responses.

    c. When Mr. Quan encounters an irrelevant or incorrect response, he puts them off to the side to deal with at a later time.

    d. Mrs. Clooney does not reread essays because she feels the initial response is always the correct interpretation of a student's answer.

11. When reporting students' scores to parents through report cards, checklists of skills and objectives are mainly used in _____. (Text Hint: See page 549)

    a. high schools

    b. junior high schools

    c. upper elementary grades

    d. kindergartens and elementary schools

12. Mr. Kouta developed a rating scale for evaluating his students' history dioramas. This rating scale is called _____. (Text Hint: See page 540)

    a. a checklist

    b. an answer key

    c. performance criteria

    d. a scoring rubric

4. Uses of assessments

1. To avoid using information about a student's intelligence in negative ways, teachers should _____. (Text Hint: See pages 109–110)

    a. base their expectations of students on IQ scores

    b. consider the students' intellectual competence in a wide range of areas

    c. develop advanced curriculum to meet the needs of students with high IQ scores

    d. not gain access to students' IQ scores

2. A standardized test is least appropriate in which of the following situations? (Text Hint: See page 488)

    a. Selecting students for entrance to a particular college

    b. Determining whether a group of students have met their teacher's objectives

    c. Comparing the students in one classroom to those in another

    d. Evaluating the quality of a new educational program

3. Mrs. Dorafill wants to use standardized test scores from the end of the previous year in planning her students' instruction for the next year. How can Mrs. Dorafill use standardized test scores from the end of the previous year to plan for the next coming school year? (Text Hint: See page 509)

    a. By using them to develop a very low or very high expectation for individual students

    b. By using them to provide her with an indication of a student's general ability.

    c. By using them to develop a very low or very high expectation for the entire class.

    d. By using them as the single indicator when grouping students

4. Which of the following is the best example of formative assessment? (Text Hint: See page 522)

    a. Observe students' nonverbal behavior to learn about their abilities and interests.

    b. Describe the extent to which students have achieved instructional goals and objectives.

    c. Communicate students' strengths and weaknesses to parents.

    d. Identify difficulties that students are experiencing and offer advice.

5. In Candace's third period algebra course, her teacher uses grading to evaluate students in need of remedial work before moving on to the next skill. Which purpose of grading does this meet? (Text Hint: See page 545)

    a. Administrative

    b. Informational

    c. Motivational

    d. Guidance

6. Mr. Riggles created a multiple-choice and essay quiz for his students after they finished reading *Roll of Thunder, Hear My Cry*. The exam tested students on the main characters, plot, setting, and climax of the book. This type of assessment is an example of a(n) _____. (Text hint: See page 523)

   a. informal assessment

   b. summative assessment

   c. formative assessment

   d. standardized assessment

5. Understanding measurement theory and assessment-related issues

1. Mr. Capadro wants all of his tenth grade students to do well on the upcoming standardized test. Because more than 70 percent of Mr. Capadro's students are minorities, what should Mr. Capadro be most aware of? (Text Hint: See page 511)

   a. The controversy of the potential for cultural bias in standardized tests may require him to give his students alternative assessments.

   b. The controversy of the potential for cultural bias in standardized tests may require him to give them extra time to finish the standardized tests.

   c. The controversy of the potential for cultural bias in standardized tests may require him to let them take the tests a few times before they are to be scored.

   d. The controversy of the potential for cultural bias in standardized tests may require him to give them a high-stakes test to determine whether or not they should take other tests.

2. Research suggests that teachers spend about how much of their professional time dealing with matters of assessment? (Text Hint: See page 520)

   a. 5–10%

   b. 10–20%

   c. 20–30%

   d. 30–50%

3. Which of the following statements best describes current views about assessment? (Text Hint: See page 520)

   a. Assessment should be integrated throughout the instructional process.

   b. Assessment should be implemented at the conclusion of a particular lesson or unit of study.

   c. Assessment should only be implemented by teachers who are specially trained in the areas of traditional and alternative assessments.

   d. None of the above

6. Interpreting and communicating results of assessments

1. Which of the following reasons is offered to explain the poor academic performance of American students, as compared to students of other countries? (Text Hint: See page 499)

   a. Standardized tests taken by American students include more open-ended items than do such tests taken by students of other countries.

   b. Inadequate time spent on schoolwork.

   c. American students spend more time doing homework than do students of other countries.

   d. American schools have smaller class sizes than do schools in countries of comparison.

2. Mrs. Williams learns that Jerome scored in the 88th percentile for reading comprehension while Terrence scored in the 81st percentile. She concludes that Jerome is a better reader than Terrence. Mrs. Williams is most likely _____. (Text Hint: See page 508)

   a. using test scores to place students in reading groups

   b. biased

   c. a test scoring expert

   d. overinterpreting test scores

3. When conducting parent-teacher conferences related to student grades, it is good practice to do all of the following EXCEPT _____. (Text hint: See page 550)

   a. be positive

   b. be objective

   c. be prepared

   d. be impersonal

4. At the conclusion of each grading term, Mrs. Jenkins writes lengthy descriptions of her students' performance on tests and assignments, behavior, and motivation. She is most likely using which form of reporting student grades? (Text hint: See page 549)

   a. Written progress reports

   b. Skills checklist

   c. Report card

   d. Parent-teacher conference

Answer Key

a. Instructional Strategies

1. Major cognitive processes associated with student learning

1. C—Feedback: Subject Category II. Instruction and Assessment: Instructional Strategies: Major cognitive processes associated with student learning: Critical thinking and creative thinking

2. A—Feedback: Subject Category II. Instruction and Assessment: Instructional Strategies: The major cognitive processes associated with student learning: Memorization and recall

3. B—Feedback: Subject Category II. Instruction and Assessment: Instructional Strategies: The major cognitive processes associated with student learning: Memorization and recall

4. C—Feedback: Subject Category II. Instruction and Assessment: Instructional Strategies: Major cognitive processes associated with student learning: Representation of ideas

5. C—Feedback: Subject Category II. Instruction and Assessment: Instructional Strategies: The major cognitive processes associated with student learning: Memorization and recall

6. A—Feedback: Subject Category II. Instruction and Assessment: Instructional Strategies: Major cognitive processes associated with student learning: Critical thinking

7. B—Feedback: Subject Category II. Instruction and Assessment: Instructional Strategies: Major cognitive processes associated with student learning: Critical thinking

8. D—Feedback: Subject Category II. Instruction and Assessment: Instructional Strategies: The major cognitive processes associated with student learning: Problem-structuring and problem-solving

9. A—Feedback: Subject Category II. Instruction and Assessment: Instructional Strategies: Major cognitive processes associated with student learning: Representation of ideas

10. A—Feedback: Subject Category II. Instruction and Assessment: Instructional Strategies: Major cognitive processes associated with student learning: Inductive and deductive thinking

11. B—Feedback: Subject Category II. Instruction and Assessment: Instructional Strategies: Major cognitive processes associated with student learning: Inductive and deductive thinking

12. C—Feedback: Subject Category II. Instruction and Assessment: Instructional Strategies: Major cognitive processes associated with student learning: Higher-order thinking

13. C—Feedback: Subject Category II. Instruction and Assessment: Instructional Strategies: Major cognitive processes associated with student learning: Creative thinking

14. D—Feedback: Subject Category II. Instruction and Assessment: Instructional Strategies: Major cognitive processes associated with student learning: Creative thinking

15. C—Feedback: Subject Category II. Instruction and Assessment: Instructional Strategies: The major cognitive processes associated with student learning: Problem-structuring and problem-solving

16. C—Feedback: Subject Category II. Instruction and Assessment: Instructional Strategies: Major cognitive processes associated with student learning: Creative thinking

17. D—Feedback: Subject Category II. Instruction and Assessment: Instructional Strategies: Major cognitive processes associated with student learning: Creative thinking

18. A—Feedback: Subject Category II. Instruction and Assessment: Instructional Strategies: Major cognitive processes associated with student learning: Critical thinking

19. D—Feedback: Subject Category II. Instruction and Assessment: Instructional Strategies: The major cognitive processes associated with student learning: Play

20. D—Feedback: Subject Category II. Instruction and Assessment: Instructional Strategies: The major cognitive processes associated with student learning: Social reasoning

21. D—Feedback: Subject Category II. Instruction and Assessment: Instructional Strategies: The major cognitive processes associated with student learning: Problem-structuring and problem-solving

22. A—Feedback: Subject Category II. Instruction and Assessment: Instructional Strategies: Major cognitive processes associated with student learning: Critical thinking and creative thinking

23. B—Feedback: Subject Category II. Instruction and Assessment: Instructional Strategies: The major cognitive processes associated with student learning: Problem-structuring and problem-solving

24. B—Feedback: Subject Category II. Instruction and Assessment: Instructional Strategies: Major cognitive processes associated with student learning: Critical thinking and Social reasoning

25. D—Feedback: Subject Category II. Instruction and Assessment: Instructional Strategies: Major cognitive processes associated with student learning: Invention

2. Major categories, advantages, and appropriate uses of instructional strategies

1. C—Feedback: Subject Category II. Instruction and Assessment: Instructional Strategies: Major categories, advantages, and appropriate uses of instructional strategies: Cooperative learning

2. B—Feedback: Subject Category II. Instruction and Assessment: Instructional Strategies: Principles, techniques, and methods associated with major instructional strategies: Student-centered models: Collaborative learning

3. B—Feedback: Subject Category II. Instruction and Assessment: Instructional Strategies: Major categories, advantages, and appropriate uses of instructional strategies: Independent study

4. A—Feedback: Subject Category II. Instruction and Assessment: Instructional Strategies: Major categories of instructional strategies: Reflection

5. B—Feedback: Subject Category II. Instruction and Assessment: Instructional Strategies: Major categories of instructional strategies: Concept mapping

6. D—Feedback: Subject Category II. Instruction and Assessment: Instructional Strategies: Major categories of instructional strategies: Whole-group discussion and Questioning

7. A—Feedback: Subject Category II. Instruction and Assessment: Instructional Strategies: Major categories, advantages, and appropriate uses of instructional strategies: Cooperative learning

8. B—Feedback: Subject Category II. Instruction and Assessment: Instructional Strategies: Major categories, advantages, and appropriate uses of instructional strategies: Cooperative learning

9. D—Feedback: Subject Category II. Instruction and Assessment: Instructional Strategies: Major categories, advantages, and appropriate uses of instructional strategies: Cooperative learning

10. B—Feedback: Subject Category II. Instruction and Assessment: Instructional Strategies: Major categories, advantages, and appropriate uses of instructional strategies: Cooperative learning

11. B—Feedback: Subject Category II. Instruction and Assessment: Instructional Strategies: Major categories, advantages, and appropriate uses of instructional strategies: Cooperative learning

12. D—Feedback: Subject Category II. Instruction and Assessment: Instructional Strategies: Major categories of instructional strategies: Small group work

13. D—Feedback: Subject Category II. Instruction and Assessment: Instructional Strategies: Major categories of instructional strategies: Reflection and Metacognition

14. B—Feedback: Subject Category II. Instruction and Assessment: Instructional Strategies: Major categories of instructional strategies: Interdisciplinary instruction

15. C—Feedback: Subject Category II. Instruction and Assessment: Instructional Strategies: Major categories of instructional strategies: Interdisciplinary instruction

16. D—Feedback: Subject Category II. Instruction and Assessment: Instructional Strategies: Major categories, advantages, and appropriate uses of instructional strategies: Direct instruction

17. D—Feedback: Subject Category II. Instruction and Assessment: Instructional Strategies: Major categories, advantages, and appropriate uses of instructional strategies: Questioning

18. C—Feedback: Subject Category II. Instruction and Assessment: Instructional Strategies: Major categories, advantages, and appropriate uses of instructional strategies: Direct instruction

19. A—Feedback: Subject Category II. Instruction and Assessment: Instructional Strategies: Major categories, advantages, and appropriate uses of instructional strategies: Discovery learning

3. Principles, techniques, and methods associated with various instructional strategies

1. C—Feedback: Subject Category II. Instruction and Assessment: Instructional Strategies: Principles, techniques, and methods associated with various instructional strategies: Direct instruction: Mnemonics

2. B—Feedback: Subject Category II. Instruction and Assessment: Instructional Strategies: Principles, techniques, and methods associated with various instructional strategies: Direct instruction: Questioning

3. D—Feedback: Subject Category II. Instruction and Assessment: Planning Instruction: Techniques for creating effective bridges between curriculum goals and students' experiences: Anticipating pre-conceptions

4. B—Feedback: Subject Category II. Instruction and Assessment: Instructional Strategies: Principles, techniques, and methods associated with major instructional strategies: Student-centered models: Collaborative learning

5. B—Feedback: Subject Category II. Instruction and Assessment: Instructional Strategies: Principles, techniques, and methods associated with major instructional strategies: Student-centered models: Cooperative learning (pair-share, jigsaw, STAD, teams, games, tournaments)

6. D—Feedback: Subject Category II. Instruction and Assessment: Instructional Strategies: Principles, techniques, and methods associated with various instructional strategies: Direct instruction: Demonstrations

7. A—Feedback: Subject Category II. Instruction and Assessment: Instructional Strategies: Principles, techniques, and methods associated with various instructional strategies: Direct Instruction

8. A—Feedback: Subject Category II. Instruction and Assessment: Instructional Strategies: Principles, techniques, and methods associated with various instructional strategies: Student-centered models: Discussion models

9. B—Feedback: Subject Category I. Instruction and Assessment: Instructional Strategies: Principles, techniques, and methods associated with various instructional strategies: Direct Instruction: Outlining and Note-taking

10. D—Feedback: Subject Category II. Instruction and Assessment: Instructional Strategies: Principles, techniques, and methods associated with various instructional strategies: Student-centered models: Laboratories

11. C—Feedback: Subject Category II. Instruction and Assessment: Instructional Strategies: Principles, techniques, and methods associated with various instructional strategies

12. B—Feedback: Subject Category II. Instruction and Assessment: Instructional Strategies: Principles, techniques, and methods associated with major instructional strategies: Student-centered models

13. D—Feedback: Subject Category II. Instruction and Assessment: Instructional Strategies: Principles, techniques, and methods associated with major instructional strategies: Student-centered models

14. B—Feedback: Subject Category II. Instruction and Assessment: Instructional Strategies: Principles, techniques, and methods associated with various instructional strategies: Direct Instruction

15. A—Feedback: Subject Category II. Instruction and Assessment: Instructional Strategies: Principles, techniques, and methods associated with major instructional strategies: Direct instruction: Mastery learning

16. C—Feedback: Subject Category II. Instruction and Assessment: Instructional Strategies: Principles, techniques, and methods associated with major instructional strategies: Direct instruction: David Ausubel's "Advance Organizers"

4. Methods for enhancing student learning through the use of a variety of resources and materials

1. D—Feedback: Subject Category II. Instruction and Assessment: Instructional Strategies: Methods for enhancing student learning through the use of a variety of resources and materials: Service learning

2. B—Feedback: Subject Category II. Instruction and Assessment: Instructional Strategies: Methods for enhancing student learning through the use of a variety of resources and materials: Local experts

3. B—Feedback: Subject Category II. Instruction and Assessment: Instructional Strategies: Methods for enhancing student learning through the use of a variety of resources and materials: Local experts

4. B—Feedback: Subject Category II. Instruction and Assessment: Instructional Strategies: Methods for enhancing student learning through the use of a variety of resources and materials: Computers, Internet resources, Web pages, email

5. A—Feedback: Subject Category II. Instruction and Assessment: Instructional Strategies: Methods for enhancing student learning through the use of a variety of resources and materials: Computers, Internet resources, Web pages, email

6. B—Feedback: Subject Category II. Instruction and Assessment: Instructional Strategies: Methods for enhancing student learning through the use of a variety of resources and materials: Computers, Internet resources, Web pages, email

7. A—Feedback: Subject Category II. Instruction and Assessment: Instructional Strategies: Methods for enhancing student learning through the use of a variety of resources and materials: Computers, Internet resources, Web pages, email

8. D—Feedback: Subject Category II. Instruction and Assessment: Instructional Strategies: Methods for enhancing student learning through the use of a variety of resources and materials: Primary documents and artifacts

b. Planning Instruction

1. Techniques for planning instruction to meet curriculum goals, including the incorporation of learning theory, subject matter, curriculum development, and student development

1. B—Feedback: Subject Category II. Instruction and Assessment: Planning Instruction: Techniques for planning instruction to meet curriculum goals, including the incorporation of learning theory, subject matter, curriculum development, and student development: Scope and sequence in specific disciplines

2. A—Feedback: Subject Category II. Instruction and Assessment: Planning Instruction: Techniques for planning instruction to meet curriculum goals, including the incorporation of learning theory, subject matter, curriculum development, and student development: Scope and sequence in specific disciplines

3. A—Feedback: Subject Category II. Instruction and Assessment: Planning Instruction: Techniques for planning instruction to meet curriculum goals, including the incorporation of learning theory, subject matter, curriculum development, and student development: Scope and sequence in specific disciplines

4. A—Feedback: Subject Category II. Instruction and Assessment: Planning Instruction: Techniques for planning instruction to meet curriculum goals, including the incorporation of learning theory, subject matter, curriculum development, and student development: Scope and sequence in specific disciplines

5. B—Feedback: Subject Category II. Instruction and Assessment: Planning Instruction: Techniques for planning instruction to meet curriculum goals, including the incorporation of learning theory, subject matter, curriculum development, and student development: Scope and sequence in specific disciplines and Units and lessons—rationale for selecting content topics

6. C—Feedback: Subject Category II. Instruction and Assessment: Planning Instruction: Techniques for planning instruction to meet curriculum goals, including the incorporation of learning theory, subject matter, curriculum development, and student development: Behavioral objectives—affective, cognitive, and psychomotor

7. A—Feedback: Subject Category II. Instruction and Assessment: Planning Instruction: Techniques for planning instruction to meet curriculum goals, including the incorporation of learning theory, subject matter, curriculum development, and student development: Learner objectives and outcomes

8. c—Feedback: Subject Category II. Instruction and Assessment: Planning Instruction: Techniques for planning instruction to meet curriculum goals, including the incorporation of learning theory, subject matter, curriculum development, and student development: Learner objectives and outcomes

9. B—Feedback: Subject Category II. Instruction and Assessment: Planning Instruction: Techniques for planning instruction to meet curriculum goals, including the incorporation of learning theory, subject matter, curriculum development, and student development: Behavioral objectives—affective, cognitive, and psychomotor

10. C—Feedback: Subject Category II. Instruction and Assessment: Planning Instruction: Techniques for planning instruction to meet curriculum goals, including the incorporation of learning theory, subject matter, curriculum development, and student development: Behavioral objectives—affective, cognitive, and psychomotor

11. D—Feedback: Subject Category II. Instruction and Assessment: Planning Instruction: Techniques for planning instruction to meet curriculum goals, including the incorporation of learning theory, subject matter, curriculum development, and student development: Behavioral objectives—affective, cognitive, and psychomotor

12. D—Feedback: Subject Category II. Instruction and Assessment: Planning Instruction: Techniques for planning instruction to meet curriculum goals, including the incorporation of learning theory, subject matter, curriculum development, and student development: National and state learning standards

13. A—Feedback: Subject Category II. Instruction and Assessment: Planning Instruction: Techniques for planning instruction to meet curriculum goals, including the incorporation of learning theory, subject matter, curriculum development, and student development: Anti-bias curriculum

2. Techniques for creating effective bridges between curriculum goals and students' experiences

1. A—Feedback: Subject Category II. Instruction and Assessment: Planning Instruction: Techniques for creating effective bridges between curriculum goals and students' experiences: Encouraging exploration and problem solving

2. B—Feedback: Subject Category II. Instruction and Assessment: Planning Instruction: Techniques for creating effective bridges between curriculum goals and students' experiences: Modeling

3. C—Feedback: Subject Category II. Instruction and Assessment: Planning Instruction: Techniques for creating effective bridges between curriculum goals and students' experiences: Modeling and Guided Practice

4. A—Feedback: Subject Category II. Instruction and Assessment: Planning Instruction: Techniques for creating effective bridges between curriculum goals and students' experiences: Activating students' prior knowledge and Building new skills on those previously acquired

5. B—Feedback: Subject Category II. Instruction and Assessment: Planning Instruction: Techniques for creating effective bridges between curriculum goals and students' experiences: Independent practice, including homework

6. D—Feedback: Subject Category II. Instruction and Assessment: Planning Instruction: Techniques for creating effective bridges between curriculum goals and students' experiences: Transitions

c. Assessment strategies

1. Types of assessments

1. A—Feedback: Subject Category II. Instruction and Assessment: Assessment Strategies: Measurement theory and assessment-related issues: Types of assessments: Achievement tests

2. D—Feedback: Subject Category II. Instruction and Assessment: Assessment Strategies: Measurement theory and assessment-related issues: Types of assessments: Alternative assessments

3. A—Feedback: Subject Category II. Instruction and Assessment: Assessment Strategies: Measurement theory and assessment-related issues: Types of assessments: Standardized tests

4. B—Feedback: Subject Category II. Instruction and Assessment: Assessment Strategies: Measurement theory and assessment-related issues: Types of assessments: Portfolios

5. A—Feedback: Subject Category II. Instruction and Assessment: Assessment Strategies: Measurement theory and assessment-related issues: Types of assessments

6. B—Feedback: Subject Category II. Instruction and Assessment: Assessment Strategies: Measurement theory and assessment-related issues: Types of assessments: Multiple choice tests

7. D—Feedback: Subject Category II. Instruction and Assessment: Assessment Strategies: Measurement theory and assessment-related issues: Types of assessments: Essays written to prompts

8. D—Feedback: Subject Category II. Instruction and Assessment: Assessment Strategies: Measurement theory and assessment-related issues: Types of assessments: Performance assessments

9. C—Feedback: Subject Category II. Instruction and Assessment: Assessment Strategies: Measurement theory and assessment-related issues: Types of assessments: Portfolios

10. A—Feedback: Subject Category II. Instruction and Assessment: Assessment Strategies: Measurement theory and assessment-related issues: Types of assessments: Portfolios

11. D—Feedback: Subject Category II. Instruction and Assessment: Assessment Strategies: Measurement theory and assessment-related issues: Types of assessments: Portfolios

12. C—Feedback: Subject Category II. Instruction and Assessment: Assessment Strategies: Measurement theory and assessment-related issues: Types of assessments: Portfolios

13. A—Feedback: Subject Category II. Instruction and Assessment: Assessment Strategies: Measurement theory and assessment-related issues: Types of assessments: Web-based assessment

14. C—Feedback: Subject Category II. Instruction and Assessment: Assessment Strategies: Measurement theory and assessment-related issues: Types of assessments: Performance assessments

15. B—Feedback: Subject Category II. Instruction and Assessment: Assessment Strategies: Measurement theory and assessment-related issues: Types of assessments: Aptitude tests

2. Characteristics of assessments

1. C—Feedback: Subject Category II. Instruction and Assessment: Assessment Strategies: Measurement theory and assessment-related issues: Characteristics of assessments: Reliability

2. D—Feedback: Subject Category II. Instruction and Assessment: Assessment Strategies: Measurement theory and assessment-related issues: Characteristics of assessments: Validity

3. D—Feedback: Subject Category II. Instruction and Assessment: Assessment Strategies: Measurement theory and assessment-related issues: Characteristics of assessments: Validity and Reliability

4. C—Feedback: Subject Category II. Instruction and Assessment: Assessment Strategies: Measurement theory and assessment-related issues: Characteristics of assessments: Mean

5. C—Feedback: Subject Category II. Instruction and Assessment: Assessment Strategies: Measurement theory and assessment-related issues: Characteristics of assessments: Mean

6. A—Feedback: Subject Category II. Instruction and Assessment: Assessment Strategies: Measurement theory and assessment-related issues: Characteristics of assessments: Mode

7. C—Feedback: Subject Category II. Instruction and Assessment: Assessment Strategies: Measurement theory and assessment-related issues: Characteristics of assessments: Validity

8. C—Feedback: Subject Category II. Instruction and Assessment: Assessment Strategies: Measurement theory and assessment-related issues: Characteristics of assessments: Reliability

9. A—Feedback: Subject Category II. Instruction and Assessment: Assessment Strategies: Measurement theory and assessment-related issues: Characteristics of assessments: Discrimination index

10. A—Feedback: Subject Category II. Instruction and Assessment: Assessment Strategies: Measurement theory and assessment-related issues: Characteristics of assessments: Norm-referenced

3. Scoring assessments

1. A—Feedback: Subject Category II. Instruction and Assessment: Assessment Strategies: Scoring Assessments: Reporting assessment results: Normal distribution

2. A—Feedback: Subject Category II. Instruction and Assessment: Assessment Strategies: Measurement theory and assessment-related issues: Scoring assessments: Reporting assessment results

3. B—Feedback: Subject Category II. Instruction and Assessment: Assessment Strategies: Measurement theory and assessment-related issues: Scoring assessments: Reporting assessment results: Standard deviation

4. C—Feedback: Subject Category II. Instruction and Assessment: Assessment Strategies: Measurement theory and assessment-related issues: Scoring assessments: Percentile rank

5. B—Feedback: Subject Category II. Instruction and Assessment: Assessment Strategies: Measurement theory and assessment-related issues: Scoring assessments: Reporting assessment results: Standard deviation

6. D—Feedback: Subject Category II. Instruction and Assessment: Assessment Strategies: Measurement theory and assessment-related issues: Scoring assessments: Reporting assessment results: Standard deviation

7. A—Feedback: Subject Category II. Instruction and Assessment: Assessment Strategies: Measurement theory and assessment-related issues: Scoring assessments: Reporting assessment results: Standard score

8. E—Feedback: Subject Category II. Instruction and Assessment: Assessment Strategies: Measurement theory and assessment-related issues: Scoring assessments: Reporting assessment results

9. C—Feedback: Subject Category II. Instruction and Assessment: Assessment Strategies: Measurement theory and assessment-related issues: Scoring assessments: Normal distribution

10. A—Feedback: Subject Category II. Instruction and Assessment: Assessment Strategies: Measurement theory and assessment-related issues: Scoring assessments: Rubrics

11. D—Feedback: Subject Category II. Instruction and Assessment: Assessment Strategies: Measurement theory and assessment-related issues: Scoring assessments: Reporting assessment results

12. D—Feedback: Subject Category II. Instruction and Assessment: Assessment Strategies: Measurement theory and assessment-related issues: Scoring assessments: Rubrics

4. Uses of assessments

1. B—Feedback: Subject Category II. Instruction and Assessment: Assessment Strategies: Uses of assessments

2. B—Feedback: Subject Category II. Instruction and Assessment: Assessment Strategies: Measurement theory and assessment-related issues: Uses of assessments

3. B—Feedback: Subject Category II. Instruction and Assessment: Assessment Strategies: Measurement theory and assessment-related issues: Uses of assessments

4. D—Feedback: Subject Category II. Instruction and Assessment: Assessment Strategies: Measurement theory and assessment-related issues: Uses of assessments: Formative evaluation

5. D—Feedback: Subject Category II. Instruction and Assessment: Assessment Strategies: Measurement theory and assessment-related issues: Uses of assessments: Diagnostic evaluation

6. B—Feedback: Subject Category II. Instruction and Assessment: Assessment Strategies: Measurement theory and assessment-related issues: Uses of assessments: Summative evaluation

5. Understanding measurement theory and assessment-related issues

1. A—Feedback: Subject Category II. Instruction and Assessment: Assessment Strategies: Measurement theory and assessment-related issues: Understanding measurement theory and assessment-related issues

2. C—Feedback: Subject Category II. Instruction and Assessment: Assessment Strategies: Measurement theory and assessment-related issues: Understanding measurement theory and assessment-related issues

3. A—Feedback: Subject Category II. Instruction and Assessment: Assessment Strategies: Measurement theory and assessment-related issues: Understanding measurement theory and assessment-related issues

6. Interpreting and communicating results of assessments

1. B—Feedback: Subject Category II. Instruction and Assessment: Assessment Strategies: Measurement theory and assessment-related issues: Interpreting and communicating results of assessments

2. D—Feedback: Subject Category II. Instruction and Assessment: Assessment Strategies: Measurement theory and assessment-related issues: Interpreting and communicating results of assessments

3. D—Feedback: Subject Category II. Instruction and Assessment: Assessment Strategies: Measurement theory and assessment-related issues: Interpreting and communicating results of assessments

4. A—Feedback: Subject Category II. Instruction and Assessment: Assessment Strategies: Measurement theory and assessment-related issues: Interpreting and communicating results of assessments

All Subject Categories are as listed in the ETS Principles of Learning and Teaching, *Tests at a Glance*, located at *ftp://ftp.ets.org/pub/tandl/0522.pdf*.

III. Communication Techniques

1. Basic, Effective Verbal and Nonverbal Communication Techniques

1. Which of the following is the best strategy for developing active listening skills? (Text Hint: See page 468)
   a. Practice paraphrasing other people's comments.
   b. Practice criticizing people with different points of view.
   c. Practice offering advice to people who need it.
   d. Practice interrupting politely.

2. Of the following modes of communication, which most accurately depicts one that is manipulative? (Text Hint: See page 466)
   a. Making demands in a hostile tone.
   b. Allowing others to have their way while keeping your own feelings to yourself.
   c. Trying to make someone else feel sorry for you.
   d. Stating your opinion directly and without apology.

3. Linus is really upset with Janice. So Linus confronts Janice and shares his displeasure and says he doesn't want her to take his book anymore without asking. In turn, he promises not to exclude her from working on his team. Which mode of communication is Linus using? (Text Hint: See page 466)
   a. Aggressive style
   b. Manipulative style
   c. Passive style
   d. Assertive style

4. Mrs. Henley makes sure to intermittently restate what students have to say when they come to her with a concern. She feels this is the most effective way to show students that their concerns are important to her as well. Mrs. Henley is using what listening skill? (Text Hint: See page 469)
   a. Paraphrasing
   b. Using "I" messages
   c. "You" messages
   d. Synthesizing

2. Effect of Cultural and Gender Differences on Communications in the Classroom

1. Research shows that teachers communicate differently with girls and boys in the classroom. All of the following suggests that classrooms are biased against girls EXCEPT _____. (Text Hint: See page 163)
   a. boys demand more attention, while girls are more likely to quietly wait their turn
   b. in many classrooms, teachers spend more time watching and interacting with boys while girls work and play quietly on their own
   c. teachers often give boys more time to answer a question, more hints at the correct answer, and further tries if they give the wrong answer
   d. school personnel tend to ignore that many boys clearly have academic problems

2. Evidence suggests that classroom environments are biased against boys because _____. (Text Hint: See page 163)

   a. teachers tend to identify more girls than boys as having learning problems

   b. teachers value behaviors such as hyperactivity, which is typically associated with boys

   c. teachers are more likely to criticize boys than girls and stereotype boys' behavior as problematic

   d. teachers are more likely to promote boys to the next grade than girls

3. Mrs. Williams' classroom is filled with books, posters, and other resources related to different American cultures. She communicates high expectations for all of her students, regardless of ethnicity or social background. Mrs. Williams is implementing effective teaching strategies for _____. (Text Hint: See page 153).

   a. multicultural education

   b. culture bias

   c. second-language learning

   d. mentoring

3. Types of Questions that can Stimulate Discussion in Different Ways for Particular Purposes

1. Mrs. Right wants to ensure that her students remember the information she is presenting in class today. Thus, after she is done with the lesson, she begins a question and answer period in which she asks the students to generate personal examples of the concepts they just learned. What is Mrs. Right using? (Text Hint: See page 252)

   a. Encoding

   b. Elaboration

   c. Retrieval

   d. Chunking

2. Which of the following questions is the best example of a thinking-based item designed to assess students' abilities to evaluate? (Text Hint: See page 522)

   a. Give one example of a situation that demonstrates Newton's first law of motion.

   b. Identify one weakness in the argument that deforestation will enhance the greenhouse effect.

   c. Were dinosaurs warm-blooded?

   d. Why do birds fly?

3. Mr. Noble frequently develops integrated curriculum units based on essential questions. His students create charts on which they mark their experiences in language and literacy, mathematics, science, social studies, music, and art. Which of the following is the best example of an essential question? (Text Hint: See 396)

   a. Who was the first president of the United States?

   b. How does a prism work?

   c. What is the effect of World War I?

   d. Does life exist on another planet?

4. Which of the following Bloom's Taxonomy objectives is most appropriate for encouraging students to think critically? (Text Hint: See page 380)
   a. Knowledge
   b. Comprehension
   c. Application
   d. Evaluation

5. To improve her students' prosocial behavior, Ms. Tilly moderates whole-group discussions when there are disagreements or misunderstandings among students. She asks questions that help students understand one another's needs, feelings, and perspectives. Which type of question would Ms. Tilly most likely ask her students? (Text Hint: See page 99)
   a. How would you feel if someone messed up your desk like that?
   b. Would you like to go to the principal's office?
   c. Why are you so destructive?
   d. Who messed up Jerome's desk?

Answer Key

1. Basic, Effective Verbal and Nonverbal Communication Techniques

1. A—Feedback: Subject Category III. Communication Techniques: Basic, effective verbal and nonverbal communication techniques

2. C—Feedback: Subject Category III. Communication Techniques: Basic, effective verbal and nonverbal communication techniques

3. D—Feedback: Subject Category III. Communication Techniques: Basic, effective verbal and nonverbal communication techniques

4. A—Feedback: Subject Category III. Communication Techniques: Basic, effective verbal and nonverbal communication techniques

2. Effect of Cultural and Gender Differences on Communications in the Classroom

1. D—Feedback: Subject Category III. Communication Techniques: The effect of cultural and gender differences on communications in the classroom

2. C—Feedback: Subject Category III. Communication Techniques: The effect of cultural and gender differences on communications in the classroom

3. A—Feedback: Subject Category III. Communication Techniques: The effect of cultural and gender differences on communications in the classroom

3. Types of Questions that can Stimulate Discussion in Different Ways for Particular Purposes

1. B—Feedback: Subject Category III. Communication Techniques: Types of questions that can stimulate discussion in different ways for different purposes: Probing for learner understanding

2. B—Feedback: Subject Category III. Communication Techniques: Types of questions that can stimulate discussion in different ways for different purposes: Helping students articulate their ideas and thinking processes

3. D—Feedback: Subject Category III. Communication Techniques: Types of questions that can stimulate discussion in different ways for different purposes: Stimulating curiosity and encouraging divergent thinking

4. C—Feedback: Subject Category III. Communication Techniques: Types of questions that can stimulate discussion in different ways for different purposes: Encouraging divergent thinking

5. A—Feedback: Subject Category III. Communication Techniques: Types of questions that can stimulate discussion in different ways for different purposes: Promoting a caring community

All Subject Categories are as listed in the ETS Principles of Learning and Teaching, *Tests at a Glance*, located at *ftp://ftp.ets.org/pub/tandl/0522.pdf*.

IV. Profession and Community

a. The Reflective Practitioner

1. Types of resources available for professional development and learning

1. The National Science Teachers Association, the National Council for the Social Studies, The National Council of Teachers of English, and the National Council of Teachers of Mathematics are all examples of _____. (Text Hint: See Ch 11)
   a. online newsgroups
   b. professional development institutes
   c. teachers' unions
   d. professional associations

2. Numerous resources are available on the Internet for teachers. What does The Educator's Reference Desk provide? (Text Hint: See page 402)
   a. Provides free, online information, articles, and research about a wide range of educational topics
   b. Free access to online encyclopedias
   c. Online professional development courses
   d. None of the above

2. Ability to read, understand, and apply articles and books about current research, views, ideas, and debates regarding best teaching practices

1. Which statement best describes the controversy in math education? (Text Hint: See page 356)
   a. Educators currently debate whether math should be taught in the elementary grades.
   b. Educators currently debate whether math should be taught online.
   c. Educators currently debate whether math should be taught using a cognitive, constructivist approach or a practice, computational approach.
   d. Educators currently debate whether the NCTM math standards should be replaced with the standards used in Japan.

2. Recent research in math shows that _____. (Text Hint: See page 356)
   a. teachers in the U.S. should emphasize basic skills and formulas
   b. teachers in the U.S. are less likely to assign math homework than teachers in most other countries
   c. teachers in the U.S. are more likely to assign math homework than teachers in most other countries
   d. assigning math homework has no positive affect on students' overall learning and performance

3. According to the recent National Assessment of Educational Progress, in the fourth grade, frequent calculator use was associated with _____. (Text Hint: See page 358)
   a. lower national achievement test scores in math
   b. higher national achievement test scores in math
   c. expert math knowledge in eighth grade
   d. full mastery of basic math skills

3. Why personal reflection on teaching practices is critical, and approaches that can be used to reflect and evaluate

1. A teacher would like to identify students' attitudes about using calculators to complete math assignments. Which of the following research methods would be most appropriate? (Text Hint: See page 17)
   a. Case study
   b. Laboratory observation
   c. Standardized test
   d. Questionnaire

2. When choosing participants for an experiment, an investigator most effectively ensures that the resultant effects are not due to any preexisting group difference by _____. (Text Hint: See page 21)
   a. assigning participants alphabetically to treatment and control conditions
   b. letting participants choose treatment or control groups
   c. assigning participants randomly to either treatment or control groups
   d. assigning students who arrive first to the treatment condition.

3. Which of the following refers to an intensive and in-depth study of one individual? (Text Hint: See page 19)
   a. Descriptive research
   b. Ethnography
   c. Case study
   d. Experimental research

4. Which of the following terms refers to an integrated, coherent set of ideas that attempts to explain a phenomenon and make predictions? (Text Hint: See page 16)
   a. Principle
   b. Theory
   c. Hypothesis
   d. Scientific method

5. A _____ describes how closely two constructs are related. (Text Hint: See page 20)
   a. correlation
   b. hypothesis
   c. theory
   d. principle

6. In a study comparing the effects of studying with music versus no music on reading comprehension, an investigator administers a comprehension test after a reading study period. She finds that scores were higher for the group who listened to classical pieces. What is the independent variable in this study? (Text Hint: See page 20)
   a. Studying
   b. Reading comprehension score
   c. Study period
   d. Presence or absence of music during studying.

7. Ms. Stevenson calculates how correlated her students' final exam scores are with the number of homework assignments during the school year and determines they are positively correlated. Which of the following is true? (Text Hint: See page 20)

    a. When students have less homework they score lower on the final exam.

    b. Having more homework causes lower scores on the final exam

    c. Having more homework causes higher scores on the final exam.

    d. When students have more homework they score lower on the final exam.

8. Which of the following is a descriptive approach to research that consists of in-depth examination of life with a group that includes direct involvement with the participants? (Text Hint: See page 19)

    a. Descriptive research

    b. Ethnography

    c. Case study

    d. Experimental research

9. Which of the following conclusions can be drawn only from an experimental study? (Text Hint: See page 20)

    a. Quantity of trips to the bathroom is associated with lower academic achievement.

    b. High teacher expectations leads to higher academic achievement.

    c. High school students think more analytically than elementary students.

    d. When the teacher drinks more caffeine he is much more animated during his lectures.

10. A _____ occurs when the researcher becomes a participant in the activity or setting in order to better understand life in that group. (Text Hint: See page 18)

    a. participant observation

    b. ethnography

    c. descriptive research

    d. experimentation

11. Which of the following would be the best example of action research? (Text Hint: See page 23)

    a. Answer a question about whether a school district has an effective classroom management approach.

    b. Improve classroom management practices in a third grade math classroom.

    c. Determine best classroom management practices that can be applied to most school classrooms.

    d. Make decisions about the effectiveness of a particular behavioristic classroom management program.

12. Which of the following is *NOT* true concerning the need to be cautious about what is reported in the popular media? (Text Hint: See page 27)

    a. Views expressed in the media are never grounded in systematic educational research.

    b. Sometimes when information to report is not sensational enough, there is a chance it might be embellished to keep audiences tuned to their programming.

    c. Most journalists are not scientifically trained in educational research, so they may sometimes not make sound decisions about reporting information.

    d. Media often do not go enough into detail about a study, so important specifics may be omitted.

b. The Larger Community

1. The role of the school as a resource to the larger community

1. Mr. Johnson utilizes an activity within his social studies class that involves students volunteering in the community. Students are given the option of helping the elderly, working in a hospital, or assisting Habitat for Humanity. This is a good example of _____.(Text Hint: See page 98)

   a. character education

   b. values clarification

   c. cognitive moral education

   d. service learning

2. In an effort to improve the literacy of its students, Washington Elementary School holds family literacy seminars for parents twice a month. The seminars include English-as-a-Second-Language classes and information about sharing language-related activities with children. This program is an example of _____. (Text Hint: page 347)

   a. character education

   b. a social constructivist approach to reading

   c. reciprocal teaching

   d. metacognitive strategies

2. Factors in the students' environment outside of school (family circumstances, community environments, health and economic conditions) that may influence students' life and learning

1. According to a recent technology survey in 2001, _____. (Text Hint: See page 12)

   a. about 30 percent of low-income students have a computer at home, compared to almost 90 percent of students from high-income families.

   b. students from low-income families are equally likely as high-income students to have a computer at home.

   c. about 10 percent of all students have high-speed Internet access in their classrooms.

   d. about 30 percent of students report they have no interest in technology use

2. A child's low self-esteem may be caused by _____. (Text Hint: See page 91)

   a. competence in an area

   b. family conflict

   c. emotional support

   d. social approval

3. Currently in the United States, what percent of African-American children live below the poverty line? (Text Hint: See page 136)

   a. Less than 20 percent

   b. Approximately 25 percent

   c. Approximately 30 percent

   d. More than 40 percent

4. Weyne Hill High School has few resources, a large number of students, lower achievement scores, lower graduation rates, and lower percentage of students going to college. According to the information provided in this scenario, where is Weyne Hill High School most likely to be located? (Text Hint: See page 137)

    a. In a higher-income neighborhood

    b. In a lower-income neighborhood

    c. In a collectivist society

    d. None of the above are correct

5. Exposure to more family conflict and violence, less social support, polluted air and water, and inferior schools are factors representative of _____. (Text Hint: See pages 136, 137)

    a. high socioeconomic status

    b. culture bias

    c. gender discrimination

    d. an impoverished childhood environment

6. Which of the following statements describes the social inequities associated with technology? (Text Hint: See page 401)

    a. Students from middle- and upper-income families are far more likely to have computers at home.

    b. Schools with high percentages of low-income minority students tend to use computers for drill-and-practice exercises.

    c. Boys are more likely to use computers for math and science applications while girls are more likely to use computers for word processing.

    d. All of the above

3. Basic strategies for developing and utilizing active partnerships among teachers, parents/guardians, and leaders in the community to support the educational process

1. Which of the following examples is the best use of tutoring? (Text Hint: See page 317)

    a. Two students working on teacher-made worksheets.

    b. A parent volunteer assisting a student with the alphabet.

    c. A parent volunteer circling the room to ensure students are on task.

    d. Both A and B are correct.

2. Who might serve as effective tutors for students? (Text Hint: See page 317)

    a. Peers

    b. Volunteers

    c. Mentors

    d. All the above

4. Major laws related to students' rights and teacher responsibilities

1. Ms. Meyers is a regular classroom teacher who has just begun working with children with special needs. Her principal has advised that she be familiarized with the Individuals with Disabilities Education Act (IDEA), since she will now be interacting with parents whose children have special needs and she will have to create individualized education plans (IEP). Which of the following is not true and therefore not one of the items that Ms. Meyers will be learning about regarding IDEA's specific provisions that relate to the parents of a child with a disability? (Text Hint: See page 191)

   a. Schools are required to send notices to parents of proposed actions.

   b. Parents are not allowed to attend meetings regarding the child's individualized education plans (IEP).

   c. Parents are allowed to attend meetings regarding the child's placement.

   d. Parents have the right to appeal school decisions to an impartial evaluator.

2. All of the following are facets of the federal *No Child Left Behind* act EXCEPT _____. (Text Hint: See page 498)

   a. by 2005–2006, teachers who are not considered "highly qualified" will receive a reduction in pay or a warning of dismissal

   b. separate objectives are to be proposed for students who are economically disadvantaged, students from ethnic minority groups, students with disabilities, and students with limited English proficiency

   c. by 2005–2006, states will be required to give all students annual standardized tests in grades 3 through 8

   d. schools that are labeled as "underperforming" must be closed if they do not show improvement after five years

3. In 1975, Congress passed the Education for All Handicapped Children Act. What does this law require? (Text Hint: See page 191)

   a. All students with disabilities receive homebound instruction.

   b. All students with disabilities receive life skills training.

   c. All students with disabilities be placed in separate, special education classes.

   d. All students with disabilities be given a free, appropriate public education.

4. The overrepresentation of minorities in special education programs has led to concern among education leaders. The U.S. Office of Education cites all of these as concerns EXCEPT _____. (Text Hint: See page 193)

   a. students may be underserved or receive services that do not meet their needs

   b. students may be misclassified or inappropriately labeled

   c. special education classes are overcrowded.

   d. placement in special education classes may be a form of discrimination

Answer Key

a. The Reflective Practitioner

1. Types of resources available for professional development and learning

1. D—Feedback: Subject Category IV. Profession and the Community: The Reflective Practitioner: Types of resources available for professional development and learning: Professional associations

2. A—Feedback: Subject Category IV. Profession and the Community: The Reflective Practitioner: Types of resources available for professional development and learning: Professional literature

2. Ability to read, understand, and apply articles and books about current research, views, ideas, and debates regarding best teaching practices

1. C—Feedback: Subject Category IV. Profession and Community: The Reflective Practitioner: Ability to read and understand articles about current views, ideas, and debates regarding best teaching practices

2. B—Feedback: Subject Category IV. Profession and the Community: The Reflective Practitioner: Types of resources available for professional development and learning: Professional associations

3. A—Feedback: Subject Category IV. Profession and the Community: The Reflective Practitioner: Types of resources available for professional development and learning: Professional associations

3. Why personal reflection on teaching practices is critical, and approaches that can be used to reflect and evaluate

1. D—Feedback: Subject Category IV. Profession and Community: The Reflective Practitioner: Why personal reflection on teaching practices is critical, and approaches that can be used to achieve this

2. C—Feedback: Subject Category IV. Profession and Community: The Reflective Practitioner: Why personal reflection on teaching practices is critical, and approaches that can be used to achieve this

3. C—Feedback: Subject Category IV. Profession and Community: The Reflective Practitioner: Why personal reflection on teaching practices is critical, and approaches that can be used to achieve this

4. B—Feedback: Subject Category IV. Profession and Community: The Reflective Practitioner: Why personal reflection on teaching practices is critical, and approaches that can be used to achieve this

5. A—Feedback: Subject Category IV. Profession and Community: The Reflective Practitioner: Why personal reflection on teaching practices is critical, and approaches that can be used to achieve this

6. D—Feedback: Subject Category IV. Profession and Community: The Reflective Practitioner: Ability to read and understand articles about current views, ideas, and debates regarding best teaching practices

7. A—Feedback: Subject Category IV. Profession and Community: The Reflective Practitioner: Why personal reflection on teaching practices is critical, and approaches that can be used to achieve this

8. B—Feedback: Subject Category IV. Profession and Community: The Reflective Practitioner: Why personal reflection on teaching practices is critical, and approaches that can be used to achieve this

9. B—Feedback: Subject Category IV. Profession and Community: The Reflective Practitioner: Why personal reflection on teaching practices is critical, and approaches that can be used to achieve this

10. A—Feedback: Subject Category IV. Profession and Community: The Reflective Practitioner: Why personal reflection on teaching practices is critical, and approaches that can be used to achieve this

11. B—Feedback: Subject Category IV. Profession and Community: The Reflective Practitioner: Why personal reflection on teaching practices is critical, and approaches that can be used to achieve this

12. A—Feedback: Subject Category IV. Profession and Community: The Reflective Practitioner: Ability to read and understand articles about current views, ideas, and debates regarding best teaching practices

b. The larger community

1. The role of the school as a resource to the larger community

1. D—Feedback: Subject Category IV. Profession and Community: The Larger Community: The role of the school as a resource to the larger community

2. B—Feedback: Subject Category IV. Profession and Community: The Larger Community: The role of the school as a resource to the larger community

2. *Factors in the students' environment outside of school (family circumstances, community environments, health and economic conditions) that may influence students' life and learning*

1. A—Feedback: Subject Category IV. Profession and Community: The Larger Community: Factors in the students' environment outside of school (family circumstances, community environments, health, and economic conditions) that may influence students' life and learning

2. B—Feedback: Subject Category IV. Profession and Community: The Larger Community: Factors in the students' environment outside of school (family circumstances, community environments, health, and economic conditions) that may influence students' life and learning

3. D—Feedback: Subject Category IV. Profession and Community: The Larger Community: Factors in the students' environment outside of school (family circumstances, community environments, health, and economic conditions) that may influence students' life and learning

4. B—Feedback: Subject Category IV. Profession and Community: The Larger Community: Factors in the students' environment outside of school (family circumstances, community environments, health, and economic conditions) that may influence students' life and learning

5. D—Feedback: Subject Category IV. Profession and Community: The Larger Community: Factors in the students' environment outside of school (family circumstances, community environments, health, and economic conditions) that may influence students' life and learning

6. D—Feedback: Subject Category IV. Profession and Community: The Larger Community: Factors in the students' environment outside of school (family circumstances, community environments, health, and economic conditions) that may influence students' life and learning

3. *Basic strategies for developing and utilizing active partnerships among teachers, parents/guardians, and leaders in the community to support the educational process*

1. B—Feedback: Subject Category IV. Profession and Community: The Larger Community: Basic strategies for involving parents/guardians and leaders in the community in the educational process

2. D—Feedback: Subject Category IV. Profession and Community: The Larger Community: Basic strategies for involving parents/guardians and leaders in the community in the educational process

4. *Major laws related to students' rights and teacher responsibilities*

1. B—Feedback: Subject Category IV. Profession and Community: The Larger Community: Major laws related to students' rights and teacher responsibilities: Appropriate education for students with special needs

2. A—Feedback: Subject Category IV. Profession and Community: The Larger Community: Major laws related to students' rights and teacher responsibilities: Equal education

3. D—Feedback: Subject Category IV. Profession and Community: The Larger Community: Major laws related to students' rights and teacher responsibilities: Appropriate education for students with special needs

4. C—Feedback: Subject Category IV. Profession and Community: The Larger Community: Major laws related to students' rights and teacher responsibilities: Equal education and appropriate treatment of students

All Subject Categories are as listed in the ETS Principles of Learning and Teaching, *Tests at a Glance*, located at *ftp://ftp.ets.org/pub/tandl/0522.pdf*.

Part IV

Practice Tests

Practice Multiple-Choice Test Based on the PRAXIS II™ Principles of Learning and Teaching Format

1. Sally is a student in Ms. Patterson's kindergarten class. One day, after accidentally kicking a beanbag chair, Sally apologizes to the chair. Which of the following developmental phenomena does the above best exemplify?

    a. animism

    b. centration

    c. conservation

    d. imaginary audience

Questions 2–3. Maya and Sharon are students in Mr. Williams' 8th grade English class. Mr. Williams has assigned his students to read *Lord of the Flies*. As they read, he has the students discuss the symbolism the author used in the book. Maya does so with ease. Sharon cannot seem to grasp any of the metaphors used in the book and merely repeats things either Mr. Williams or another student has said.

2. Which of the following is the most plausible explanation for why Maya does understand the symbolism in the book?

    a. Maya is more intelligent than Sharon.

    b. Maya is able to think in a formal operational manner regarding literature.

    c. Maya is a concrete operational thinker.

    d. Maya lacks the ability to think concretely.

3. Which of the following is the most plausible explanation for why Sharon does not understand the symbolism in the book?

    a. Sharon lacks the ability to think concretely.

    b. Sharon has not been adequately reinforced for demonstrating her understanding of symbolism in the past.

    c. Sharon is a concrete operational thinker.

    d. Sharon is a pre-operational thinker.

4. Mr. Johnson believes that Vygotsky had the right idea when it comes to how students learn. Given this, which approach is Mr. Johnson likely to take in helping Bobby, who is struggling in reading comprehension?

   a. Mr. Johnson will give Bobby numerous worksheets regarding each reading selection to complete on his own.

   b. Mr. Johnson will have Bobby make dioramas reflecting his understanding of each book he reads.

   c. Mr. Johnson will pair Bobby with an older student who is a better reader. They will read selections together and the older student will ask Bobby questions to monitor his understanding, guiding him to correct responses when he does not understand.

   d. Mr. Johnson will have Bobby take a test after each reading selection and will reward him for each correct response with a piece of candy.

Questions 5–7. Sam finishes his math work long before most of the other students in Ms. Castle's class. When Sam gives Ms. Castle his work, she gives him another sheet with similar problems on it to complete. Sam looks perplexed, but dutifully goes to his seat and completes the extra problems. This pattern continues for the next three days. On the fourth day, Sam dawdles over his work. He looks out the window, sharpens his pencil, plays with his eraser, and doodles until the last five minutes of math time, and then he buckles down and completes his math work.

5. What would Vygotsky say about the math work that has been assigned for Sam?

   a. The work is below Sam's zone of proximal development.

   b. The work is within Sam's zone of proximal development.

   c. The work is above Sam's zone of proximal development.

   d. The work is too abstract for Sam.

6. Which of the following is the most plausible explanation for Sam's behavior?

   a. Sam no longer understands his math work.

   b. Sam was punished for finishing early by receiving more work.

   c. Sam is lazy.

   d. Sam dislikes math.

7. Which of the following would be the best course of action for Ms. Castle?

   a. Ms. Castle should continue to give Sam extra work when he finishes his assigned work.

   b. Ms. Castle should contact Sam's parents regarding his inappropriate classroom behavior.

   c. Ms. Castle should give Sam an alternative assignment if he has mastered what she is teaching.

   d. Ms. Castle should take away Sam's recess privilege unless he buckles down to work.

8. Steve memorizes things quite easily, yet struggles with connecting ideas or understanding the meaning of what he has learned. Which of the following is the most likely explanation for this?

   a. Steve is high in linguistic intelligence.

   b. Steve is lazy.

   c. Steve is a surface learner.

   d. Steve is a formal-operational thinker.

9. Kurt loves to design and build things. At the age of 10, he has already designed and built his own tree house. He has designed and built elaborate buildings as projects for book reports. He has built a raft that actually floated down the local creek. What would Howard Gardner say about Kurt?

   a. Kurt is high in verbal skills.

   b. Kurt is unlikely to be successful in school.

   c. Kurt is high in visual, spatial, and logical mathematical skills.

   d. Kurt is high in naturalist skills.

Questions 10–11. You overhear a student coming out of class saying, "A D! I knew it! I've never been any good at science!"

10. How would Bandura explain this student's reaction to her poor grade?

    a. The student has low self-efficacy in science.

    b. The student has not been adequately reinforced for prior success in science.

    c. The student has a performance goal orientation.

    d. The student views ability as malleable.

11. How would Weiner explain this student's reaction to her poor grade?

    a. The student has low self-efficacy in science.

    b. The student's attributions are focused on ability, which is internal, stable, and uncontrollable.

    c. The student has a performance goal orientation.

    d. The student has not been adequately reinforced for prior success in science.

12. Mark and Shelly are very good students in Mr. James' class. They regularly get the two highest scores in the class on tests. They always compare their scores and boast about out-performing the other. What goal orientation do these students exemplify?

    a. failure orientation

    b. mastery orientation

    c. performance orientation

    d. anxiety orientation

13. A first-grade teacher is covering a unit on animals. She wants her students to understand the purpose blubber serves in marine mammals. To this end, she has her students place their latex-gloved hands in icy water, using a stopwatch to see how long they can leave their hands in the water. Then she has her students place their gloved hands in a plastic bag filled with lard so that the lard surrounds their hands. She has them place their hands in the icy water and times them again. All of the students could leave their hands in the icy water longer when their hands were encased in lard. Students then discussed their findings and determined that the lard kept their hands warm. The teacher then described blubber as the "lard of marine mammals". Students then indicated that blubber helps keep marine mammals warm. Which of the following teaching strategies does the above best exemplify?

    a. cooperative learning

    b. demonstration

    c. guided discovery

    d. jigsaw

14. When Ms. Wilkerson teaches math, she wants her students to do more than memorize basic math facts; she wants them to understand *why* 6x5=30 and to be able to use that information in their everyday lives. To this end, she begins teaching multiplication by showing the students that it is actually repeated addition. She uses manipulatives to illustrate. She then gives the students many real world problems, which they often work together to solve, using the same manipulatives she used. Which of the following instructional approaches does the above exemplify?

    a. behavioral

    b. constructivist

    c. discovery

    d. information processing

15. Mr. O'Neil has several students in his class who struggle with reading. He is trying to decide how to best approach helping them. Which of the following would be his best choice?

    a. Help the students to pick out minute details in what they have read.

    b. Use the better readers in his class to tutor those who are struggling.

    c. Use older students to tutor those who are struggling.

    d. Leave them alone. They will catch up eventually.

16. Which of the following is the best example of Mager's behavioral objectives?

    a. Students will learn to love math.

    b. Given 30 multiplication problems on a test, students will solve them with 80 percent accuracy.

    c. Students will understand the process of multiplication.

    d. Students will work hard to solve their math problems.

17. Ms. Matty's objective is for her students to list and describe Piaget's stages of cognitive development. According to Bloom's taxonomy, at what level is this objective written?

    a. Analysis

    b. Application

    c. Comprehension

    d. Knowledge

Questions 18–20. Mark, a fifth grade student, receives the scores from a standardized test. According to the results, Mark's percentile rank score in math was 99 and his percentile rank score in reading was 50. His grade equivalent score was 7.3.

18. What does Mark's grade equivalent score mean?

    a. Mark should be placed in the 7th grade.

    b. Mark performed as well on this test as an average 7th grade student in the third month of the school year would have performed on the same test.

    c. Mark scored as well or better than 7 percent of others taking the test.

    d. Mark performed as well on this test as an average student who is 7 years, 3 months old would have performed on the same test.

19. What does Mark's percentile rank in math mean?

    a. Mark scored as well or better than 99 percent of others taking the test.

    b. Mark's math achievement is about average for his grade.

    c. Mark answered 99 percent of the items on the math portion of the test correctly.

    d. Mark really needs to work on his math skills.

20. What does Mark's percentile rank in reading mean?

    a. Mark does not read well in comparison to others taking the test and is probably in need of remediation.

    b. Mark answered 50 percent of the items on the reading portion of the test correctly.

    c. Mark's reading achievement is about average for his grade in comparison to others taking the test.

    d. Mark's reading achievement in comparison to others taking the test is very advanced for his grade.

21. Mr. Jacobs assigns quarter grades based on the normal bell curve. What kind of grading is he using?

    a. Criterion-referenced grading

    b. Informal assessment

    c. Authentic assessment

    d. Norm-referenced grading

22. Which of the following is a practice Piaget would most likely advocate?

    a. Give young children the opportunity to manipulate all sorts of objects and experiment with them.

    b. Give young children tangible reinforcements for correct answers in class.

    c. Provide young children with an older mentor to scaffold their learning.

    d. Give young children worksheets designed to help them learn to color within lines and form letters and numerals.

23. Which of the following is the best strategy for helping students transfer what they have learned to new situations?

    a. Give frequent quizzes based on memorization of facts.

    b. Work on real-world application of material in class.

    c. Prepare structured lectures that give students much information.

    d. Focus on one narrow aspect of the curriculum at a time.

24. Which of the following is the best strategy for fostering critical thinking?

    a. Discourage student questions during lecture.

    b. Seek elaboration of student responses to questions.

    c. Ask fact-based, closed-ended questions.

    d. Use flash cards.

Question Number	Correct Answer	Explanation	Where to review in *Educational Psychology*	Subject Category
1.	a.	Sally appears to believe that an inanimate & the Learning Process	p. 42	I. A. Student Development object has feelings similar to those of people.
2.	b.	Maya is able to think in abstract terms, a characteristic of formal operational thinking.	pp. 46–47	I. A. Student Development & the Learning Process
3.	c.	Sharon is unable to think in abstract terms, a characteristic of concrete operational thinking.	pp. 45–46	I. A. Student Development & the Learning Process
4.	c.	This is an example of scaffolding.	p. 52	I. A. Student Development & the Learning Process
5.	a.	The zone of proximal development consists of what the student can do with the aid of a more advanced peer or adult.	p. 51, ch 10	I. A. Student Development & the Learning Process
6.	b.	Regardless of Ms. Castle's intentions, the consequence of receiving additional work resulted in Sam no longer finishing his work early.	p. 216	I. A. Student Development & the Learning Process
7.	c.	Much as she would for a student who has a disability, Ms. Castle needs to understand that Sam's learning needs are not being met by the assignments she has given. He needs something different within his ZPD.	pp. 51; 200–202	I. B. Students as Diverse Learners
8.	c.	Steve fails to tie what he is learning to a larger framework.	p. 124	I. B. Students as Diverse Learners
9.	c.	Logical-mathematical and spatial skills are necessary to design and build things. Kurt's ability to do these things is advanced for his age.	p. 111	I. B. Students as Diverse Learners
10.	a.	Bandura's concept of self-efficacy is the belief that one can master a situation and produce outcomes. Clearly this student has low self-efficacy	p. 226	I. C. Student Motivation and the Learning positive Environment
11.	b.	Weiner's Attribution Theory focuses on to what people attribute their successes and failures. This students' attribution is ability, an internal, stable, and uncontrollable trait.	p. 423	I. C. Student Motivation and the Learning Environment
12.	c.	Performance oriented students focus on their performance relative to others. They tend to be competitive.	pp. 424, 425	I. C. Student Motivation and the Learning Environment
13.	c.	The teacher has carefully planned an experiment that will help her students to "discover" a basic principle.	p. 398	II. A. Instructional Strategies
14.	b.	The focus on understanding and real-world problems makes this approach constructivist.	p. 357	II. A. Instructional Strategies

Question Number	Correct Answer	Explanation	Where to review in *Educational Psychology*	Subject Category
15.	c.	Peer tutors can be effective, but cross-age tutoring is generally more beneficial for all students.	p. 319, 321	II. A. Instructional Strategies
16.	b.	Mager specified that the behavior, the context, and the performance criteria should all be present.	p. 378	II. B. Planning Instruction
17.	c.	Students need only to remember the information.	p. 380	II. B. Planning Instruction
18.	b.	Grade equivalent scores are for average students at that grade on the test given.	p. 507	II. C. Assessment Strategies
19.	a.	Percentile rank scores indicate that a person did as well or better than that percentage of people taking the same test	p. 506	II. C. Assessment Strategies
20.	c.	Percentile rank scores indicate that a person did as well or better than that percentage of people taking the same test.	p. 506	II. C. Assessment Strategies
21.	d.	Norm-referenced grading is based on the normal curve. Student performance is compared to the performance of others.	p. 547	II. C. Assessment Strategies
22.	a.	Piaget believed that with appropriate materials, young children would develop cognitively and construct their own learning.	p. 44	I. A. Student Development & the Learning Process
23.	b.	Students are more likely to transfer information that is relevant to their lives, and which they have learned to apply.	p. 307	I. A. Student Development & the Learning Process
24.	b.	All but b are based on memorization and correctness rather than on thinking	pp. 288–290	I. Student Development & the Learning Process

Practice Short-Answer Test Based on the PRAXIS II™ Principles of Learning and Teaching Format

Scenario 1: Ben

Scenario

Mr. Joyner teaches algebra and geometry at Prairie View High School. Most of his students take these two classes because of the state requirement of two years of math, not out of any interest in math. While this doesn't thrill Mr. Joyner, he accepts it and does his best to ensure that his students learn. They have to show at least minimum competency to pass the class. The grading scale at Prairie View is rather rigorous: 94 percent for an A; 88 percent for a B; 82 percent for a C; 70 percent for a D.

Ben

Ben is a sophomore in Mr. Joyner's geometry class. He has struggled in math since second grade, when he had trouble memorizing facts. Now Ben has trouble memorizing formulae. Mr. Joyner thinks that knowing the formulae is very important, so he doesn't allow his students to use notes or books when taking exams. Ben generally does fairly well on homework, but does very poorly on quizzes and tests.

Ben dutifully does his homework each night. While he occasionally asks his father for help, he generally completes most of it on his own. With examples and formulae in front of him, he can generally figure out what to do. On tests, however, he has a very tough time. They appear to be written in a foreign language. He simply can't remember the formulae, so he finds other ways to work the problems that seem logical to him. The results are rarely correct and Ben often doesn't even receive partial credit because the process he used was wrong.

Ben earned a C– during the first quarter and felt fairly satisfied with this. His second quarter grade was a D. He began to worry. "I really need to pass this class. I sure don't want to take it again! Geometry stinks!"

At the beginning of the third quarter, Ben contracted a nasty virus that kept him out of school for two weeks. He tried to keep up in his classes, but without seeing problems worked in class, his understanding plummeted even further. He failed the third quarter of the course with a quarter score of 58 percent. With the report card also came the results of a standardized test. Ben scored below the 50th percentile in algebra but at the 85th percentile in geometry.

While his parents were aware that he was struggling, he certainly hadn't told them that he was failing. He'd led them to believe that he'd probably get a C or D for the quarter. His teacher did not apprise them of his failing grades either.

Upon seeing the F on his report card and his score on the standardized test, Ben's mother becomes upset with both her son and Mr. Joyner. She talks with Ben about his problems. "How can you fail a class and be at the 85th percentile in the state, Ben? Aren't you trying?"

Ben tells her that he is doing well on the homework, but that he "bombs" the tests. When she asks him why, he replies that he can't memorize formulae. Ben's mother then calls his school counselor, Ms. Patterson, to talk about his problems.

She tells the counselor, "Ben has problems memorizing. He simply can't memorize things that have no real meaning to him. It's not unusual for him to spend six hours memorizing vocabulary words for English, and those he can use contextually. But math formulae are impossible for him. It's been this way since he got sick in second grade. He does well on the homework, but not on the tests because he just can't memorize formulae. Something is clearly wrong here. How can he score at the 85th percentile and yet fail the class?"

Mr. Joyner's opinion regarding Ben's performance

The disparity between Ben's performance on homework and tests is so great that Mr. Joyner sometimes wonders how much help Ben gets on his homework. Mr. Joyner suspects that perhaps one of his former students provides a little too much "scaffolding" in a misguided effort to help Ben.

Parent-Teacher Conference

A meeting is set up between Ben, his mother, Mr. Joyner, and Ms. Patterson to discuss Ben's problems. Due to everyone's schedules, two weeks pass between the phone call and the meeting. At the meeting each teacher indicates how Ben is doing in class. He is earning an A in English, Bs in his small engines and agriculture classes, and a C in chemistry. His only failing grade is in geometry. Ben's mother has both his report card and the results of the standardized test with her. She explains Ben's problem to Mr. Joyner and hands him the results of the standardized test. Mr. Joyner looks at the test score in amazement.

Short Answer Questions

1. What are two explanations for the discrepancy between Ben's performance on the standardized test and his performance on classroom assessments?

2. What errors has Mr. Joyner made?

3. What are two strategies that Mr. Joyner could use to help Ben?

4. How should Mr. Joyner respond to Ben's mother?

Scenario 2: Clarissa

Scenario

Clarissa is entering eighth grade at Monroe Middle School. She has always enjoyed school and is a good student whose name consistently appears on the honor roll. She is particularly good at math and excels at taking multiple-choice tests in other subjects. This year she has Mr. Crenshaw for science. Clarissa has always done quite well at science, as she is adept in memorizing scientific facts. She is looking forward to repeating this performance. However, after listening to Mr. Crenshaw's introduction, she is a bit apprehensive.

Science

"Students, this may not be like other science classes you've taken. This year you won't be memorizing facts and regurgitating them on a test. This year, you're going to become scientists! You will come up with a problem to research and engage in real scientific research regarding it from start to finish."

Clarissa raises her hand. "You mean like a science project?" she asks.

"Sort of, except that you're not going to follow one out of a book and merely replicate it, Clarissa. YOU are going to be the primary researchers of real-life problems that might be researched and solved through science."

"All right!" yells Jonah. "We finally get to DO something!"

Clarissa stares down at her desk in disbelief. She can't understand how it is possible that she could solve a scientific problem.

The next day, Mr. Crenshaw's students brainstorm possible problems they could research. The list becomes quite extensive. After developing their list, they begin to eliminate those that would require resources beyond the district's means (such as travel to foreign lands), are too complex (such as global warming), or too simplistic (which chewing gum's flavor lasts the longest?). Clarissa is upset about the elimination of the chewing gum problem because it is one she thinks she might have been able to handle.

After narrowing the list, students are allowed to choose the problem they would like to investigate. They are allowed to work independently or in teams of up to three scientists if they choose. Clarissa chooses to investigate the pollution of a near-by creek. She also chooses to work independently.

Over the next week, Mr. Crenshaw spends time teaching his students various problem-solving strategies. They develop heuristics. They also learn about the scientific process, from problem-finding, to questioning, generating hypotheses, testing those hypotheses, and finally drawing conclusions. Clarissa is stymied.

"Mr. Crenshaw, why don't you just tell us what you want us to do?" she asks.

"Well, I have, Clarissa. I want you to become a scientist and investigate a problem. How do you think you should approach the problem of Bluff Creek's polluted waters?"

"Phooey, I don't know. How about if we just put clean water in it from the water tower?"

"Do you really think that will help? You'll have to use the scientific process to convince me."

"Groooooooaaaaaaaaaaaaaaan, can't we just take a test about water pollution?"

Short Answer Questions

1. What are two possible explanations for Clarissa's preference for tests over the approach Mr. Crenshaw has taken?

2. What would you explain as to Clarissa's idea regarding how to solve the pollution problem?

3. What are the advantages and disadvantages to the instructional approach Mr. Crenshaw has taken?

4. How could Mr. Crenshaw assess his students' understanding, given his instructional approach?

Scenario 3: Adam

Scenario

Adam is a student in Mr. Potter's fourth-grade class. He is the youngest of 6 children in a blended family. His mother and step-father both work long hours to support their family. His father moved to another state recently. Adam is a bright child, but is not always well behaved. He enjoys entertaining his classmates by making jokes, often at Mr. Potter's expense.

Mr. Potter's opinion regarding Adam

Mr. Potter views Adam's disruptive behavior as a cry for attention. He doubts that Adam gets much attention at home due to having so many siblings and because his parents are rarely home. He tries to ignore Adam's behavior because he does not want to reinforce it.

The bad day and beyond

One day during language arts, Adam began talking very loudly to the other students in his area. He was also laughing and telling jokes. Mr. Potter chose to ignore Adam's behavior, hoping that he would stop on his own. Adam didn't stop. Instead, his behavior became more raucous. Still Mr. Potter ignored it. Soon Adam was making enough noise that Mr. Potter was afraid that students in the neighboring classrooms would be disturbed. He verbally reprimanded Adam.

Adam was a bit quieter for the next few minutes. After that, however, he once again became loud and disruptive. Again Mr. Potter verbally reprimanded him. This time he also told Adam that if he continued with his disruptive behavior, he would have to go to the office. Adam's behavior became even more disruptive. Mr. Potter sent him to the office.

When Adam arrived at the office it was full of people—teachers getting their mail and making copies, volunteers signing in, students who were ill, students sent on errands, and other students who had been sent for disciplinary reasons. The school secretary told Adam to have a seat, which he did. He conversed with every person who entered the office as well as those who were there when he arrived. Half an hour after his arrival, he was sent back to class. He behaved quite well for the rest of the day, to Mr. Potter's relief.

The next day, when students were assigned to write a paragraph, Adam once again became disruptive. He loudly told jokes to his classmates, laughed until tears were streaming down his face, and threw a paper airplane across the room. Mr. Potter reprimanded him and asked him to stop. When Adam didn't comply, Mr. Potter sent him to the office, which was once again bustling with activity.

The problem spreads

Over the course of the next two weeks, Adam was sent to the office for disrupting class each day, always during a writing assignment. Mr. Potter was perplexed. Even more perplexing was that within three school days other children were becoming disruptive as well, requiring that they too be sent to the office.

Short Answer Questions

1. How would you characterize Mr. Potter's classroom management techniques?

2. Why did Adam's behavior persist in spite of the fact that Mr. Potter's attempts not to reinforce it with attention?

3. What are two explanations for Adam's continued disruptive behavior after being sent to the office for discipline?

4. What should Mr. Potter try in the future to prevent Adam from being disruptive?

Scenario 4: Ms. Murphy

The scenario

Ms. Murphy teaches second grade in an economically disadvantaged elementary school. Many of her students read below grade level and are not meeting state standards, according to the standardized test administered the year before. All of the teachers in Ms. Murphy's school are under pressure for their students to meet state standards.

Some of Ms. Murphy's students have had little exposure to reading outside school, and most do not choose to read during their free time at school. Knowing that reading skills are important to future success in school, Ms. Murphy is justifiably concerned.

The incentive program

In an effort to entice her students to read more, Ms. Murphy develops a reading incentive program. She places a large chart on the classroom wall to track student progress. Each time a student completes a book, he or she tells Ms. Murphy, who then places a star next to the student's name on the chart. Each student who reads five books per month receives a small prize from the class prize box. The student who reads the most books in any given month receives a larger prize.

Student response

When Ms. Murphy tells her students about the new incentive program, most are very excited.

"This is great!" says Joey. "I'm gonna get the most stars!"

"No you won't," says Peter, "Sámi will. She's always got her nose stuck in a book. She's the best reader in the class."

Sámi is a very good reader. She is reading well above grade level and generally favors novels from the young adult section of the library. These books are rather lengthy and take her quite some time to finish. However, she really enjoys them. Ms. Murphy has brought her several from her own collection as well, since none of her classroom books seem to interest Sámi.

The first week of the program is quite exciting. Every day students tell Ms. Murphy about the books they have read. The chart begins to fill with stars. By the end of the week every student has at least one star next to his or her name except Sámi. During the last week of the month many students choose reading as a free-time activity. The students are eager to ensure that they will earn at least one prize and many are devouring books in anticipation of being the month's "top reader." At the end of the month, 23 of Ms. Murphy's 25 students have five stars on the chart. The only exceptions are Sámi, who has only one star, and Michael, who had the chicken pox during the month. True to his word, Joey receives the most stars—fifteen. The students excitedly choose their prizes.

The following month the reading frenzy continues. This time Sámi joins her classmates in their accumulation of stars and receives 30, making her the top reader. Joey is right behind her with 25. Every student in the class earns at least five stars, entitling all to a prize. Because they are all reading so much, Ms. Murphy gives them a Friday afternoon party at which they watch an animated movie and eat popcorn.

A similar pattern is repeated over the next several months. The star chart fills quickly. Ms. Murphy believes that the students are reading enough that they will do quite well on the annual state achievement test. She is thrilled with their progress. She decides that after the test, she will drop the incentive program and just quietly keep track of how much her students read. After doing this she notices that once again very few students are reading during their free time. Even Sámi is no longer reading when she is finished with her other work. Now she draws instead.

Short Answer Questions

1. What are the advantages and disadvantages to incentive programs such as the one Ms. Murphy designed?

2. Why does Sámi no longer read for pleasure?

3. What are some other ways in which Ms. Murphy could help her students to improve their reading?

4. What are some strategies Ms. Murphy could use to prepare her students for the standardized test?

PLEASE USE THE INFO BELOW TO POPULATE RESOURCES FOR EACH QUESTION (USING CONTENT FROM THE 2ND TWO CATEGORIES)

Case	Question	Where to review in *Educational Psychology*	Subject Category
Ben	1	Ch. 15 & 16	II. Instruction and Assessment
Ben	1	Ch. 4 & 6	I. Students as Learners
Ben	2	Ch. 15	III. Communication Techniques
Ben	2	Ch. 16	II. Instruction and Assessment
Ben	3	Ch. 8, 9, 11	II. Instruction and Assessment
Ben	3	Ch. 13, 14, 15	I. Students as Learners
Ben	4.	Ch. 3, 14, 15	III. Communication Techniques
Clarissa	1	Ch. 4, 8, 9	I. Students as Learners
Clarissa	2	Ch. 2, 9	I. Students as Learners
Clarissa	3	Ch. 10, 11, 12	II. Instruction and Assessment
Clarissa	4.	Ch. 16	II. Instruction and Assessment
Adam	1	Ch. 14	I. Students as Learners
Adam	2	Ch. 7, 13	I. Students as Learners
Adam	3	Ch.4, 6, 7, 13	I. Students as Learners
Adam	4.	Ch. 6, 11, 12, 13, 14	II. Instruction and Assessment
Ms. Murphy	1	Ch. 11, 12, 13, 15, 16	II. Instruction and Assessment
Ms. Murphy	2	Ch. 13	I. Students as Learners
Ms. Murphy	3	Ch. 11	II. Instruction and Assessment
Ms. Murphy	4.	Ch. 15	II. Instruction and Assessment